To: Dr. Patrick O'Connell

Thank you for your service!

Peace & Blessings.

John

"*Secretary of the Navy John Dalton led the Navy and the Marine Corps through one of the most challenging periods of modern times. He 'righted the ship' for the Navy in the aftermath of the Tailhook scandal, the major cheating scandal at the Naval Academy, and the tragic and premature death of the Chief of Naval Operations. His leadership was values based, and he led with passion and compassion, discipline and toughness, and an unwavering concern for sailors and Marines. He was matched by his extraordinary spouse, Margaret, whose impact on family issues was profound. John tells the tale of a life molded in service to our country through the lens of some very tough and visible leadership successes and failures: great lessons for us all. His is a wonderful narrative of a life well lived. This is a fun, serious, compelling memoir every leader should read.*"

—**MIKE MULLEN**, ADM, USN, 28th Chief of Naval Operations,
17th Chairman Joint Chiefs of Staff

"I have known John Dalton since 1975. We share a long history, beginning with his service in my administration and his active support of the Carter Center since its inception. John's memoir is brimming with valuable lessons from his full life, and I encourage everyone to read it!"

—**President Jimmy Carter**, 39th President of the United States

"John Dalton has lived a fascinating life—from Shreveport to submarines, public service to the private sector—guided by faith, family, patriotism, and purpose. After I appointed him Secretary of the Navy, his vigorous leadership made our naval forces stronger, more modern, and more diverse. *At the Helm* is an interesting, enjoyable portrait of a life well-lived."

—**President Bill Clinton**, 42nd President of the United States

"There are lives worth reading about and there are lives worth learning from. John Dalton's memoir will fascinate you, inspire you, and ultimately remind you of how one person can truly make a difference. As Dalton says, 'little things do add up.'"

—**The Most Rev. Michael B. Curry**, Presiding Bishop of The Episcopal Church and author of *Love is the Way* and *Songs My Grandma Sang*

"A plainspoken and detailed affirmation of the eternal verities of love of God, love of country, and respect for others that enabled John H. Dalton to rise from humble beginnings to become a fine naval officer, a successful entrepreneur, a high government official, and an honorary canon of the Washington National Cathedral. There is much in this memoir that can help us overcome the antagonism of our intensely partisan country. Dalton and his wife Margaret recognized problems, such as racial injustice and income disparities, and worked on remedial actions to make the world a better place."

—**Paul R. Ignatius**, Secretary of the Navy in the LBJ Administration

"Oh, the places he's been and the things he's done! John Dalton went from an Annapolis graduate to Secretary of the Navy and beyond in a rich and eventful life. In this memoir, he writes of the hard times—business and other setbacks—as well as the successes that have made him among the most respected and well-liked public servants in Washington. He draws lessons for policymakers and identifies what he sees as the critical traits for leaders. *At the Helm* is a must-read!"

—**Susan Page**, *USA TODAY* Washington Bureau Chief and Author of
*Madam Speaker: Nancy Pelosi and the Lessons of Power*

"For four years, I served with John Dalton—a rare privilege with a remarkably reliable leader of our Navy and Marine Corps. This dear (and fiercely competitive) friend and I annually cross Army-Navy swords. That said, anyone reading this delightful, fast-moving book about John's upbringing, his faith, and life travels will know why so many of us consider John to be one of the most principled and inspirational leaders to have ever served our country."

—**Joe R. Reeder**, 14th Under Secretary, United States Army (1993–97)

"*At the Helm* is a thoroughly enjoyable account about an extraordinary American patriot and humanitarian—John Dalton. The country is indebted to John for his dedication to the principles of freedom and democracy. I am fortunate to have had John as a role model and friend for more than four decades."

—**David Rubenstein,** former Chairman of the Carlyle Group and Philanthropist

"I have known John Dalton since we were midshipmen at the Naval Academy, and I knew he was a sports enthusiast when I first met him. He lived in Dallas when I was with the Cowboys. From a modest beginning in Louisiana, John has enjoyed an exciting life in the public and private sectors. His life is an example of the American dream and a portrait of a life well-lived. There is much to be learned from reading this book."

—**Roger Staubach**, Heisman Trophy Winner and MVP of the Super Bowl,
where he led the Cowboys to victory twice

# AT THE HELM

## My Journey with Family,
## Faith, and Friends
## to Calm the Storms of Life

## JOHN H. DALTON

### 70TH SECRETARY OF THE NAVY

KNOX PRESS

A KNOX PRESS BOOK
An Imprint of Permuted Press

At the Helm:
My Journey with Family, Faith, and Friends to Calm the Storms of Life
© 2023 by John H. Dalton, 70th Secretary of the Navy
All Rights Reserved

ISBN: 978-1-63758-515-3
ISBN (eBook): 978-1-63758-516-0

Cover photo by Terry Cosgrove
Interior design and composition by Greg Johnson, Textbook Perfect

This is a work of nonfiction. All people, locations, events, and situation are portrayed to the best of the author's memory.

Permuted Press, LLC
New York ✦ Nashville
permutedpress.com

Published in the United States of America
1 2 3 4 5 6 7 8 9 10

*I dedicate this book to my claim to fame, Margaret.*
*She has been an invaluable help in writing this book.*
*The happiest moment of my life was when she agreed to marry me!*

# CONTENTS

# PREFACE

The USS *George Washington* dropped anchor off Omaha beach where she stayed overnight in 1994. The next morning during the early hours of June 6, President Bill Clinton, much of the crew, and I stood on the carrier's large hanger deck elevator to conduct the sunrise wreath-laying ceremony to commemorate the fiftieth anniversary of D-Day. At the same time of day that thousands of allied soldiers braved the rough waves of the English Channel in 1944, we spoke of their memory, their bravery, and their sacrifice. After Rear Admiral Al Krekich, I was second to speak that morning, and when I took the podium, I praised the heroism of those who had risked everything to defeat the scourge of fascism:

> *Fifty years ago, allied vessels brimming with determined warriors, uncertain of their fate, but clear of their purpose, sailed across these very waters. Today, we honor them.... By the end of that day, the wall of tyranny had been breached, but the price had been high. On behalf of the Department of the Navy, I welcome all our honored guests to the commemoration of the allied invasion of Normandy.*

When I finished, I introduced a D-Day Navy veteran who had received the Navy Cross during World War II, Dean Rockwell, to speak. He had brief remarks and then introduced President Clinton, who proceeded to the podium and was respectful and measured in his words. When the speeches were finished, the president and several Navy veterans escorted the wreath and cast it ceremoniously off the hangar deck into the dark, turbulent waters of the channel below. Following this first ceremony of D-Day, President Clinton and a large contingent of officials flew ashore. There they presided over events at Pointe du Hoc, Utah Beach, the French-hosted Omaha Beach ceremony, and finally, the capstone event of the day: the ceremony at the American Cemetery in Normandy, attended by government officials from the UK, US, France, and Canada and thousands of D-Day veterans.

It was truly a beautiful ceremony, and I am grateful to have had the opportunity to attend. President Clinton was the principal speaker and did an outstanding job. On a side note, my wife, Margaret, happened to sit next to Walter Cronkite's wife and, apparently, they had a great time together. It was all a terrific way to honor the courage and sacrifice of our veterans. The large fleet of Navy ships of the George Washington Carrier Battle Group and an Amphibious Ready Group was a grand sight to behold. As the ships weighed anchor and sailed past the cemetery in majestic procession, I was never prouder to be the Secretary of the Navy and delighted that, prior to leaving the ship, I had told the crew there that I was using my secretarial authority to award the Navy Unit Commendation to the USS George Washington and all of her sailors. (See the appendix for more about the D-Day anniversary events.)

First event of the 50th D-Day Ceremony on the USS George Washington at dawn on June 6, 1994.

This was just one example of the honor and privilege I enjoyed as the seventieth Secretary of the Department of the Navy. It wasn't all pomp and circumstance; I had more than my share of scandal and upheaval to address. But I wouldn't have changed a thing. As a Louisiana boy of modest means, growing up to attend the US Naval Academy and eventually becoming the top civilian at the helm of that venerated institution—as well as the Navy and Marine Corps—was a dream come true. This is my story.

As I began to write this book and reflect upon my life, one particularly poignant line stuck out to me. Phil Lader, former American ambassador to the United Kingdom in the Clinton administration and a good friend of mine, once said something in a speech that really resonated with me. "Everyone in this room is very busy and has a lot of balls in the air. Three of those balls are crystal, and if you break one of those, you have a big problem. They are your family, your friends, and your faith. Be sure and nourish them. If so, they will be there for you when you need them." I believe that he is absolutely right, and as one will see in this book, they have been there for me when I needed them most.

# CHAPTER 1

# 335 MERRICK STREET

New Orleans was bright and sunny on December 13, 1941, when I joined the family of William Carl and Jaunice Davenport Dalton. Those who know their history can see that I was born six days after the attack on Pearl Harbor and our nation's entry into World War II. I sometimes joke that the Japanese heard I was coming and bombed Pearl Harbor!

My parents named me John Howard, after my paternal grandfather, Peter John, and my maternal uncle, Howard Davenport. I was the youngest of three children. The eldest was my late sister, Margaret, who was ten years my senior, followed by my brother, William Carl, Jr., who is six years older. Looking at the difference in ages among us, I believe my parents thought they were finished having children, and then I showed up. My family showered me with love from the day I was born, and I do not recall serious fights or sibling rivalry between us.

Though I was born in New Orleans, our family moved for my father's work when I was three years old. He was a railroad man with the Louisiana & Arkansas Railway Company, known as the L&A (later acquired by Kansas City Southern Railway Company), and they transferred him 330 miles northwest to Shreveport. It was there, in the city that runs along the west bank of the Red River, that I would grow up.

My father was a native of rural Stephens, Arkansas, but, through work and family, had come to call Louisiana his home. Choosing to go by his middle name, Carl, he was the eldest of eight siblings. He was a tall, handsome, and jovial man, standing about 6'1". He worked hard at his profession and was very successful for someone who lacked even a high school diploma. He loved to laugh and sometimes laughed so hard at his own jokes that the vein in the middle of his forehead was easily visible. He may have been a little too old to serve when our country joined the Second World War, and he may have had only an eighth-grade education, but he never let anything hold him back.

While my father was the oldest of eight, my mother was the youngest of seven. She was nine years younger than her husband, whom she had married when she was eighteen, a mere one month after she graduated from high school. She was very much like my father in some respects: tall, attractive, and fun-loving. However, if you ever wanted to get on her bad side, just say something negative about one of her children!

My parents were wonderful role models for us. Despite the difference in their ages and upbringings, my mother and father had much in common. They were kind, honest, fun-loving, salt-of-the-earth people of great faith. They both enjoyed a good party and cared deeply for those close to them, always going above and beyond to help those they cared about. Sometimes they could be strict, something most kids don't appreciate at the time, but they taught me many good lessons. The most important of those were to love God, love your neighbor as yourself, and treat everyone with dignity and respect.

We moved to 335 Merrick Street in Shreveport. That was our three-bedroom

*Baby Johnny with curls.*

family home, and I lived in that house from the day we moved from New Orleans until my service in the US Navy. Our family was active in the neighborhood, and I would play with friends my age while my parents went to house parties and joined in barbeques during the hot Louisiana summers.

The nature of my father's work with the L&A Railway meant that he was rarely home during the week. Normally, he would leave on Sunday night or early Monday morning and return on Friday night or early Saturday. Because of this, my mother was the queen of the castle most days. She ruled with a loving and fair hand, always making time for Margaret, William, and me but never letting us misbehave too badly.

We didn't typically take vacations and our family rarely left Louisiana, so we spent most of what free time we had in Shreveport. I still clearly remember going to the state fair on autumn days with friends or family to enjoy the rides and the times my mother gave me fifteen cents so I could go to the YMCA and back on the electric trolley, with enough money left over for a soft drink.

We made annual trips to Arkansas, usually for Christmas, to see the relatives on my father's side. During those visits I would sometimes see one of my father's brothers, Roy Bale Dalton. I never knew my uncle well, but he would have a huge impact on my life.

Uncle Roy was eighteen years younger than my father and had volunteered to serve during the Second World War. During the war, he had enlisted in the Navy and served in the Pacific theater, first as a seaman recruit and later as a naval aviator. Like many of his generation, he rarely spoke about his experiences, and along with the fact that we were never very close, I knew better than to pry.

Having returned from the war with a number of medals, it was clear that he had served with great honor and distinction. I remember staring at his collection with awe, especially his Silver Star and Navy Cross—the two highest awards the Navy could bestow. In those decorations I could picture fleets of ships sailing on wide blue oceans. I imagined the adventures there, out over the horizon and wondered

*With my family: father, Carl; mother, Jaunice; sister, Margaret; brother, William.*

what serving my country would be like. While the notion that the US Navy and public service would be in my future was still many years away, my uncle Roy definitely planted that seed in my mind, whether he intended to or not.[1]

As a kid I had a paper route, and I would wake up early every day of the week, braving neighborhood dogs, to deliver newspapers to people in the area. I also used to scavenge along the sides of the streets and major roads for discarded glass soft drink bottles. I would return the used bottles to vendors for two cents each for their refilling. Luckily there were enough of them around to make this a lucrative enterprise for a young boy. I also had a job at the bowling alley of the First Presbyterian Church one night a week where I set pins for seventy-five

---

[1] Others were also inspired by my uncle's legacy. Roy Bale Dalton III, his grandson, followed in his footsteps and served in the Navy after graduating from the Naval Academy in 2002. He was the senior military advisor to Senator Bill Nelson from Florida and was the commanding officer of one of the two reserve helicopter squadrons in the US Navy. Bale serves as the deputy chief of staff to the NASA administrator, the Honorable Bill Nelson, in the Biden administration. His father, Skip, is the federal judge in Orlando representing central Florida.

cents per game for two games. I saved that money and frequently used part of it to take my mother for hamburgers at the Toddle House. As I matured, I would move on to more conventional jobs; but those early experiences taught me the value of being entrepreneurial and taking the initiative, skills that would serve me well later in life.

One of the many things my parents had in common that they passed on to us was their faith. To this day, my faith in the Lord has been a constant in my life. It is something I have nurtured, something that has given me strength and comfort in my darkest moments and has helped keep my moral compass true north.

My mother and dad were devout Christians. My dad was a Methodist, and my mother converted from Baptist to Methodist when they married. Some of my earliest memories are of my family around the table saying the blessing for every meal and prayers at bedtime.

My Christian upbringing extended beyond our home. Every Sunday, rain or shine, our family walked about ten blocks to Noel Memorial Methodist Church, listened to the sermons, sang hymns, and took part in the church's other activities. The church has always been a very important part of our lives.

My father was active on the board of stewards and the men's Bible class and also involved with the Gideons, believing Bibles should also be accessible to people in hotels whenever they needed the wisdom of the good book. He attended Gideons-hosted breakfast events on Sunday mornings, occasionally taking me along. My mother taught Sunday school and encouraged me to join the Methodist Youth Fellowship (MYF), where she was a chaperone. It was there that I took my first small steps into leadership when I was elected president of the MYF. It was mostly an administrative role: greeting those coming to Sunday school and running a general meeting before we went to our respective classes, but I learned from that responsibility.

The church and the example my parents set at home went a long way in forming my faith in those days, but one event would more clearly define my Christian belief. I always enjoyed my time at church and the

Bible lessons my parents gave to all their children, but I felt as if some small piece of knowledge was just out of reach. It wasn't doubt; I just didn't fully "understand."

Then, in 1951, the Billy Graham Crusade came to Shreveport and stayed for three weeks; preaching was offered to over two hundred thousand people during what later was called the Shreveport Revival. My father was away working on the L&A, but I went with my mother to hear one of his messages.

The crusade had begun at the Municipal Auditorium in downtown Shreveport, but the crowds became so large that they had to relocate to the state fair stadium at the fairgrounds. (This site is now the Independence Bowl.) We were among the thousands who had flocked to hear Billy Graham. His charisma and conviction were unforgettable, and it was there, at that service, that I first felt that I understood the gospel.

Graham closed his sermon with a prayer, inviting everyone wanting Jesus to be the Lord of their lives to raise their hand, which I did. All who raised their hands were invited to come down and approach the stage to profess their faith in God. Needing no further encouragement, I quickly made my way to the front. I was counseled by a member of Billy Graham's crusade team, who led me in another prayer.

When we finished, the team member turned to me and said, "Do you commit yourself to Jesus Christ and recognize him as the Lord of your life?" I agreed with no hesitation, and the volunteer, smiling, gave me a paperback copy of the Gospel of John, asking me to go home and read it.

Every night before going to bed, my mother and I would read aloud a chapter of the Gospel of John they had given me. We probably had read parts of the Gospel of John before, both at Noel and at home, but after hearing Billy Graham, it was different somehow. On the third night, I reached John 3:16.

*For God so loved the world that he gave his one and only Son, that whoever believes in him shall not perish but have eternal life.*

After reading that verse, my mother looked up and said, "Johnny, read that verse again."

That happened over seventy years ago, but I still recall the moment as clearly as if it were yesterday. My mother told me that verse was the foundation of our faith. To this day, it helps me to follow our Lord's example and treat others—no matter who they are—with dignity and respect. Remembering that God loves us and cares for us, even during the most trying times in our lives, He can help us endure anything.

Looking back at my childhood, I can appreciate how blessed I was growing up the way I did and with the family that I had. Mother and Dad worked hard and sacrificed for us, especially to provide us the education neither of them had the opportunity to access.

Others were not so lucky. Like much of the south at the time, Louisiana was not an equal place, and Jim Crow was the order of the day. The civil rights movement did not pick up steam until I was at the Naval Academy, and so I grew up in a society that was, tragically, institutionally racist. I confess that at the time it seemed normal to me, and as a child I did not consciously question why people treated African Americans so badly. I can clearly recall an occasion when I was eight or nine years old when my parents, another couple, and I went to an eatery called Morrison's Cafeteria. We had a very polite and efficient black waiter serving us, and when he brought the food, I expressed my gratitude.

"Thank you, sir," I said. I had been taught to treat my elders with respect, and he was, as far as I was concerned, an elder.

The husband of the other couple sternly scolded me in front of the waiter saying, "We don't say sir to *him!*"

Looking back at it, I feel a profound mixture of embarrassment and shame at how things were. The way society discriminated against African Americans was beyond disgraceful. I never participated in the racism that then was so widespread, nor as a child could I have done anything about it. My eyes were opened wide with my education outside of Louisiana, thanks to the efforts of friends and the selfless actions of civil rights leaders like Martin Luther King, Rosa Parks, John Lewis, and others. Beginning as a young adult, I have tried to fight for equality for everyone, in my own way.

Having been blessed with a wonderful childhood, I can't think of anything more important. Every child wants and needs to be loved. I truly believe that a child who is cherished and reared with strong values is far more likely to be successful in life and to treat others with dignity and respect.

# CHAPTER 2

# CLASSROOMS AND SPORTS FIELDS

While spending time at home and church was important to me, there was a lot more to my childhood than that. Like most kids, my school was a very formative experience, and those years would go on to help define me. My mother and father both understood the value of a good education and encouraged William, Margaret, and me to study hard and always do our best.

When I was ten years old (around the same age as when Billy Graham came to town) I ran for president of my fifth-grade class at Alexander Elementary School. Similar to the Methodist Youth Fellowship, I gave a speech to my classmates to announce my candidacy. I was nervous as the election went forward but thrilled when our teacher, Mrs. Tauzin, announced I had won. We all know that an elementary class president is small potatoes, but that experience helped show me the value of reaching out to my peers, working to earn their trust, and the basics of seeking leadership in a competitive setting.

Meanwhile, other events closer to home marked the beginning of one of the most important aspects of my life. My brother, William, was a good athlete. It was amazing to watch him play sports, and as I got a little older, I wanted to emulate him and get involved in athletics, too. At first it was practicing in the front or backyard, throwing footballs, baseballs, or dribbling and shooting a basketball. William gave me a good grasp of the basics, and he strongly fostered my interest in them. Without his example and encouragement, I do not know if sports would have become such an important part of my life.

William got me into football and basketball, but my enduring love for America's pastime, baseball, came from a different source. Sometime in the late 1940s Shreveport suffered through an outbreak of polio two summers in a row. During that time, kids like me were made to take naps during the afternoons. Don't ask me how napping was supposed to protect you from polio, but I did as I was told. Instead of whining, I found a way to distract myself. We owned a radio, and during "naptime" I would turn it on and look for an interesting program. One day, as I was dialing through stations, I found the frequency for the St. Louis Cardinals baseball team. Even though they were hundreds of miles away in Missouri, their broadcasts reached all the way down to the Gulf of Mexico. I spent hours listening to broadcasts of their games and became so involved that I would forget about the polio outbreak outside. I immensely enjoyed listening to Harry Caray because of the exciting way he covered the games, particularly when he exclaimed "Holy Cow!" whenever the Cardinals hit a home run or did something else exciting. I never needed any encouragement to "nap" on days when the Cardinals were playing.

Because my school didn't have a football team, I was able to play for the nearby Creswell Elementary. I played different positions on the Creswell team and, by doing so, I got a better understanding of how the sport was played and how to work as part of a team. We played a lot of games, and while we did not win the championship, we did well enough that they let me stay on and join their 85-pound team in the fifth grade. I loved playing football, and I was in my element.

Having had a taste for leadership and sports in elementary school, I was determined to do more of both and keep pushing my boundaries. I became president of the student council at Hamilton Terrace Junior High (HT). Like before, I went out of my way to speak to my classmates who were elected as part of the student council, getting to know their thoughts and convincing them why I would be the right choice. The hard work paid off, and, when the vote came, I was comfortably elected president. Much like my presidency at Alexander, the powers of student council president were far from sweeping. But it helped me better understand the interpersonal skills I had picked up when I was younger and confirmed to me the importance of leading with confidence and compassion.

It was at Hamilton Terrace that I began emerging into my own when it came to athletics. At Hamilton Terrace I met one of my major role models. Nicky Lester was our football coach in junior high. He was about my sister's age and part of her wider circle of friends, so I had met him before I got to Hamilton Terrace.

Despite his brusque, no-nonsense personality, Nicky was an absolutely terrific football coach. I had some experience as a quarterback from my Creswell days, but under coach Nicky's watchful eye, this became my main position. Nicky even gave me a book entitled *Split T Football* by Bud Wilkinson, the man who coached the Oklahoma Sooners, who were the national champions. I read the book cover to cover more than once, eager to learn all I could about the tactics I could use and signals I could call.

My three years with the Hamilton Terrace team were more than just fun and games, though it goes without saying that I was having a great deal of fun. That time was also very useful in helping refine my budding leadership skills. One of my most vivid recollections was the time that my friend Bob Hamm was going to be the team captain for a game against Broadmoor Junior High School, and the referee asked the coach if Bob would make the decisions on the field with respect to penalties. Coach Nicky Lester said, "No, my quarterback will make those decisions. He's ninety-nine pounds of quarterback dynamite!" Coach Nicky Lester was famous around the school for those kinds of comments, though they weren't always as good-natured as that one. Still, his confidence in my judgment and abilities meant a lot to me and filled me with pride.

My time at Hamilton Terrace seemed to fly by, and before I knew it, I had finished with junior high and was on the way to Byrd High School. It was one of the best public schools in Louisiana, and it was also renowned for its sporting prowess. Several of its students received college athletic scholarships. Gene Newton, my brother's classmate and another of my role models, would win a football scholarship to Tulane University. So I was excited to start there and was anxious to get onto the football field.

Like my time at Alexander and HT, I continued to participate in school politics at Byrd. In my sophomore year I was elected to the student council and later that year ran for Sgt.-at-Arms but lost. In my junior year I was elected treasurer of the student council and served in that capacity for my senior year. As treasurer, I learned basic but important budgeting skills and discovered that I was good at working with money. This would influence my future career choices, and it was a rewarding experience.

The student government at Byrd was more active than that at Hamilton Terrace. One of our interesting experiences was going to Jacksonville, Florida, for the Southern Student Council Convention. It was student politics 101, and we met many interesting people while we were there. What made the trip stand out even more was that we flew to Jacksonville in a private plane. The father of one of our executive council members, our secretary Jane Cunningham, was an officer at the United Gas company, and he made it possible for us to travel on the company plane to the convention. The only other time I had been on a plane was a short hop to Little Rock, Arkansas, to see a good friend, so flying in such style was exciting to say the least.

I was also blessed with other leadership opportunities in high school. My junior year I was chosen as one of ten students to represent Byrd at Pelican Boys State during the summer before my senior year. We went to Baton Rouge along with over three hundred other students from around Louisiana to learn about politics and how the government worked. We stayed at Louisiana State University in a dormitory nicknamed "The Pentagon." Looking back, I find this quite funny, considering where I would end up working years later. Over the next several days we did everything from having elections to running "campaigns."

I was elected a senator, president pro tem of the senate, and chairman of my party. My friend Bubba Rasberry, the vice president of Byrd's student council, would be selected Outstanding Citizen of the Year at Pelican State, allowing him to participate in Boys Nation in Washington, DC. Even though it was all fiction, I think we represented Byrd very well with our charisma and ambition, and I loved the experience, especially when we took over the state capitol on the final night.

My Christian faith continued to be an important part of my life when I was a teenager. I was not the only one who took it seriously at school, and this was particularly true in the years after Billy Graham had come to Shreveport. His crusade had inspired not just me but other people my age. At Byrd, a number of students had set up prayer and Bible study groups, and I was quick to get involved. I was selected as one of the prayer group leaders, and we would regularly meet at each other's homes to discuss the Bible and our faith and to pray.

We would also all come together once every two or three weeks before school for a chapel service. One of us would usually speak at those services, and I had the honor of doing so on a couple of occasions. The prayer groups were very special to me, as was the chance to explore and talk about our faith as peers. That complimented the traditional services at Noel Church nicely.

Just because I was getting more involved in student politics and participating in faith groups did not mean I was neglecting sports, though. I was a pretty good athlete and loved it as much as ever. Not long after I started at Byrd, I set my sights on earning my way into college on a football scholarship. I was good enough at the game that the idea was not a far-fetched one, as long as I kept practicing. It would also keep the financial responsibility of paying for college off my parents, who had already done so much for me. I had seen the sacrifices my parents made to put my older brother and sister through college, and I didn't want to place that burden on them for a third time.

Fate, however, had other plans.

It was early in the tenth grade, only a few months after I entered Byrd. I had tried out for and made the football team, and I was having a great time. I had continued in my quarterback role from my Hamilton Terrace days, and while I missed Nicky Lester a great deal, the coaches at Byrd were very capable. We continued playing the Split T formation, just like we had done at HT.

One day at practice, I had the ball and was going down the line of scrimmage when it happened. Some defensive players managed to break through the line and tackle me. The impact caused me to fall badly, and I felt a terrible pain shoot through my left knee. Considering how much I played football, I was no stranger to being knocked about or taking a few licks, but I immediately knew this was different.

The pain in my knee was absolutely awful, and I was quickly stretchered away to seek medical attention. I went to see our team doctor, Dr. Don Overdyke, a serious and somber man who inspected me and x-rayed my knee. After the results came back he let me know, in no uncertain terms, that this was a bad injury and not something I could just walk off or bounce back from. "You can forget about athletics." He said bluntly, "When you are grown, you might be able to dance with your wife or play nine holes of golf, but you are through with athletics."

Dr. Overdyke's prognosis was crushing! In just a few moments, sports, one of the biggest parts of my life, was taken away from me. I was devastated, and for a while, I didn't know what to do with myself. Part of me refused to accept Dr. Overdyke's assessment, and as soon as it was time to get my cast removed, I decided to ask for a second opinion.

That time, I saw his partner, Dr. Ed McPherson. The results were better than I feared, but worse than I had hoped. After checking my knee, he explained that I could rehabilitate it through swimming.

However, he hammered the final nail in the coffin when he confirmed that I could no longer play contact sports.

I was thankful that my knee wasn't as bad as had first been said and that I could make it better if I worked on it. But I also felt dejected, because I could no longer play the sport I loved. It was a painful lesson for me, physically and mentally, and it made clear that I wasn't invincible. From then on, any time I went to a football game, it was only as a spectator.

Just like that, my dreams of going to college on a football scholarship were lost forever.

What on earth was I going to do now?

# CHAPTER 3

# FROM THE RED RIVER TO THE CHESAPEAKE

For a good while after I injured my knee, I was despondent. I felt rudderless, because I could never play contact sports again, and any chance of a football scholarship evaporated. My family, faith, and friends were there for me, telling me that it was not the end of the world, but this was still perhaps the darkest time of my life up to that point.

As bitterly disappointing as it had been, Dr. McPherson's consultation and encouragement had offered a dim light at the end of a long tunnel. If I had any chance of rehabilitating my knee, even if it would never completely recover, I was determined to take it. Almost as soon as I was out of his office, I made my way to the YMCA swimming pool to begin the long process of rehabilitation.

I was not a stranger to the water. At Lake Bistineau during our Fourth of July family gatherings, we often would swim in the lake as an escape from the sweltering heat. However, it had never been a passion for me in the way other forms of athletics had been. Now the road to rehabilitation led through the swimming pool, and I was going to see that journey through.

As the weeks passed, my knee slowly began to feel much better. Eventually, I even got back into basketball, which I would play through my senior year.

Now that I had recovered, I decided to see if I could use my new-found aquatic abilities for something more than my physical health. I landed a job as a lifeguard, first at the YMCA camp (where I was also a camp counselor) and later at the Palmetto Country Club. At the country club, a colleague and I would take turns each week serving as lifeguard and waiting on tables around the swimming pool.

That was not the only job I had at the time. During my senior year, thanks to a good recommendation from my close friend and neighbor Bob Hamm, I was hired at Selber Brothers in the Young Executive Shop selling suits, sport coats, ties, shirts, and other attire for young men. It was a straightforward job and, from it, I learned how to improve my salesmanship skills. I also learned the importance of being properly attired, and I improved my taste in clothing. There was good money involved in the way of commissions, particularly around holiday seasons like Christmas or Thanksgiving.

One Black Friday, the day after Thanksgiving, Leonard Selber, our boss, came to us salesmen with a challenge: there would be a twenty-dollar bonus for whoever sold the most clothes that day, and we were staying open until 9:00 PM.

As the evening wore on and we neared closing time, the contest was almost too close to call. I knew I was one of the top contenders for the bonus, but it was far from a done deal. An elegant older lady came into the store, and I happened to be nearest to the entrance in our part of the store. I approached her in as dignified a manner as I could.

Putting on my best salesmanship skills, I politely asked her if I could be of any assistance, and she explained that she was interested in buying some sport coats for her grandsons. I was happy to oblige her, and three coats later (two for thirty-five dollars each and one for forty-five dollars) she walked out as a satisfied customer, and I left later that day with a very sweet bonus. I felt like J. Paul Getty!

While I relished the victory and the cash, it turned out that I would see that lady again, but under very different circumstances. I discovered that she was the paternal grandmother of Margaret, my future wife and

17

the love of my life. Now to those who do not know me, let me clarify. As I said before, I had a sister named Margaret. However, the wonderful woman I would go on to wed also shares the same name.

Margaret was the younger sister of my friend Bucky Ogilvie, and we all went to Byrd together. I was a senior, Bucky was a junior, and Margaret was a sophomore, and I occasionally would go to their house to visit. Margaret also had a brother six years younger named Staman, with whom I would build a strong relationship several years later. I have great respect for both of her brothers. I had a steady girlfriend for most of my time in high school, but at one point we broke up, and I decided to ask Margaret out on a date.

I arrived at their house in our family car and was greeted at the door by Margaret's mother. I asked her what time she would like me to have Margaret home, and she answered around eleven that night. It was a nice date, but it did not lead to anything serious at the time. We would continue this for another decade, dating other people but occasionally seeing each other in a noncommittal way. Margaret and I may not have been an item during high school, but I had clearly made a good impression on her mother. I think she figured out that we were meant to be together long before we did, and she would do what she could to bring us together in the years to come!

Even though I continued making lemonade out of the lemon life had handed me, there was one problem that no amount of swimming, lifeguarding, or working at Selber Brothers could answer. It was the elephant in the room: the question of what I was going to do after high school. I knew that I wanted to go to college, but the injury meant any chance I had of a football scholarship was completely out of consideration. There was a big question mark hanging over my future like a dark cloud.

All this changed one day during a school assembly at Byrd when I was fifteen. We usually had a whole-school assembly once a week in the main auditorium, where the principal or other teachers would make announcements. Sometimes there would also be guest speakers, who would come in and talk about a variety of subjects.

The guest speaker that day was Dr. W. B. Worley, the chairman of the Building and Grounds Committee of the Caddo Parish School Board. He was an intelligent and accomplished man, who was more inspirational than any other speaker we had had so far. He talked about a number of topics but finally caught my attention when he spoke about the United States Naval Academy. He said that he wanted his son to go there because, in his opinion, it was "the best overall education a young man could receive." He said that he would be proud if any of his children had the opportunity to go there.

A lightbulb switched on in my head. I thought back to my Uncle Roy, his service in the Navy and his medals, and suddenly all of the pieces started falling into place. "Aha, that's what I'll do!" I thought. It felt like divine providence, and from that moment forward, the Naval Academy became my new goal. It gave me an objective that I could strive toward and a renewed sense of direction that I had been missing since my injury. I left that assembly full of energy and determination. I knew what I wanted to do and where I wanted to go to college.

That did not mean things were going to be easy, but nothing meaningful ever is. Applying to enter the United States Naval Academy was similar to trying to get into West Point––and just as difficult. You needed excellent grades, proven leadership skills, a track record of taking the initiative, and you had to be physically fit. I checked most of those boxes, now that my leg had healed, including the strong grades. My Achilles' Heel (or perhaps more accurately, my Achilles' Knee) was arguably my SAT scores, which, while respectable, were not highly competitive.

The biggest challenge would be receiving the principal appointment from my congressman. Without it, I would not be seriously considered, no matter how athletic I was or how good my grades were. On his own initiative, my brother, William, wrote a letter to our congressman, a man by the name of Overton Brooks, asking for an application. It was the first time either of us had written to someone as important as a congressman, and I was excited and very grateful when Will wrote the letter. All I could do was wait and hope that I would be admitted.

The reply I got back was not a no, but it definitely took the wind out of my sails. I was assigned the position of first alternate, which was a fancy way of saying that if their first choice backed out or otherwise became unavailable, then the opening would go to me. Needless to say, that was not the response I had hoped for!

By that time, I was running out of options. No football scholarship, no placement at the Naval Academy, and graduation was fast approaching. Again, I felt both like I had failed and that I did not have a clear plan or objective to focus on. With the support of my family, my faith, and friends, I am relieved to say that I didn't wallow in that sad place for long.

After talking it over with my parents, I decided that I should apply to Louisiana State University. At the time, a diploma was sufficient for admission. It was in-state, and it was a fine college. It also had the added bonus of being in Baton Rouge, LA, which was less than four hours away from Shreveport, so I could visit home regularly. Realizing that I had nothing to lose and everything to gain, I applied, and to my excitement, I got a letter weeks later that confirmed my admission. Even if it had not been my first choice, at least I knew what I was going to do next.

After I had been accepted at LSU but before graduation from Byrd, I was invited by a fraternity at LSU to a rush party. As I drove down to Baton Rouge to attend the party, I made a stop in Alexandria, LA, to visit with my sister, Margaret. I remember my brother-in-law, Bob Ratelle, coming to my room to visit with me and telling me how sorry he was that I had not been admitted to the Naval Academy. He consoled me and said that if I really wanted to go there, I should apply again next year.

Going to college was something of a culture shock for me, as I am sure anyone leaving home for the first time can attest. It took me a couple weeks to get acclimated, to meet new people and learn my way around the green parks and red-roofed buildings of the campus. After that settling in period, though, I began to enjoy my time at LSU. I may have only been a freshman, but I was determined to seize this opportunity by the horns and get the most out of it that I possibly could.

This may not come as a surprise by now, but I was not content with going with the flow. I wanted to take the initiative, succeed, and make an impression. My political aspirations had not dimmed from my days at Alexander, Hamilton Terrace, or Byrd, and when opportunities came to run for president of my fraternity pledge class and to represent the freshman class in the student government, I seized them. Running for those elected positions at college was definitely a change in gear from the days at high school, but I was still able to draw on those skills and run both campaigns successfully. I enjoyed being in a position of responsibility, speaking on behalf of my classmates so that their voices were heard, and leading. But I also understood the responsibility of it and did my best to see that they were represented in the manner they deserved.

The ethics of hard work and determination that my parents had taught me also paid dividends at LSU. After who knows how many nights writing papers and long hours at the library poring over books, I earned my way into Phi Eta Sigma. It was, and is, a prestigious freshman honor society that required nearly perfect grades to be selected. I was elected president of my pledge class at Kappa Sigma fraternity and separately elected to represent the freshman class to the Student Government Association, which made me feel good about my first year in college.

Now, while I worked with great diligence and grit to earn those things, I still looked for chances to unwind and have fun. I played on the fraternity touch football team against other fraternities, and I attended as many college football games as I could. LSU was also renowned as a party school—and for good reason! There were raucous parties, usually at fraternity houses, seemingly every week. The music was great, people danced, the drinks flowed, and good times were had by all.

However, despite the great time I was having at Louisiana State, my thoughts often drifted back to the Naval Academy. Even though I had not managed to get in the first time, the dream had not died, and as time passed at LSU, I endeavored to try again. Most of my friends and family were supportive and encouraged me to chase my dream, but I do remember one fraternity brother at LSU, Jim Thompson, questioning me and telling me that I was crazy to do it. He had spent two years at the Naval Academy and transferred to LSU to finish his undergraduate degree and go to law school there. "You'll be a nobody at the Academy, and you've got a great thing going here. Why give it up?" he said.

Even though I disagreed with him, I could understand his perspective. It was true that things were going well, but in my mind, I was not throwing anything away. If anything, I was trading up. I had no regrets about going to LSU; I learned a great deal, and I had matured a lot as a person. It prepared me in ways that my previous experiences had not. In hindsight, I think it was a critical step in my life's journey. Had I had been admitted to the Naval Academy at seventeen years old, I do not know whether I would have been ready for it.

The second time I applied I felt more prepared, submitting the application in good time and with a fresh set of very good grades and accomplishments from my freshman year. My chances looked better than before, but success was far from guaranteed. This time, however, I would be blessed with a stroke of luck.

Our next-door neighbor on Merrick Street was a woman by the name of Clara Clancy, known affectionately in the neighborhood as Miss Clara. She was a kind and friendly woman who lived alone for as long as I had known her. She worked at Glenwood Drug store, a small café and pharmacy across the street from Byrd High School. It was a nice if unremarkable place, but it suddenly became relevant to me for one very important reason.

Miss Clara told me that Overton Brooks, our Member of Congress, would go to Glenwood Drug every day for breakfast whenever the Congress was in recess and he was back in Shreveport. Without the principal appointment from him, my chances of a Naval Academy education were less than slim. This time, I would approach him directly.

And that is exactly what I did! One morning when he was back in town, I marched over to Glenwood Drug after a tip from Miss Clara that the congressman would be there. Sure enough, as I walked in the drug store, I saw him sitting at a table, sipping a cup of coffee and reading the newspaper. This was my best shot, and I would not get a chance like this again. I was nervous but knew that I had to take advantage of it.

I do not recall exactly what was said when I sat down with him; it is a bit of a blur. However, I know I explained my situation to him, what I had done, and why I thought I was the best qualified for the principal appointment. It was a not a long conversation, and truth be told, I suspect I caught him off guard. I think he was probably accustomed to scheduled appointments in the comfort of his office. I told him what I had accomplished at LSU, and that if he gave me his principal appointment, he would not regret it. Toward the end of our conversation, he seemed impressed with me and agreed to give me the principal appointment. I could not believe it; it was too good to be true!

When the congressman left, I went over to Miss Clara and thanked her profusely. She had been the one to tip the scales for me, and I would be grateful to her forever after that day. After that I ran home as fast as I could and barged into the living room to tell my mother. I was not at the Naval Academy yet, but I was much closer.

It took time for everything to fall into place, and I was itching with impatience. Finally, I received the acceptance letter from the Naval Academy. All that hard work had paid off, and I felt a sense of accomplishment and gratitude that is still difficult to describe. My family was overjoyed. Not only because I had been accepted into such a prestigious institution, but also because they knew it had been my dream, and they were happy and proud to see me realize it.

Even though I was keen to get to the Academy, leaving LSU was an emotional experience. I had many good friends there, especially my fraternity brothers Clint Pierson and Tommy Watts and my roommate, Tommy Lolley.

I made a final stop on the Fourth of July at the old family stomping grounds at Uncle Howard's Lake Bistineau camp to see everyone on my mother's side of the family. Finally, the time came for me to leave, and for only the third time in my life, I boarded a plane. A good number of my high school classmates from Byrd came to see me off at the airport. I was touched and grateful by this outpouring of support and teared up when the plane took off for Atlanta. It was Senator Russell Long from Louisiana who once said, "When I die, I don't know whether I'm going to heaven or to hell, but I know I will change planes in Atlanta." It was certainly true for me as I made a connection there to our nation's capital. I had planned to take a bus to Annapolis when I arrived in DC, but as luck would have it, I ran into four others who were also on their way to the Naval Academy.

Together we realized that it would be cheaper and faster if we all pitched in for a taxi. So, we all bundled into a cab, which with five athletic young men and their bags was a tight squeeze! It felt like both the longest and shortest ride of my life, but finally, we reached the beautiful Yard of the Naval Academy.

We were taken to Bancroft Hall, and I was introduced to my Plebe Summer roommates. I think we flipped a coin to see who got the single rack (bed), and I won. Things were off to a good start!

I was not sure what to expect, but I was excited and eager to begin the journey.

# CHAPTER 4

# THE PROBLEM WITH GALOSHES

My four years at the United States Naval Academy in Annapolis, Maryland, were some of the most formative of my life, and they would play a huge role in molding me into the person I would become. I always had a reverence for the selflessness of public service, even as a kid in Shreveport, but it would be during this time that this, my second fundamental value, came into sharp focus.

Like all of the incoming plebes (freshman class), I arrived July 5, 1960, when many of the upperclassman were either on leave or participating in various summer programs off campus (or the Yard, as we called it). That meant that we were the only class there for about eight weeks before classes began. I soon learned that this was known as "Plebe Summer," and that each year had its own nickname: sophomores: third-class or youngster; juniors: second-class or *segundo*; and seniors: first-class or firsty.

When I went to my room on the first day, I found that my roommates were Mike Martin from West Virginia and Ed Farrell from Rhode Island. I had never met anyone from either state before. They were nice guys and had just graduated from high school a month or six weeks before. We were in civilian clothes and went to Tecumseh Court in front of Bancroft Hall for the Induction Day Ceremony. A unique thing about the induction ceremony was that Chief of Naval Operations, Admiral Arleigh Burke, was the principal speaker and administered the oath of office to us. Our squad leader was Midshipman Mel Chang, a second classman and a member of the class of 1962. (They now use first-class-men for the plebe summer detail.) Bancroft Hall, the largest dormitory in the world, which housed all 3,800 members of the brigade at that time, loomed large and grand before us. I was officially Midshipman J. H. Dalton now, a proud member of the great class of 1964!

Despite the unflattering moniker used to label freshman like me, Plebe Summer was a good introduction to life at the Academy, and it allowed us to get our feet wet before the upperclassman could return and harass the new faces. Beyond some orientation classes, there were plenty of opportunities to sign up for activities, and I jumped at the chance to join a sports team.

I quickly went out for the crew team, as I was eager to meet new people and scratch my itch for athletics and team sports. Unfortunately, I did not have much knack for rowing crew, and I was cut from the team not long after plebe summer began. However, I had much more success with soccer. Even though it was not a contact sport in the strict sense of the term, I knew I had to be careful. Playing it was a risk to my knee, and fear of injuring it again was always a concern, especially when such an injury could cost me the place I had worked so hard to achieve.

To my immense relief, it was never a problem, and I took advantage of any chance I got to get on the field. I made the plebe team and was even good enough to make the varsity soccer team as a sophomore and junior. For the spring season I went out for the plebe lacrosse team and made it. I did not play first string, but I was happy to make the team at all, because I had never played the game before or even been familiar with it. Life was good!

My parents made the long drive from Shreveport to Annapolis that August to visit me at the Academy for Parents' Weekend, over 1,200 miles each way. I was deeply touched that they traveled so far for Parents' Weekend, and I eagerly showed them around the Academy's beautiful grounds. They were awed, and I could sense their pride in me that I had made it that far. It felt good to earn that recognition, and I was determined to show that it was not misplaced.

"It is wonderful you are here," my Dad said, "but for you to graduate four years from now would be really special!"

The weeks flew by, and, before I knew it, September was upon us, and Plebe Summer was over. That meant two things: first, that actual classes were about to start,

*My parents visiting me at the Naval Academy for Parents' Weekend.*

and second, that the upperclassmen were returning to the Academy in force. Being a plebe meant that we were at the bottom of the pecking order, and while the upperclassmen were not mean-spirited, they certainly made that fact abundantly clear! Making the soccer and lacrosse teams meant that I played my way onto the training tables in the mess hall. If you were on one of those, you were not hassled during meals like the plebes who were not as athletic.

That harassment rarely crossed the line into genuinely hostile or demeaning behavior. We had each been given a small handbook when we started at the Academy, called *Reef Points*. It is a small satirical book filled with arbitrary and comical answers to questions like:

**Q:** *How long have you been in the Navy?*

**A:** *All my bloomin' life, sir! Me mother was a mermaid, me father was King Neptune. I was born on the crest of a wave and rocked in the cradle of the deep. Seaweed and barnicles are me clothes. Every tooth in me head is a marlinspike, the hair on me head is hemp. Every bone in my body is a spar, and when I spits, I spits tar! I'se hard, I am, I is, I are!*

Every plebe had to know the menus for each meal, the officer of the watch, the names of the captains of every athletic team, and many other things like the number of days until the Army-Navy game, Christmas leave, the Ring Dance, and Graduation Day. They were known as plebe rates.

We plebes had to commit whole extracts of Reef Points to memory, because at any time an upperclassman could quiz us on it. If you got it wrong, you were typically given a "come around," which was definitely not enjoyable! It required being in the upperclassman's room about half an hour before breakfast formation or before evening meal formation. I studied the handbook hard, and after a while, I was able to recite verses anytime someone tried to ambush me, and I always made a habit of knowing my rates. Impressed at my recounting and knowing there were easier targets, I was soon spared this hazing. Little did they know that an upperclass midshipman from Shreveport had sent me a copy of Reef Points shortly after my appointment was approved, and I was able to study it front to back for about two months prior to my arrival at the Academy. I can still remember some of those Reef Points many decades later.

Notwithstanding these unusual traditions, the biggest hurdle to me in those early days was the culture shock. It was like night and day compared to any schooling or lifestyle I had experienced before, even more so after transferring from a renowned party school like LSU. Everything at the Naval Academy was regimented, disciplined, and coordinated. Being a military institution, I had anticipated that they would run a taut ship, but expecting and experiencing are two very different things.

It took me some time to get used to how things were done there, and, like all young people, I sometimes chafed at the strict discipline. Starting from day one at the induction ceremony, we learned to march, do various drills, participate in athletics, and move from one place to the other very rapidly. It was relentless, with people screaming at us all the time, and nothing you ever did was right or good enough.

After only a few days at the Academy, I was utterly depressed! *What in the world have I done?* I thought. Maybe my fraternity brother Jim Thompson had been right, after all. I had a good life at LSU, and here I was a lowly plebe at the US Naval Academy. It took me a while to get used to the regimen, but eventually I began to embrace it, and this was made easier because I was not going it alone. I soon formed strong friendships with some other midshipmen, including Ken Fusch, Craig Clark, and Mike Murray.

We came from diverse backgrounds, which colored the way we saw things and the opinions we held. That sometimes led to heated debates on all kinds of subjects, but, at the end of the day, I learned so much from them. They challenged me to be a better person and helped me see the world in a new light. We always had each other's backs through the trials and tribulations of life as a midshipman, and they remain my dear friends to this day. One of the most important things we learned as plebes was, "Never bilge a classmate!" In other words, never do anything to make one of your classmates look bad.

We were also assigned a senior, or firsty, who showed us the ropes and to whom you could go if you had a major problem. Mine was a midshipman by the name of Tom Case, a capable leader who was our company commander in the third set (trimester). He was a good mentor, and I think his advice was a huge help throughout my time at the Academy.

I was also deeply impressed by the Superintendent of the Naval Academy, Rear Admiral Charles C. Kirkpatrick. He had served as a submarine commander who won the Navy Cross during the Second World War and ran the Academy from 1962–64 with incredible talent, integrity, and leadership. He frequently spoke to us at pep rallies or when we gathered in small or large groups. He always concluded his remarks by saying, "You can do anything you set your mind to do, and don't you forget it," which greatly inspired me! He was a fantastic role model whose palpable charisma and force of will taught me to set ambitious goals for myself and to work tirelessly to accomplish them. It is timeless, priceless advice: to believe in oneself and not to rest on one's laurels. I will always be grateful to him for that, and I encourage the reader to take strength and inspiration from his words, as well.

To no one's surprise, the Naval Academy also challenged us academically. Reflecting on my time there, I believe plebe year was the most challenging for me in most regards, including the academic side of things. The first time they posted the unsatisfactory list, my name was on it for the "Bull" subject of the history of Western Europe (we called any nontechnical subject Bull). It was particularly frustrating and disappointing to see that unsat list publicly posted in the passageway (hallway) of our company area.

Being unsat was a mark of shame against you, no matter what subject it was, and you would be held back if you did not improve it by passing that subject by the end of the year. That was known as turning back, and the midshipmen this happened to were known as "turnbacks." So I buckled down hard, even going to see the instructor for extra instruction.

It took time, but not only did I claw my way off the unsat list, I also made it onto the Superintendent's List of freshmen, the Academy's equivalent of the Dean's List. What I am saying is this: sometimes, you will find yourself in situations that are very different from what you are used to and can be hard to deal with. Remember that friends, faith, good role models, and some old-fashioned hard work can get you through almost anything, and you will learn a great deal in the process.

The Army-Navy football game my first year at the Naval Academy was a big deal. If we won the game, the plebes would get "carry-on" from then, which at the time was the Saturday after Thanksgiving, until Christmas leave about four weeks later. Carry-on was a Navy term that meant that plebes were not required to walk in the center of the hallway or passageway braced up in an exaggerated form of standing at attention and squaring every quarter at ninety degrees. It was another part of being a plebe, and it was another unusual convention that we had to endure.

That was a huge incentive for the plebes to cheer for a Navy victory. Not that we needed one, because beating Army is ingrained into every midshipman from the day one first walks onto the Yard. In the fourth quarter of the Army game we had a lead of 17–12 and Army was moving the ball and inside the twenty-yard line. Their quarterback threw a pass to the end zone, but Joe Bellino intercepted it and ran it back to midfield. That sealed the game for us. The class of '64 had carry-on for four weeks, which seemed like a lifetime! We won all four of the Army-Navy games when I was a midshipman.

Christmas leave was the first time the plebes had had the opportunity to go home since the first week in July. A group of midshipmen chartered a plane to Dallas for those who lived in North Texas and North Louisiana. My brother met me at Dallas Love Field, and we drove to Shreveport. It was great to be home! The first Sunday I was there, my dad took me to the men's Bible class at Noel Church, and I decided to wear my uniform for the occasion. After the lesson they asked me to read the prayer of a midshipman to his class of about two hundred people. (The prayer is in the appendix.)

We lost the national championship game to Texas on January 1, 1964, but the team played well. Navy's only two Heisman Trophy Award winners, Joe Bellino and Roger Staubach, both played while I was there. They were incredible to watch, and I was gratified to have them represent us. The year I went to LSU, Billy Cannon won the Heisman trophy, and he was the only LSU Tiger to ever win it until Joe Burrow won it in 2019. So in five years of college, I had observed three Heisman Award winners who were representing my team. I was in hog heaven!

I also happened to go to the Naval Academy in 1960, the year John F. Kennedy was elected president. I do not think I have to give a history lesson on that man and his importance, but the election was particularly close to our hearts as midshipmen. JFK was a Navy veteran (the first one to be elected president) who was proud of his service in the Second World War and very vocal in his support of the branch of the armed forces in which he had served. Kennedy credited the Navy for a big part of the leadership skills that he demonstrated.

Kennedy gave a speech to the plebes on August 1, 1963, at the Naval Academy, where he said,

> *"I can imagine no more rewarding a career. And any man who may be asked in this century what he did to make his life worthwhile, I think can respond with a good deal of pride and satisfaction, 'I served in the United States Navy.'"*

Those words, and others like them, greatly inspired us. We were huge JFK fans, watching him on television or listening to his speeches on the radio whenever we could. His leadership and magnetism helped spark my interest in national politics.

We learned when we returned from Christmas leave that the brigade would be marching in President Kennedy's inaugural parade and that he wanted a big Navy presence for the occasion. PT 109, which he commanded in World War II in the Pacific, was part of the parade, and the entire Brigade of Midshipmen, 3,800 strong, was to take part. We could not contain our excitement. We drilled hard in the preceding weeks, wanting our performance to be flawless.

President Kennedy's inauguration gripped the nation. His short, fourteen-minute inaugural address is still best remembered for that single line:

> *My fellow Americans: ask not what your country can do for you— ask what you can do for your country.*

This was a call to public service, to whom JFK called the "new generation of Americans—born in this century, tempered by war, disciplined by hard and bitter peace, and proud of our ancient heritage."

Now it was time for the inaugural parade, and for the Brigade of Midshipmen, it was our time to shine. However, what we did not count on was the inclement weather. The day of JFK's inauguration was very cold, snowy, and slushy. Of course, this would not stop us from marching, but it did cause one unforeseen problem. The galoshes we were issued were ill fitting at best, and as we marched, we inevitably trod on each other's heels, causing them to slide off our feet.

There was no time to stop to pull them up, no opportunity to adjust the fit, and soon many of us were missing one or both galoshes. Daunted but undeterred, we continued our stoic march in good cohesion, leaving a trampled trail of thousands of over-shoes in our wake. We all laughed about it later, but in the heat of the moment it was tense. Who ever heard of a military parade almost being disrupted by galoshes?!

A couple weeks after the Inaugural Parade, we had a long weekend or winter break. Our classmate in the Seventeenth Company John Klein lived in the Queens borough of New York City, and he invited several of his classmates to the Big Apple. It was my first time in the city. With its towering skyscrapers, it was unlike anyplace I had ever been before, and courtesy of the USO, I went to my first Broadway play, *The Music Man*, with Bert Parks playing the lead role. I remember it like it was yesterday!

The summer of 1961 heralded the end of my first year at the Naval Academy. That meant that there was a very special tradition ahead of us, an event sacred to the Naval Academy and laden with symbolism: the No More Plebes ceremony. When the graduation ceremonies concluded, we all hustled over to the Herndon Monument, a mighty granite obelisk standing over twenty-one feet tall on the Yard across the street from the chapel.

The objective was simple: replace a midshipman dixie-cup hat that had been placed on top of the monument with a midshipman dress cap, known as "capping the monument." However, the obelisk had been smeared all over with a thick coat of grease by the upperclassmen earlier that morning, making an already challenging climb all but impossible to do.

We all had to work together to scale its sheer, slippery surface, so we formed a human tower. We linked arms and pressed our backs against the monument, allowing our comrades to clamber over us and stand on our shoulders to repeat the process. The leaning tower of Plebes rose and fell, only to rise again, inching closer and closer to the top with each attempt. Finally, someone replaced the cap, and we all cheered. It was loud, chaotic, and hot, but incredibly fun!

More importantly, it officially meant that we were no longer plebes, and there would not be any more until the new class arrived in July. Now we were sophomores, also known as "youngsters" or third-classmen.

From then on, summers involved a mix of learning and leisure activities for the midshipmen. For my part, I was excited to see what was in store and happily joined Youngster Cruise. Not long after the No More Plebes ceremony, many of us packed our seabags and boarded the USS *Independence* (CV-62), a Forrestal-class aircraft carrier with a crew of about five thousand sailors. Commissioned just two years before, it was a marvel of engineering, and it took my breath away to experience first-hand life on a ship like that.

I had the terrific opportunity to be taken on a flight in an A3D Skywarrior, a strategic bomber designed for the Navy to be used on aircraft carriers. It was unlike anything I had seen or done before, and I was awed as we roared into the air to fly high above the ocean and the clouds. The plane and others like it had little resemblance to what my uncle Roy had flown almost twenty years before, but I could not help being reminded of him. I had actually hoped to be a naval aviator, but my vision deteriorated when I was a midshipman, and my eyes were not 20/20 by the time I graduated, so I had to pursue another branch of the Navy. However, from the time of Youngster Cruise, I was convinced that I had made the right decision in choosing the US Navy.

As well as learning what life was like on a Navy ship, the USS *Independence* also steamed into New York Harbor for the three-day Fourth of July weekend. Back in the Big Apple for a second time, our arrival happened to line up perfectly with a major league baseball series at Yankee Stadium. The New York Yankees were playing a home series against the Detroit Tigers, and there was no way on earth that I was going to miss that. The first day we had liberty from the ship, my buddy Ken Fusch and I hopped on a subway and headed to the game.

That was my first opportunity to see a major league baseball game. We saw Roger Maris hit home run number thirty-one of the sixty-one that he would need to break Babe Ruth's all-time home run record in a season. He broke that record in September 1961, and we had seen him hit one of those home runs. It was a great way to start my love of major league baseball, and I will never forget it. We also saw my second Broadway musical, *My Fair Lady* starring Audrey Hepburn and Rex Harrison. Ken and I still laugh about the wonderful time we had that weekend in New York City.

The beginning of youngster year came around quickly, and soon we were all back in Bancroft Hall studying away, and there were important events that came to define the next twelve months.

For the Army-Navy game that year I invited Margaret to come up for the game. She was in her freshman year at Newcomb College in New Orleans. I fixed Ken Fusch up with Margaret's best friend, Francye Willoughby, and she came as his date for the occasion. They came up on Friday afternoon, and Ken and I went "over the wall" illegally to see them at the drag house. (Midshipmen referred to their dates by the affectionate term of drags, and the residences where they stayed were called drag houses.) We won the game 13–7, had dinner at a Polynesian restaurant to celebrate, and rode back to Annapolis on the midshipmen bus. I met Margaret for church off the Yard on Sunday morning before making sure she left safely. All in all, it was a great weekend!

After the academic year had ended, I was officially no longer a youngster. Now I was a second-classman, or segundo. That summer involved a great deal of training and travel. We were split into three groups of over three hundred each, and we engaged in a rotation of activities. I was selected as our group commander. It was an honor but also a significant responsibility—overseeing several hundred young men as a young man was no easy feat!

*Margaret visiting me for the 1961 Army-Navy game.*

It was in Jacksonville that problems began to rear their ugly and unwanted heads. For one reason or another, the discipline in our group began to break down, and several midshipmen had become less professional. It was mostly small infractions rather than gross violations of conduct such as having too much to drink, not showing up on time, or the occasional inappropriate comment to superiors. However, even if they were minor offenses, they were occurring frequently and still had to be dealt with.

Because I was in charge of our group, I felt that I was responsible for trying to fix the situation. I approached the officer in charge of our group and asked if I could attempt to sort out the situation before it got out of hand. Thankfully, he decided to let me try. He called a meeting of all the midshipmen in our group, introduced me, and left the auditorium.

As I stood before them. I could feel their eyes on me, wondering what I was going to say. I had been pondering that myself since taking the initiative and requesting the gathering: what should be my approach, and was I doing the right thing? Even though I was the group commander, I was still a midshipman and one of their classmates. Coming down on them too hard or trying to pull rank could have backfired.

Instead, I chose to address them as classmates and to appeal to their sense of responsibility, rather than admonishing them. I made it clear that such behavior not only reflected poorly on us, but on the Academy and the Navy as a whole. There was nothing wrong with blowing off steam, but we represented the Naval Academy even when we were not on duty, and therefore, we should behave in a respectful and professional manner. However, I was careful not to mention names or list specific examples, so that no one would feel targeted or insulted.

It worked, and my classmates took my concerns on board. The number of infractions dropped considerably, and discipline improved for the rest of the summer. I was thankful that they had listened to me and relieved that my decision to call this meeting before things got out of hand had paid off. It also reaffirmed to me the importance of speaking sincerely and respectfully to people. They are much more likely to listen and respond to you when you do so.

# CHAPTER 5

# 5 STRIPER

It was only a couple of months into my second-class (junior) year when the country was rocked by what we later called the Cuban Missile Crisis. From their air surveillance, our intelligence officials had discovered numerous Soviet missiles in Cuba, ninety miles from our coast. For thirteen days in October, we watched, transfixed with awe and fear, as Kennedy and Russian President Nikita Khrushchev brought the world to the brink of nuclear war. At the time, it appeared as if the conflict was inevitable, and being midshipmen at a military institution, we were all too aware what this could mean for us if the Cold War became hot.

As the crisis dragged on, we learned that there was a contingency plan in place. If, God forbid, events escalated into a full-blown conflict, then our education would be expedited. We would still be the class of 1964, but we would graduate in 1963 and immediately enter the service to fight against the Red Menace. I do not think that there was a single midshipman at the Academy who was not anxious when we experienced that crisis. However, I also knew, if the time came, we would do our duty and shoulder our share of the responsibility.

It already felt very close to us at the Naval Academy, considering that the Navy was blockading Cuba. I happened to be acquainted with the daughter of the three-star admiral who was in charge of the blockade, Vice Admiral Alfred Gustave "Corky" Ward. I had met him a couple of times, and I was proud to know the naval officer who was responsible for the entire blockade. I can remember distinctly listening to President Kennedy's address to the nation and being very nervous about what he was going to say.

After almost two weeks of excruciating tension, the Crisis was resolved diplomatically, with the establishment of the Nuclear Hotline and the Soviets agreeing to remove their weapons from Cuba while we clandestinely did the same with our missiles in Turkey. I cannot praise President Kennedy highly enough for bringing that situation to a peaceful resolution. Cataclysmic war had been averted, and the country breathed a sigh of relief, but I am sure no one more than the midshipmen at the Naval Academy!

My junior year was perhaps the toughest for me academically, surpassing even the struggles I had as a plebe. It seemed as if we were learning more and more technical subjects, referred to as "Skinny" by the midshipmen. As the years went by, they were definitely more in my wheelhouse than the Bull classes like English or history, but they were tough. I remember electrical engineering being especially hard, and it took a frustratingly long time before I could decipher the complex diagrams or successfully complete a practical test. The importance of the topic was not lost on me; Navy ships were packed full of electrical equipment, big and small, but that subject regularly gave me headaches.

Though my studies could be a source of frustration during my third year at the Academy, sports continued to be a welcome escape. The Navy football team got off to a rough start early in the season, losing three of the first four games. Our fifth game was against Cornell, and our offense was not doing well at all. Our backup quarterback, Roger Staubach, came into the game and was instrumental in scoring a touchdown right before the half. Navy won the game 41–0. From then on, Roger was our starting quarterback, taking over from Ron Klemick. Staubach was a joy to watch, especially during the annual Army-Navy game, where we trounced them with a resounding 34–14 victory!

I was still playing soccer as a segundo, and I made the varsity team, again, though I was not part of the starting lineup. While I did not love the game as much as football, I still enjoyed it (maybe I was one of the few Americans to do so back in the sixties), and it always helped me unwind after a gruelling day of academics.

It was during my time as a junior that I finally had my exchange with West Point. The Army Academy had been founded forty-three years before the Naval Academy and had all the traditions and rituals that came with age. And, of course, our institutions had that timeless, friendly rivalry with one another, which meant we were more personally invested in the trip. An exchange with the Air Force Academy the previous year in Colorado Springs had been fun, but traveling to New York State to learn how they did things on the Hudson River excited me.

The busload of midshipmen and our overseeing Marine officer, Major B. F. Reed, Jr., drove up the coast and arrived at West Point on a Thursday. West Point was beautiful and had many more acres of land than the relatively small footprint of the Naval Academy. In addition to attending some of their classes, which were very interesting, I also went out of my way to attend a Bible study with a group of West Point cadets and attend a service at their chapel, which was almost as grand as ours, on the Sunday before we left. I thoroughly enjoyed my few days there, and I was impressed by the professionalism, friendliness, ability, and integrity of the cadets. However, just like my time at the Air Force Academy, I remained confident in my decision to choose the Navy.

I was chosen to lead the busload of midshipmen, which like any leadership position, I took seriously. We had to be in top form, especially in enemy territory! One day while we were there, Major Reed gave me an order. I do not remember what the order was all these years later, but it involved the other midshipmen, and like any order, he expected it to be carried out. However, it is what he said after he observed how I communicated his order to the other midshipmen that Major Reed wanted something more.

"Don't just tell them that I want it done. Do not pass the responsibility on to me, take charge of it, own it, and get it done." I learned an important lesson. If you are part of the chain of command, regardless of the context, it is your responsibility to do your part and make sure the request is carried out. Do not pass the buck or play the blame game, but be accountable.

In the latter half of the academic year, a new opportunity came down from on high for any midshipman interested in seizing it. It was a chance to be considered for a Rhodes Scholarship: a postgraduate program to study at the prestigious University of Oxford in the UK. I had heard of the program, but truthfully had not given it much thought until that point. I was busy enough at the Academy, I had not seen an avenue to apply, and England was far away.

But now that avenue was open, and having never been one to let an opportunity pass me by, I quickly decided to test my luck and see if I could compete. A chance to study in England for three years after graduation could be the chance of a lifetime, and it would be an honor to be enrolled in such a prestigious program. The way I saw it, there was no downside to trying. As they say in hockey or basketball, you miss 100 percent of the shots you do not take.

After being selected to compete, I was nominated as one of five midshipmen whose names would be put forward by the Academy for the scholarship. I was proud to represent the Naval Academy in the Rhodes Scholarship competition. I would compete in the State of Louisiana. That was the first time I had been interviewed by a panel of such important people, but it would not be the last.

As our junior year drew to a close, choosing the stone for our class rings was an important decision to make, and every midshipman would get his ring at the Ring Dance. Each midshipman would have the privilege of wearing his ring on first-class cruise and all of our last year. Every graduate from the Naval Academy is very proud of that ring. Each has the United States Naval Academy inscribed around the stone at the top of the ring. On one side of the ring the Naval Academy crest is proudly displayed, and the class crest is on the other. At the bottom of the ring is an inscription: *Ex Scientia Tridens* (meaning: From Knowledge, Sea Power). Finally, the inside of the ring is inscribed with the name of the midshipman who owns the ring.

The rings were presented to us during Commissioning Week, or June Week, and they were just as beautiful as we had hoped. However, there was still one more symbolic step to go before we could claim them as our own, and that was the Ring Dance.

The Ring Dance is one of the most important social events for each class at the Naval Academy. It is a formal ball, where all the midshipmen of that class (and their dates) gather to commemorate their time at the Academy and to receive their rings. With a lovely girl on my arm and flanked by Ken, Mike, and their girlfriends, I went to the Ring Dance in my service dress formal uniform.

When we arrived, the rings were presented to us. In true USNA tradition, the ring was first given to our date, who wore it around her neck on a long blue ribbon, like a necklace. We all danced and celebrated our accomplishments and everything we had been through together. It was touching to watch Mike and Ken enjoy that time with their future wives. Their love for each other was clear, and I was happy for both couples.

As fun as the party was, everyone at the Ring Dance was impatiently waiting for the main event: the Christening of the Rings ceremony. Finally, when it was your time to step into the large replica of the ring with a binnacle filled with water, the deed was done! According to Academy legend, the binnacle was filled with water from each of the seven seas. It is a fine tale and emblematic of our connection to the ocean, though I do not know how much truth there is to this claim. One by one, the women approached the binnacle and leaned forward, submerging the rings in those worldly waters.

My date played her part perfectly, and she turned to me holding the glistening golden ring with a big smile on her face. I gently took it from her, dried it off and put it on. Now the rings were truly ours. We were wed to the Navy; it was the embodiment of everything we had strived for and everything we represented. I still have my ring, and I always have it on my left hand next to my wedding ring.

We had our usual summer of activities, and the Naval Academy had been saving the best for last. I was selected as one of five midshipmen from my class, along with an ROTC midshipman from Iowa State, to take part in a foreign exchange program. However, this was nothing like the brief trip to the Air Force Academy or West Point that I had been selected for previously. This time, we were doing an exchange with the British Royal Navy in Singapore for six weeks!

We flew Pan Am from Los Angeles via Honolulu to Singapore, which was a pale reflection of the modern metropolis it would eventually become. Singapore was then part of Malaysia, with the Honorable Lee Kuan Yew as mayor. The country had experienced an insurrection in 1962, and Kuan would later become prime minister of an independent Singapore in 1965. Today, Singapore is a good friend of the United States and a valuable ally, but at the time it was little more than a third-world country. When we landed there, we drove miles and miles through undeveloped territory before we arrived in downtown Singapore.

I reported for duty to the HMS *Albion*, a British amphibious carrier that was part of the Royal Navy's Far East Fleet. That would be my home for the next three weeks. By then, I was no stranger to naval vessels, but that was my first time on board a foreign ship. The Royal Navy has a storied history and a well-earned reputation for professionalism. I was excited to spend time with one of the world's great navies, and the experience did not disappoint.

I found the British to be excellent mariners, but the culture on board was certainly distinctly different from what I had experienced on our ships. For example, I remember clearly that British sailors ditched their khakis and dressed up for dinner, wearing what the Brits called the "Red Sea Rig": a uniform consisting of dark pants, a cummerbund, and a short-sleeve white shirt with shoulder boards; I thought it was a neat uniform. I was also surprised to learn that the HMS *Albion* had a happy hour in the wardroom. There is a strict no-alcohol policy aboard ship in the US Navy, so this was a pleasant change. The perk was not abused, and I do not recall witnessing any instances of anyone having too much to drink or disorderly conduct among the crew. I was included in this, and I enjoyed the occasional drink while I was on board at the end of a hard day.

I also had the pleasure of developing a good relationship with the commanding officer, Captain William Staveley, while I was there. He seemed to me, at the time, to be the stereotype of a British officer: high class, very professional, calm, and well-spoken with a penchant for euphemisms. He was a very good leader and interacted with me and the other Americans frequently and made us feel that we were a significant part of the wardroom.

One evening I was speaking with him, and the conversation turned to my future after the Naval Academy. I told him that I was one of five midshipmen in my class that had been selected to compete for a Rhodes Scholarship. As that conversation proceeded, he asked me if I would like for him to write a letter of recommendation for me. "Absolutely, sir, I would be most grateful!" I replied. His recommendation would not automatically get me the scholarship, but it would certainly put me on the map for consideration.

The three weeks on the HMS *Albion* passed too quickly, and before we knew it, we disembarked and moved on to our next ship. We spent the next two weeks aboard the cruiser HMS *Lion*, before ending our exchange with a final week on the minesweeper HMS *Puncheston*. Not long after I boarded the HMS *Lion*, two of us were in the wardroom with the ship's chaplain. As the cruiser got underway from Singapore for exercises at sea, the chaplain smiled and said something I will never forget: "Ahhh, there are two places for a ship to be…at sea or in Hong Kong harbor!" I knew right away that I was going to enjoy my time on the HMS *Lion*!

I was impressed with all three ships, and I really enjoyed having the great experience of sailing with the Royal Navy. Throughout history, that service was considered the "sister of the seas" or the "creme de la creme" of the navies of the world, especially when we were a young country. I learned a lot in a short period of time, and we experienced exciting events that showed how varied and multifaceted a career in the Navy could be.

When our five weeks ended, we disembarked back in Singapore. However, rather than head straight home, my classmate Joe Prueher, Tom Jones (the midshipman from Iowa State), and I decided to make the most of the situation and spend some of our leave in Asia. After all, our Pan Am tickets were open-ended, and it seemed a shame to waste an opportunity to explore that part of the world while we were there. When else would we get a chance like this?

Over the next week or so, we traveled from Singapore to Hong Kong (still a British colony at the time), to Bangkok and Tokyo before we went home. That was my first taste of the Western Pacific and Southeast Asia, and it was beyond anything I could have imagined. At the time, I could not envision anything more different from Shreveport or our country as a whole. The sights, the sounds, the smells, the food, the people, it was like we were explorers on a completely different planet. The only thing that was similar was the hot, humid climate...I was more than familiar with that from long hot summers in Louisiana.

Considering how much these places have developed since I visited them all those years ago, it now feels like a world lost in time. It broadened my horizons, showing me firsthand how huge and diverse our world is.

In Hong Kong I went to a tailor who had been recommended to me and had clothes made for myself, my brother, and my father (I had taken their measurements with me, because I had been told that tailor-made clothing was very cheap and well-made there, and I wanted to take them something). In Tokyo, I bought some Noritake china for Mother. I also bought some of the beautiful Chinese silk for my mother and sister, and Mother made dresses for both of them. I bought a beautiful bolt of golden silk for Margaret. We were not an item yet, but I thought she might like it. Maybe that was a subtle sign from the man upstairs that we were meant to be! Finally, we flew back home via Honolulu, where we relaxed for a couple of days on the pristine sands of Waikiki Beach. What an unforgettable adventure!

After the wonderful experience of a first-class cruise with the Royal Navy, I went back to Shreveport for the rest of my leave. As always, I enjoyed my time in Shreveport. As they say, you can travel the world over, but there is no place like home! One August evening, I was enjoying dinner at the officers' club at Barksdale Air Force Base, which was across the Red River in Bossier City. A member of the staff approached me and informed me that I had a call from home, which was the first time that had ever happened. My dad said that I had received a call from the Naval Academy, and they asked me to return the call as soon as possible. I thanked him for letting me know, and as soon as we hung up, I immediately called the Naval Academy. I had no idea what they wanted, and as I talked to them, I realized that it was terrifically good news. The call was to inform me that I had been selected to be the deputy brigade commander when I reported back to the Naval Academy for the fall set. That was the number-two position in the Brigade of Midshipmen, second only to the brigade commander, who was to be Walt Kesler. (My position is now referred to as the brigade executive officer.)

Walt Kesler's appointment did not come as a surprise to anyone. He was the best of us, standing number one in our class by a significant margin. He was an outstanding midshipman and a role model for everyone in the brigade. His rank was midshipman captain, the only one to wear the coveted six stripes. My rank was midshipman commander and I was one of three, along with the two regimental commanders, who wore five stripes. I was highly honored to be selected for that position, and it was a genuine pleasure to work with Walt. It was the culmination of countless hours of study, taking exams, drilling, leading, and dedication to the values that the Naval Academy espoused. I was excited to see what life as a first-classman would bring.

*Brigade of midshipmen staff officers.*

At that time, there were three sets of stripers first-class year. One was the fall set, which started when we got back from first-class cruise and leave and went through the Army-Navy game. The second set was the winter set, and it went from the Army-Navy game until spring break. The first two sets were based on class standing, aptitude for the service, and leadership skills. The third set was dependent on those guidelines and how one performed in the first two sets. The first three years I was there, the brigade commander and the deputy brigade commander were never the same two people in the third set. Walt and I remained in the same positions in the third set, and we were delighted!

One night, Walt and I were back in our room, which was on the first floor of Bancroft Hall overlooking Tecumseh Court. As brigade commander and deputy brigade commander, it was required that we room together, and we were preparing for the next day's classes. We had one subject in common, so we were studying together. We had a lesson to read and several problems to solve for the next day's class. As I was just starting to begin the first problem, Walt finished and folded his book and put away his papers. I was amazed at his brilliance! He may be the smartest person that I had ever been around. Walt and I enjoyed a great relationship and had a lot of wonderful experiences our first-class year. Like me, Walt has always been a person of deep and abiding faith. After leaving the Navy, he would go to seminary and become an Episcopal priest.

I had also been selected president of the Naval Academy Christian Association (NACA). Chapel was mandatory back then, but midshipmen were given some flexibility in how they practiced their faith, like being allowed to go into Annapolis to attend the church of their denomination. I had been part of the NACA since I was a youngster and attended most of the meetings on the Yard, becoming good friends with the chaplains in the process.

NACA was an amazing group, strengthening my faith and offering solace during times of stress or difficulty. About twice a month on Sunday nights, they invited a diverse range of speakers to the Naval Academy. Some of the speakers included Vincent Godfrey Burns, the poet laureate of Maryland; Dr. W. Robert Smith, head of the department of philosophy at Bethel College; Bud Collyer, a well-known television personality; Raymond Berry, a star receiver for the Baltimore Colts; and Billy Wade, quarterback of the NFL champion Chicago Bears in 1963. I was very pleased to be president, because I wanted to give back to the NACA, an organization that had been such a significant part of my life there.

As president, I made an effort to extend the association's outreach to the other midshipmen, regardless of which year they were in or what flavor of believer they were. I also had a say in what we would discuss at our regular gatherings, a reminder of my Bible study group back at Byrd, and I had a hand in finding and inviting speakers to our functions. Not surprisingly, I pushed for getting more sports figures as our guest speakers.

Navy's football season in 1963 was outstanding. My senior year or first-class year we beat West Virginia, Michigan, Pitt, Notre Dame, Maryland handily, and Army 21–15.

We played for the national championship against the Texas Longhorns in the Cotton Bowl. They surprised us with their passing game and beat us 28–6. Walt Kesler and I saw every game during the regular season except the one against SMU, which we lost. The only two games we lost were in Cotton Bowl Stadium in Texas, so we were undefeated in forty-nine states. Our team captain, Tom Lynch, did a great job in leading the team our senior year, and he has done a superb job of keeping the team together through the years.

Sadly, my senior year was tainted by national tragedy. On November 22, 1963, President Kennedy, the first president with a naval background and an inspiration to me and millions of others, was assassinated by Lee Harvey Oswald in Dallas, Texas. That day I had been preparing for the arrival of my parents, who were again making the long drive from Shreveport to be with me for the annual Army-Navy football game that weekend. Just as they were getting to Washington, DC, they heard the news on the radio that the president had been assassinated.

My parents and many other midshipmen were just as shocked and saddened as anyone. A pall of disbelief and sorrow cast a long shadow over the Naval Academy. Even as we all struggled to come to terms with what had happened, my parents and I had another problem to deal with. The assassination had caused the game to be canceled, which meant my parents had driven all the way to Annapolis for nothing. However, First Lady Jacqueline Kennedy, composed even during a time of immense national and personal grief, intervened. "Jack would have wanted this game to be played," she said, and it was rescheduled for a week later.

Thankfully, the senior chaplain Captain James Reeves invited my parents to stay with him and his family on the Yard for that week on the street right behind the superintendent's quarters, which was a big relief for me. With that resolved, I focused on preparing for something I never thought I would have to do: march in the funeral procession of a president of the United States.

Because I was a deputy brigade commander, I was tasked with leading sixty-eight midshipmen on the solemn march from the White House to Arlington Cemetery on November 25, 1963. I suppose that it was honor to do so, but considering the situation, it did not feel like one. The streets of Washington were thronged, with some people even climbing into the trees to get a better view of the funeral procession. Many were crying as we marched in silence on that cold, sunny November day. All of us wished that this had never happened, but we were resolved to give that great man the sendoff he deserved.

A few days later, the delayed Army-Navy game was played, and I watched it with the brigade. My parents were proud to see me with the brigade staff as we stopped before marching into Memorial Stadium in Philadelphia. It was an emotional game, and, despite our grief, we were determined to do President Kennedy proud. It was a close, hard-fought game, but Navy honored his memory with a 21–15 victory. Maybe he was looking down on us, and if he was, I'm sure he would have smiled at our athletic tribute to him.

On a fine day in the spring of 1964, one of the senior officers at the Academy told me that President Lyndon Johnson's daughter, Lynda Bird, wanted to go sailing and was going to be coming over to Annapolis to sail with some midshipmen, and I was asked to escort her. I agreed to do so; however, she had a change of plans and never came. She may have heard that I was going to escort her and wanted no part of that! She may have also met Capt. Chuck Robb, USMC, who was stationed at the Marine barracks in Washington—they fell in love and married at the White House. In the years since, we have all become good friends.

My late nights of hard study paid off, and when graduation finally came, I was proud be in the top 10 percent of the class...barely! My entire family came to Annapolis for the ceremony, including my

Photograph by Don McCoy for *National Geographic Magazine*, March 1964.

*Leading the Naval Academy company at President Kennedy's funeral procession.*

parents, my sister and her family, and my brother. I almost could not believe that it was all coming to an end; what an incredible four years it had been. Dr. W. B. Worley had spoken truthfully at that assembly at Byrd, because I had learned and experienced so much. I was pleased to be leaving the Naval Academy behind me, and I was also excited to see what life had in store for me next. It was the end of the beginning for me. I was at the age of twenty-two by the time I graduated, but it was that milestone that truly made me feel I had graduated into adulthood.

As a graduation present, my parents surprised me with $1,000 (over $8,300 today) to use as the down payment for my first car. I was absolutely blown away by the generosity of their gift, as I knew that was not a trivial amount of money for them. With that cash I purchased an Impala for about $2,500 and drove with my brother, William, into DC to celebrate graduation.

I then drove up to Exeter, New Hampshire, to pay a visit to Walt Kesler before we were both deployed. His father was the dean of Philips Exeter Academy, the boarding school Walt himself had attended, and I was invited for a visit and tour of the school. I was very impressed with the place, and Walt was a living example of the high academic standards it produced. If I ever have a son, I thought, I would like him to attend a place like this. The next day his father drove us down to Boston where I saw the second major league baseball game of my life. It was the Red Sox versus the New York Yankees; you could not ask for a more competitive matchup!

The Naval Academy was truly a formative experience for me. My values of faith, sports, and public service began while I was growing up in Shreveport. However, my time in that venerable institution refined those principles, tempered my ambition with discipline, broadened my horizons, and clarified the importance of responsible and ethical leadership. I feel truly blessed that I was afforded the opportunity to go there.

I wish everyone could benefit from that kind of education, but it was the morals and principles I grew up with that were the most important. I do not think that I would have excelled at the Naval Academy if it were not for what I had been taught growing up. Sports, faith, friends, family, and public service are things we all benefit from, and if you embrace them, I believe you can lead a more fulfilling life.

# CHAPTER 6

# IN THE NAVY

After weeks of cruising up and down the east coast in my brand-new Impala to celebrate my graduation, it was finally time to get back to real life. It had been an amazing time, especially serving as best man in the wedding of my friend Ken Fusch, but now duty was calling. Public service waits for no man, and I was excited to officially begin my time in our great Navy.

Not long before I wrapped up my studies at the Naval Academy, I had spoken to our battalion officer, Commander W. C. Amick, about my future career. Even though graduation was looming, my Rhodes Scholarship application would not be resolved until December. Amick had been a submariner and convinced me that I should follow in his footsteps. Submarines were a great posting, and he sweetened the deal by saying he would help me with my selection. He made it clear that it would not be difficult for me to go to Oxford if my application was successful, and, in the meantime, I could begin my journey in one of the most prestigious career paths the Navy had to offer. He gave me excellent advice.

With Amick's help and guidance, I was selected to report to the USS *Blueback* (SS-581) in Pearl Harbor, Hawaii. It was the last diesel electric submarine the Navy built and one of the "B-Girls" trio, along with her sister ships, the USS *Bonefish* and the USS *Barbel*. I was thrilled to have gotten such a posting. Not only was Pearl Harbor a great place to be, but I would be serving on one of our nation's most cutting-edge submarines.

With the date I was due to report for duty rapidly approaching, I drove cross-country to San Francisco, with some leave in Shreveport along the way. From there, I would fly to Hawaii, but I still had a little time to explore San Francisco. I happened to arrive during the 1964 Republican National Convention, which was being held at a place called the Cow Palace, a big indoor arena that was a short drive outside the city. It was an election year, and being the politically engaged young man I was, I decided to go there.

Security has become much tighter since those days, and I managed to just wander in without anyone questioning who I was or asking for credentials. I would not have had a good answer for them if they had, so I just tried to look busy and important, which seemed to pay off. I moseyed through the throngs of applauding delegates who had come from all corners of our great country, taking in the spectacle and atmosphere of our democracy at work. It seemed I timed my arrival perfectly. While I was on the floor, Senator Barry Goldwater, the Republican candidate for president, took the stage to accept his nomination:

> *"Instead of meaningful jobs, our people have been offered bureaucratic make-work. Rather than moral leadership, they have been given bread and circuses. They've been given spectacles, and yes, they've even been given scandals.... Those who elevate the state and downgrade the citizen must see ultimately a world in which earthly power can be substituted for divine will. This nation was founded upon the rejection of that notion, and upon the acceptance of God as the author of freedom."*

At the time, with the Soviet Union an ever-present international threat and simmering civil unrest at home, I felt that Senator Goldwater made sense. I will always have the deepest reverence for JFK, and

I respected Lyndon B. Johnson too, but I had not sworn allegiance to either political party. I had sworn allegiance to the Constitution of the United States. Later that year, LBJ carried forty-four of fifty states in a landslide victory over Goldwater.

I did not stay in San Francisco for long. After arranging for my car to be shipped to Hawaii, I boarded a flight to Honolulu. I could still vividly recall the brief stay I had there on the way back from my cruise with the Royal Navy. There would be fewer chances to relax on those tropical beaches now that I was on active duty, but I was looking forward to being stationed in such a beautiful place.

After we touched down, I made my way to the twenty-square-mile military installation that was Naval Station Pearl Harbor. Now that I had arrived, it suddenly felt much more real. As a graduate of the Naval Academy, I was entering the Navy as a junior officer of the lowest rank, an ensign. At the time, it was customary for new officers to report themselves to their commanding officer's residence for introductions. Without wasting any time, I immediately set about finding the USS *Blueback*. My superior officer was Captain Don Wikeen, a seasoned submarine commander. Our conversation was formal, yet cordial: he was happy to have me on board, but he did comment on my unique situation.

Because of my Rhodes Scholarship application, and Commander Amick pulling some strings, I had managed to land myself in an unusual position: I was about to serve aboard a submarine, but I had never been to the six months of submarine school. Such a thing was not completely unheard of, but it was certainly rare. However, I had no intention of being a burden to my fellow sailors. I made it clear to Captain Wikeen that I would do my very best to learn on the job, and, in doing so, I hoped to earn the coveted Golden Dolphins, the insignia worn by qualified submarine officers (enlisted sailors wear silver ones). He officially welcomed me aboard.

The USS *Blueback* itself was an incredible feat of engineering and a testament to American ingenuity. Commissioned in 1959 and filled with the most modern equipment of the day, the submarine was 219 feet long and 29 feet wide at its broadest point. Its innovative teardrop profile allowed it to glide through the water with little resistance, reaching a top speed of over twenty knots when submerged. It was designed as an attack submarine, tasked with hunting down and destroying enemy ships and other submarines. At the time, I found this thrilling. No reasonable person wanted a war, but if one were to break out, we would be at the tip of the spear.

There was a crew of eight officers and sixty-nine enlisted men. Needless to say, things were a little cramped aboard. Because of that, sharing your bed when you were on duty, known as "hot bunking," was not uncommon. The officers rarely had to do this, but our conditions were far from extravagant. I shared a cabin (known as a stateroom) barely larger than a closet with two other officers. It had two fold-down desks and not enough storage space to go around, and as the most junior officer in the cabin, I often got the short end of the stick. On top of this, there were only two showers on the *Blueback* (one for the officers and one for enlisted men), and these were only available at specific times. I took full advantage whenever I could, but things could get fragrant in the submarine—and not in a good way!

My initial assignment was assistant engineer, and there was so much to learn and do. I was also assigned to be our submarine's Protestant lay leader. It was my responsibility to plan and conduct our weekly church services, if and when we were at sea on Sundays. On top of that, I was also our voting officer for the 1964 election, and I made sure that every sailor voted. My time on the *Blueback* was blessed with great comrades, and there were three men in particular I greatly enjoyed serving alongside: Dan Richardson, Peter Graef, and Dudley Carlson.

Lt. Dan Richardson was the navigator and one of the my cabinmates. A Naval Academy graduate, he was friendly, smart, and excellent at his job. I also had a lot of respect for him because he had earned both his golden dolphins and the wings of a certified naval aviator. Considering that my initial ambition was to be an aviator, I found it intriguing that he had chosen to leave that behind in favor of becoming a submariner. Nonetheless, I was happy to have him at my side, and it came as no surprise to me that he rose to the rank of rear admiral during his career.

The second of these men was Pete Graef, who reported for duty in April 1965. He was an ensign, and along with a third ensign, Bob McGee, we would all earn our Lt. Junior Grade promotion on the same day. We made a pact to always help the other one out if he were in a bind, and we always had each other's back. Later in his career Pete would become the commanding officer of the USS *Parche*, a special forces submarine.

Finally, there was the executive officer (XO), Dudley Carlson. The XO is the most senior position on a submarine after the captain. The captain is sometimes referred to as "the old man," though never to his face! Carlson was a truly fantastic senior officer. He was charismatic, approachable, knowledgeable, and just a terrific mentor for junior officers like me.

The fall of 1964 brought about my first nonlocal mission with the *Blueback*, when we cruised almost 1,600 miles across the Pacific to Wake Island. Yet it was in early 1965 that the Blueback and her crew participated in something both unique and exciting. Our submarine had been selected to take part in testing a new weapon, the UUM-44 Submarine Rocket (SUBROC) Missile. It was an experimental anti-submarine weapon carrying a small nuclear warhead. It would be fired from a submarine torpedo tube, rising to the surface and flying toward its prey. When it reached its destination, the missile would reenter the water and ignite its atomic payload in the vicinity of its hapless target as a type of depth charge, known as a nuclear depth bomb.

Our role in the test was to serve as the target ship. As scary as this sounds, there was no lethal payload. It was a test of SUBROC'S accuracy and reliably, not its destructive potential. We aboard the *Blueback* were happy to be involved. If this turned out to be a viable and successful weapon, it would provide us with a significant advantage against Soviet subs, which were regarded as a considerable threat. We were excited to play a part in this endeavor. Little did we know, however, that the mission would become a terrifying experience.

The test was repeated a number of times, with changes in conditions such as depth and speed. Everything seemed to be progressing smoothly, and, as planned, we adjusted our submarine for the next assessment. We took the *Blueback* to about four hundred feet below the surface, a significant depth for any submarine, and maintained a steady velocity of two-thirds our maximum speed. We were all at our stations, ready to conduct the next phase of the test.

There was a sailor on watch in the engine room whose duty was to traverse and monitor a myriad of different gauges and meters. Suddenly, water started spraying wildly in the room, mostly onto the shaft (the large pipe that goes through the engine room to the propeller for propulsion). The sailor, understandably, thought we had a serious issue on our hands—had the water pressure caused us to spring a leak? Wasting no time, he ran over to the loudspeaker and radioed the emergency to the control room.

"Flooding in the engine room! Flooding in the engine room!"

Next to a fire, water rapidly pouring in has the potential of being one of the most dangerous things that can happen onboard a submarine. The officer of the deck acted decisively, ordering an emergency blowing of the ballast tanks, full rise on both sets of planes, and full speed ahead. This was an extremely unusual protocol, but if we were in danger of sinking, we had to surface as quickly as possible. His order was heeded, and, with a lurch and shuddering of metal, water was immediately blown from our ballast tanks.

We began to rise rapidly at a rate of over fifteen knots, with the nose of the submarine tilted upward. At the time, I was desperately trying to get from my stateroom to the control room, and I remember as clear as day struggling up the narrow passageway that was slanted at a twenty-five-degree angle. I made it, but that was not the end of the disarray. No sooner had we surfaced with a big splash than we began to sink again! It was like a fish jumping out of water. We were scrambling to get the circumstances under control even as the *Blueback* descended to 50 feet, 100 feet, 150 feet. Finally, at 200 feet, and after what felt like an eternity, we stabilized the situation and cautiously rose to periscope depth.

With the panic over, we asked for a pause in the SUBROC test while we took stock of what had happened. We had a meeting in the wardroom and afterwards in the crew's mess to review the situation and have a good debrief about what happened and why. Thankfully, we had not suffered any damage, nor had the engine room actually been flooding. As it turned out, some tubing that had been attached to a gauge had split open, causing it to spew water onto the shaft. This was a not a life-or-death issue and could be fixed relatively easily, but we all understood why it seemed that way to the sailor when the source of the water was unknown.

We went on to complete the SUBROC tests without any more issues, but I will never forget that incident. For a short period of time, it looked like it would be curtains for all of us!

A few weeks after we returned from Wake Island, the time had come for me to complete the last stage of my Rhode Scholarship application. As I was the one Naval Academy applicant from Louisiana, I flew to New Orleans in December 1964 for the panel interview. As always, I tried to put my best foot forward; however, as I left the interview, I knew that it had not gone as well as I had hoped. I had worn my uniform to the selection board. The Vietnam War was already starting to become very unpopular, and being identified with the military no longer carried as much respect. Sure enough, in January I heard that I had not been selected: in fact, none of the five applicants from the Naval Academy had won the competition. While I did not get the scholarship, I do not regret making the attempt, and I encourage everyone never to let an opportunity pass you by because of inaction.

Now that I had closure about the Scholarship, I began to reassess my future plans. I was thoroughly enjoying my time as a submariner, and my studies to earn my golden dolphins were going well, but I wondered how much of a future I had on a diesel submarine. It was an amazing experience, and I was learning a great deal, but I was ambitious. I wanted to broaden my skill set and move on to even bigger and better things. After weighing the various options, I decided that I would apply for the Nuclear Power Program.

It was a prestigious but difficult course which, if passed, would qualify me to serve on any nuclear-powered submarine in the fleet, of which there were more and more. However, it was not as simple as just signing up. I had to apply and be accepted to the program. That meant having the infamous interview with Admiral Hyman Rickover. Admiral Rickover is a name that is not well known outside of military circles, but he was a very important man who has had a lasting legacy with the US Navy. He was largely responsible for modernizing our fleet and has since been referred to as the "Father of the Nuclear Navy." In 1965, this process was still well underway, and anyone who wanted to be a part of it had to be accepted into the Nuclear Program, which meant being approved by Admiral Rickover himself.

In the spring of 1965, not long after expressing my interest in signing up for the program, I was summoned to Washington, DC, to be questioned at the old Navy Annex on Constitution Avenue. Over the course of several interviews that went smoothly, I met captains, civilians, and commanders who worked for the Admiral. However, I had yet to meet the Admiral himself. This was standard procedure, and Rickover's interviews were notorious throughout the Navy. All kinds of stories circulated about them, like shortening the front legs of your chair to literally throw you off balance, abrupt dismissal if he didn't like an answer, and questions that were blunt or seemingly irrelevant (like telling the interviewee to ask his secretary out on a date). I was feeling confident about my chances, but I will not deny that I was a little nervous when I finally went to his office.

As I entered, I greeted Admiral Rickover, and he abruptly told me to sit down. Luckily, I was spared the uneven chair, but the interview turned out to be one of the most peculiar meetings I have ever experienced. Admiral Rickover thumbed through some papers on his desk, then looked at me, his large eyes inscrutable.

"Mr. Dalton, why are you so late applying to my program?" he asked bluntly. It had been almost a year since I had graduated, so it was a legitimate question. I replied that I had been competing for a Rhode Scholarship.

"Why did you want to do that?"

I gave him what I thought was a responsible answer about the broadening of my horizons and so on.

"What would you want to study at Oxford?"

"Philosophy, Politics, and Economics, sir."

"What do you know about the British education system?" He pressed.

"Very little, sir. However, I believe that studying at Oxford University would be a great experience, and it would be helpful to me in my Navy career."

"Have you read my book on education?"

"No, sir." I answered. I did not even know he had written such a book.

"You read it. Now, get out of here."

And like that, the interview was over. I was completely bewildered. Had I passed? Had I failed? Would there be a call back? Feeling uncertain and confused about my future, I returned to duty on the *Blueback*. I would learn a few weeks later that I had passed the interview and would start the nuclear program at the end of the year, which was a huge relief. I was also excited because it meant I could spend the time in between with the *Blueback*, earn my dolphins, and continue to serve alongside my friends. For the record, I never got around to reading Admiral Rickover's book.

My remaining time on the *Blueback* would be defined by one more major excursion outside of Hawaii. We were deployed to the Western Pacific (West Pac) and the far east for several months. We made port calls at Yokosuka, Japan; Hong Kong; and Subic Bay in the Philippines.

During that deployment, we patrolled the South China Sea, bringing us into the theater of the escalating Vietnam War. It was there that we counted ships, mostly Chinese, going into and out of the port of Hanoi, and we relayed this information back to our superiors. It was important to get a gauge of how much support the North Vietnamese were getting from their allies.

We returned from this deployment in June and resumed our local patrols around Pearl Harbor until September. It was about that time that, after being thoroughly tested (including firing a torpedo toward a target ship), I earned my dolphins; I was now a fully qualified submariner! The wardroom officers gave me a wetting-down party, at which my dolphins were put at the bottom of a glass filled with all different types of alcohol, and I had to drink it to retrieve them. It was a hoot! By then, I had also become the supply and commissary officer.

In September of 1965, the *Blueback* left Pearl Harbor to transit to the Puget Sound Naval Shipyard in Bremerton, Washington, for a scheduled submarine overhaul. As we made our way to the West Coast, Captain Ray Jones, our new commanding officer, decided that I should be the officer on deck when we were coming into port at the shipyard. This meant it was my responsibility to guide our vessel through the Strait of Juan De Fuca.

I had the conn and was transmitting information to the crew below. Captain Jones stood on the bridge beside me as I guided the submarine, on the surface, through the narrow strait. His presence there was a matter of procedure; the captain had to be able to step in if the officer on deck made a mistake. He did not interject or cut me off once, and as the *Blueback* came into the pier, he remarked how professionally I had handled the situation.

There were routine fitness reports from the commanding officer, reviewing your performance at that command. That happened every six months for an ensign, and it came annually once you were promoted. Captain Jones was a good leader who ran a taut ship, and he gave me a glowing report.

"John Dalton, in my opinion, is one of the finest, if not THE finest, ensign in the US Navy," he said. (That fitness report was conducted shortly before my promotion.)

This was high praise! He even said he would recommend me to be an aide to a flag officer (an admiral). I was truly honored that he thought so highly of me. Sometimes, I wonder how events would have turned out if I had followed that path, but as things stood, I was destined for the Nuclear Power Program and excited about it. Diligence, teamwork, and drive were proving to be the bedrock of my success in the Navy. My naval service was shaping me into a better man with every passing day.

That was the first time a submarine had ever been overhauled at Bremerton, and the overhaul was not due to be finished for a year. As I was scheduled to begin nuclear training in January, that meant my last few months with the *Blueback* were quiet. I tried to make the most of that idle time. I took a weekend trip across the border to Vancouver with a friend, joined the Elks Club, and shot my first deer. It was also refreshing that I could regularly attend church and call home every Sunday. Each week, I would call home on Sunday afternoon, and my dad would always ask me, "Johnny, where did you go to church today?" I knew I was going to get that question from him. These calls were luxuries that were sorely missed when we were beneath the ocean waves.

This relative downtime was pleasant, but as the wet and cold winter weather of the Pacific Northwest closed in, I was getting restless. The day I left was one of mixed emotions for me. I was certainly eager to begin the Nuclear Program, but I was also going to miss my friends, my shipmates, and, of course, the *Blueback* itself. The *Blueback* would go on to serve honorably until its decommissioning in 1990. It is the only surviving B-Girl and can be visited today in Portland at the Oregon Museum of Science and Industry (OMSI). Ironically, the sub was also used as a set for the famous submarine thriller movie, *The Hunt for Red October*, something all her former crew are proud of.

Before I left the *Blueback* in December, Graef, McGee, and I were promoted to Lt. junior grade. We had all spent the required eighteen months on active duty to earn our new half stripe, and receiving them together is something I will never forget. My navy career was going from strength to strength, and I could not wait to see what the future would bring. It is amazing to me that of the eight officers who served together in the *Blueback* wardroom, two would make admiral, and I would have the privilege of serving as the seventieth Secretary of the Navy. That may be a record in the history of the US Navy!

Leaving the *Blueback*, I drove down from Bremerton to the Mare Island Naval Shipyard in Vallejo, near San Francisco, to begin the first half of the nuclear training. Other than knowing the school was going to be difficult, I was uncertain what to expect. Oh boy, was I in for a shock. The first six months of the classes were strictly academic, involving long hours in the classroom studying subjects like nuclear physics, electrical engineering, and math. It was incredibly rigorous and difficult. It had been over a year and a half since I had last been in a classroom, and clearly, I was not in a scholarly state of mind.

About three weeks after beginning my classes, we had a test in each subject. I flunked all three! While I had sometimes found education difficult, that was the first time I had struck out like that. It felt like I had been punched in the gut. I was reluctant to call my parents, but I did call my brother, William, about it. I was in tears, and my brother, always a source of understanding, compassion, and steadiness, talked me through it. Just keep studying and try again; he said everything will work out.

He was right. I was never a star pupil there, but with his moral support and lots of late nights studying, I managed to pull through and pass the academic section of the course. It had been six frustrating months of stress and headaches, but I had done it. The only silver lining of that time for me was that San Francisco was so close. It was easy to drive there on the weekends for a date or a much-needed night out. Nevertheless, I was thankful when it was done.

The second half of the Nuclear Program was the practical part, and it would take me all the way across the country to Saratoga Springs in upstate New York. One of the three nuclear prototypes was located there, and I was looking forward to swapping the classroom for more hands-on experience. The practical training at the prototype turned out to be almost as laborious as the classroom back in Vallejo, but I forced my way through it.

As my training was nearing completion, I received terrible news from home. Sometime in November of 1966, my mother called me. She told me that my father had suffered a heart aneurysm and asked me to come home, because things were not looking good. My father had suffered a heart attack in 1954, from which he never fully recovered, and had been in poor health ever since. My mother did not need to say that it might be the last time I would see him, so I took emergency leave and rushed back to Shreveport as quickly as I could.

I was the last of our family to arrive at the hospital. My mother, brother, and sister were all there and had been comforting him the best they could. I was relieved that I had arrived in time, but it was clear that my father did not have long to live. I stayed by his bedside as long as I could, recalling all the good times: our fishing trips to Lake Bistineau and Caddo Lake, services at Noel Memorial Methodist Church, and much more. I was there for a couple days, and I wish that I could have stayed with him until the end, but I had to return to the Nuclear Program. My father, composed and serene in his final days, was remarkably understanding. As I was about to leave, he took my hand in his and said, "Always trust in God." Those were his last words to me. He was a good man, and I'm very proud of him!

A few weeks after I returned to Saratoga Springs, my father, at the age of sixty-seven, passed away. I was in mourning and not in the mindset to study. I failed to pass the oral exam but was allowed to retake it a couple of weeks later. Thankfully, I managed to pass that oral exam, but I was in no mood to celebrate. I officially graduated from the Nuclear Program in late 1966. Finally, that ordeal was over.

I was relieved to put it behind me and get back to sea, yet I could not help but feel disappointed by the whole affair, especially not being able to stay by my father's side for as long as it took. On top of that, the course had not been as I had pictured it. A part of me wondered if I had made the right decision, if this grind was what Navy life was actually like. Maybe the honeymoon period that I had so enjoyed on the *Blueback* was over. Upon reflection, I think that the Nuclear Power Program was where the seeds of my disillusionment with my Navy career were planted.

I did not have the time to dwell on those thoughts, though, for within days of completing the training, I was given my new orders. I was assigned to the USS *John C. Calhoun* (SSBN 630), a James Madison-class nuclear-powered fleet ballistic missile submarine based in Charleston, South Carolina.

After driving south to the Palmetto state, I did the same thing I had done in Pearl Harbor and reported to my new commanding officer. The *Calhoun* had two crews that would switch over every hundred days, and I was assigned to the "Gold Crew" under Captain Frank Thurtell. Like my previous commanders, I found him to be professional and capable. I was assigned the role of main propulsion assistant in the engineering department and was again chosen to be the Protestant lay leader for the crew.

The *John C. Calhoun* dwarfed the *Blueback*: 419 feet long and 33 feet wide at its broadest point with a crew of 130, including 13 officers. Like the *Blueback*, it was a new submarine, having been commissioned the year I graduated from the Academy, but it served a very different purpose. The *John C. Calhoun* operated in a strategic capacity, rather than a tactical one. It was equipped with sixteen Polaris nuclear missiles, capable of traveling 2,500 nautical miles to rain nuclear fire on the target. We were a component of America's Nuclear Triad strategy, alongside strategic bombers and intercontinental ballistic missiles, designed to deter an attack from the Soviet Union or Communist China. It was an altogether different mission than that of the *Blueback*, and I was excited to be aboard.

*Sailors on patrol on the USS* John C Calhoun *in 1968.*

Patrols would typically last ten weeks, during which we would prowl beneath the North Atlantic waves, never once coming to the surface. After seventy days submerged, we would finally surface and come into port at Charleston, South Carolina. The Blue Crew would take over within about four days and have a total thirty-day refit, which meant that we typically spent one hundred days ashore at any one time.

In order to make these long periods on land less tedious, I joined with a group of other classmates to find a nice place in town to live while in port. After some searching, we found the perfect place, an apartment on the second floor of the beautiful peach-colored residence at 11 Meeting Street, a block away from White Point Garden in the older, wealthier part of Charleston, south of Broad Street. Combining our housing allowances, we could comfortably afford it, and it became my home away from home for two years. Our group soon earned the name of the EMS (11 Meeting Street) Boys by other sailors on the *Calhoun* and my house mates' ships, and we became the go-to hosts for parties and other social gatherings, sometimes inviting the neighbors and some of the local southern belles. In addition to me, there were originally three other classmates: Geoff Kirkland, Joe Ince, and B. J. Haynes. Eventually seven lived there, including Bob Sutton, Rich Shapack, and Fred Tollison. Six of us were classmates from Annapolis, and Fred was a naval ROTC graduate from the University of South Carolina.

In the fall of 1968, Margaret, along with her parents, her aunt, and uncle came to Charleston on the way to visit her brother at Washington and Lee University in Lexington, Virginia. I showed them around Charleston and invited them to view our new Meeting Street digs. It was great to see them. I invited Margaret to join me for the Navy game in Annapolis that weekend, but she had other plans. At that time, I realized that she would be a great "catch," but, to be continued....

Years later in 2002, Geoff Kirkland, who originally found the well-located apartment, would reach out to all of us along with our spouses, suggesting a reunion to celebrate old times. Since then, we have met every couple of years. At the first reunion we stayed in a bed and breakfast right around the corner from 11 Meeting St. It is a wonderful group of great friends that I enjoy as much now as I did back then.

On the *Calhoun*, when the time came for us to report for duty, after the first patrol, we typically flew to Rota, Spain, where the Blue Crew would usually finish their patrol. After the standard thirty-day refitting, we took to the seas for our own long deployment. Spending ten weeks at a time under water, the days begin to blend into one another. In essence, our mission was always the same: remain hidden, keep moving, and be ready to strike the enemy in case the Cold War heated up. Because of this, I do not recall many specifics of our deployments, but we always fulfilled our duty with diligence.

There was one event, however, that I remember vividly. The Gold Crew had flown to Rota to take over from the Blue Crew, and before we set sail on our deployment, I decided to grab a bite to eat in town with some of my shipmates from the wardroom. I had a large plate of delicious Pescaito Frito: whole fried anchovies. Within a week or so of leaving port, I began to be unbelievably sick. I felt awful, and so much so that I was unable to stand watch. After examining me, the medical officer confirmed that I had contracted hepatitis. I was quarantined in my state room for a good while and had to eat by myself in the wardroom. That meant that the other officers in our ward room would have to stand watch in place of me, which meant standing port and starboard watches, six hours on and six hours off. I was very happy when that illness had run its course and so were they! When I was originally diagnosed with hepatitis, my skin was as yellow as a canary!

In terms of creature comforts, the *Calhoun* was more pleasant than the *Blueback*. For instance, there was plenty of fresh water because of the water purifiers that could be run freely with electricity provided by nuclear power, so we could shower whenever we wanted, and there was more space. However, I did not enjoy my time on it as much. The crew was, without doubt, professional and highly capable. And yet, it lacked the same sense of camaraderie and brotherhood. For example, while they were undoubtedly good at their jobs, I did not have the same rapport with our captain or the XO that I had had with Ray Jones or Dudley Carlson.

The main exception to this was Dave Stryker, the weapons officer. He was not a member of the EMS Boys because he was married, nor did we share a stateroom, but we became good friends during our two years serving together. We shared an interest in finance and investment and, in private, had both begun to question whether we, in fact, wanted to make the Navy a career.

That uncertainty had remained with me since the nuclear prototype program, a small but nagging doubt in the back of my mind. It was not that I did not love serving in the Navy, but it was all consuming, especially being part of a nuclear submarine crew. There was little time for family or nonmilitary friends. Tedious and bureaucratic red tape sometimes made the service trying, as well. These frustrations were genuine, but they had not tarnished my desire to keep serving, and I held out hope that things would improve with time.

Those hopes were dashed in 1968. It was four days before we were due to ship out on another deployment, when I again received heart-wrenching news from home. My sister, Margaret, and her husband, Bob Ratelle, an Episcopal priest, had been in Europe, taking the opportunity to enjoy a couple weeks of vacation there after his sabbatical at Oxford University. They had left their daughter, Lynn (my niece), in the capable hands of my mother. Lynn had been spending her summer days at a camp in Asheville, North Carolina. One day, during arts and crafts, she had complained to a camp counselor that she was feeling weak and was told to go lie down in her cabin.

She was found sometime later, dead in her bed. The autopsy indicated that she had died from acute myocarditis, a form of heart failure. She was such a sweet and very bright child, gone to heaven far too soon. I wanted to go back home for the funeral and be with my family, so I asked our new captain, Bill Cossaboom, for emergency leave. He listened to me explain the situation and sighed.

"I really am sorry for your loss, John, but we sail in four days. I can't replace you in that time, and I need you here. I'm sorry, but you can't have leave."

I could completely understand the situation. As far as the Navy and the mission were concerned, it was the correct call. Nonetheless, I was deeply hurt by the decision. I did not hold it personally against Captain Cossaboom, but this was the turning point. It soured me on making the Navy a career, and I decided to pursue a vocation where I could balance my work and private life. Not long after that deployment, I submitted my letter of resignation from my active-duty service.

The Navy did its best to convince me to stay. With the Vietnam War becoming increasingly unpopular, voluntary enlistment was down across all branches of the military, including the Navy, and they were desperate to retain as many enlisted men and officers as possible. They made me an attractive offer, but by that time, my mind was made up.

I would complete my service to the end with diligence and dedication, but after that I would start a new path. However, I did agree to remain an officer in the Naval Reserve.

Before leaving Charleston, I was a part of a mixed Blue/Gold crew to take the *Calhoun* to Mare Island Naval Shipyard on the West Coast to have its weapon component refitted from Polaris to Poseidon missiles. We went through the Panama Canal, which was very interesting. Though largely uneventful, it was a refreshing change of pace to work alongside some new faces for a while.

In December 1969, five and a half years after I had first reported to the *Blueback* in Pearl Harbor, I bid the Navy a fond farewell as an active-duty officer. Despite my share of negative experiences, my time in the US Navy had been overwhelmingly positive. I have no regrets about my Navy service, because I learned so much and met many wonderful people. It was an opportunity to serve my country and lead enlisted men by example. I lived and breathed the values of honor, courage, and commitment, both to my fellow sailors and to the country we all love.

The unvarnished truth is that the Naval service is hard, long, and sometimes thankless work. You may find yourself far from home and the ones you love for extended periods of time. Long stretches of boredom can give way to protracted phases of exhausting and stressful work, and vice versa. But it is worth it. You will forge friendships that last a lifetime and learn skills and values that will benefit you for decades to come. You will develop a new appreciation for the freedoms we sometimes take for granted and experience adventures others can only dream of. Even if you only serve for a few years, like I did, you will come out a better and more confident person than when you began, so long as you give it your all. I encourage every young person to seriously consider service in the military.

That would not be the only way in which I served my country, and the Navy would see me again one day! In the meantime, though, I had a thirst for knowledge and a budding curiosity of finance and investing.

It was time to see where this interest would take me.

# CHAPTER 7

# LOVE AND MARRIAGE

I wanted a rapid transition from the Navy to starting a new career, so during the last six months of my service, I decided to take the initiative and interviewed with a number of companies where I thought I might work, including IBM and Merrill Lynch in Atlanta (along with Dave Stryker). The interviews were informative, but I quickly came to the conclusion that my lack of relevant experience or education left me at a disadvantage. The employer interest was certainly there, but I needed credentials to back it up.

Therefore, I decided to go back to school for an MBA degree. I had some apprehension in making that decision since the "school" part of the Nuclear Program had left a bad taste in my mouth regarding academics, but I knew it had to be done. So, I applied to the Wharton School of Finance and Commerce at the University of Pennsylvania, one of the best business schools in the country. The results of my entrance exam were competitive. I did not do as well as I would have liked, but, undeterred, I decided to soldier on and push for an interview on campus. How could I have known that the man interviewing me would be an acquaintance from the Naval Academy? David F. Jones was a 1962 USNA graduate and had been in the seventeenth company with me. Our talk was equal parts catch-up and interview, and he gave me a resounding recommendation, which was enough to ensure my acceptance. I was going back to school!

I was due to start in January 1970, so, in the fall of 1969 I asked David if there were any other USNA alumni enrolling in Wharton at the same time as I. He told me about Don Smith and Bill Gregg, who were both classmates of mine from the Naval Academy. Don and I decided to share an apartment in Secane, PA, not far from Bill, and the three of us carpooled to school every day. While I felt good about heading back to the classroom, I was thankful to have a couple of friends on the journey with me.

The studies were challenging, but, unlike the Nuclear Program, I enjoyed the subject matter much more, and I took to it like a duck to water. I had some unspent income from my Navy days but not enough to carry me through my education. So, I applied for a VA loan and made use of the GI Bill to help cover the costs (another reason to consider military service, as it will help pay for a veteran's education). I also landed a part-time job with Walston & Company, an investment banking firm, which gave me a little expendable income as well as a small taste of the industry I was so excited to enter.

Though I was no longer in the Navy, I was still part of the Naval Reserve. That continued to be a valued commitment for me, as well as a way to stay connected to the organization I still viewed with great affection and respect. I participated in training and other events on a regular basis and became friends with my instructor. Like me, he was an avid baseball fan, and his company had four season tickets for the Philadelphia Phillies at Connie Mack Stadium.

The problem was, the Phillies were "cellar dwellers" who were typically near the bottom of the National League standings, and the stadium was in a rough area of the city. That meant he was hard-pressed to make use of all four tickets, and rather than let them go to waste, he told me that I could have them anytime I wanted. Being a cash-strapped student with a love of baseball, this was a real plum for me. Sure, they may not have been as good as the Yankees or the Red

Sox, but they were a spirited team of underdogs, and watching them play was a thrill.

I also saw the last game ever played at Connie Mack Stadium. The Phillies were playing the Montreal Expos, and the winner of the game avoided last place of the National League, or the cellar. You would have thought it was game seven of the World Series. The stadium was packed and the Phillies won the game and avoided the cellar. The fans ransacked the stadium, and I had a souvenir for many years, a piece of the seat that I was sitting in, but it was lost in one of our moves.

The first semester flew by, and, before I knew it, it was already summer. It was a busy time, with both summer school and a two-week active-duty engagement with the Naval Reserve on board a submarine. By the time mid-August came around, however, I finally found myself with some free time on my hands, so I decided to drive back home, making a stop along the way to visit my brother in Meridian, Mississippi.

On May 27, 1967, William had married a former high school classmate of mine from Byrd, Pam Stewart, and I had not seen him much since their wedding, where I had served as his best man. As always, it was great to catch up with him. Before I was there, he invited me to go to an exhibition football game with him and Pam. It was the New Orleans Saints versus the Boston (now New England) Patriots, and it promised to be an excellent matchup. Of course, there was no way that I was going to miss a game like that, and I asked if I could bring a guest, to which he happily agreed. I knew that Margaret Ogilvie was a big Saints fan, so I invited her. Maybe God had decided it was finally time for things to get going and bring us soulmates together! At any rate, I called and invited her. She accepted the invitation and flew from Shreveport to Meridian to join the three of us for the game and the weekend.

As much as I enjoyed the game, that day was one of the most important of my life for an altogether different reason. We may have known each other since high school, and we may have dated casually and hung out as friends for years, but, for some reason, that was the first time things truly clicked between Margaret and me. She was captivating, and I found myself focusing far more on her than the football game, and anything that could take my attention from one of my favorite sports was a rare situation indeed!

After the game, we spent the rest of the weekend in Meridian, and Margaret drove with me back to Shreveport in my 1967 MGB. I was heading in that direction anyway, and it gave me the perfect excuse to spend more time with her. We spent almost the entire week together in Shreveport, going out every night and spending time with our respective families. We even went to a double-A minor-league baseball game together to watch our local team, the Shreveport Captains, play the Arkansas Travelers. Like before, I found myself much more interested in Margaret than the game itself, but it did give me a chance to express my newfound affection for her in a manner that was quintessentially John Dalton. Anyone who would go with me to see a minor league game with 232 people in the stands is my kind of girl!

That week, we also drove with my mother down to Alexandria, Louisiana, to see my sister, Margaret, and her husband, Bob. In hindsight, I think that was my way of introducing Margaret to my family as my serious girlfriend. They were anything but surprised; most of them seemed to have known it was a matter of time, *when* we would become an item, rather than if.

It was a magical week, and as it came to an end, I knew without a shadow of a doubt that I loved her. Unfortunately, it was time to head back to school, but I was determined not to let distance hinder our blossoming relationship. I knew that September 24 was Margaret's birthday, and from the City of Brotherly Love, I ordered a dozen red roses to be delivered to her. Margaret would tell me later that her mother had been home when they arrived, and had said, with a coy smile, "It looks like Johnny has made up his mind!"

Margaret's mother had always been in my camp, and I think she had been subtly scheming to bring us together since our first date as teenagers. She often invited me for dinner when I was in town, and it had been her idea for the family to visit me in Charleston when they were heading to Lexington, Virginia, even though it was a considerable detour. I know that she was happy for us and knew we were meant to be, but I also bet she was excited to see her efforts finally pay off.

Along with the roses, I also invited Margaret to come visit for the annual Navy Homecoming football game. She accepted, and I excitedly awaited her arrival over the next several weeks. It was a close game, but Navy lost to the heavily favored Pittsburgh Panthers 10–8. We spent another incredible few days together. By now I had made up my mind: no more playing the field; Margaret was the one for me. As the long weekend drew to a close, I knew what I had to do. I got down on one knee and asked Margaret if she would marry me...and she said yes!

We may have known each other for years, but our actual romance was a whirlwind, and our engagement would be no different. Margaret and I did not want to waste any time, so we agreed to marry during the Christmas break. We called our families to share the big news, and everyone was so excited and happy for us. Margaret's father, Buck, picked up the phone after we had told Margaret's mother, Carolyn, the good news, but he was confused and asked, "Wait a minute, are y'all already married?" We were not, but it would have been better for his pocketbook if we had already completed the marital process. Cleary, it seemed everyone knew that we were meant to be together before we did. Still, as they say, better late than never!

There was one person who was completely clueless, though. I had been friends with Margaret's brother Bucky since high school, and we had stayed in touch since graduation all those years before. I called him to tell him I was getting married and wanted to invite him to be one of my groomsmen. Excited, Bucky congratulated me and asked who the lucky lady was. His shock when I said, "Your sister," was absolutely priceless!

Margaret went back to Shreveport the next day, but now that we were engaged, we needed a place to live in or near Philadelphia. I invited Margaret back to Philly for the Thanksgiving weekend. We would enjoy

Thanksgiving on Thursday, search for an apartment all day on Friday, and go to the Army-Navy game on Saturday. Margaret and I found the ideal apartment, but there was some concern about whether we could rent it or not. On Saturday, at the game, Navy was ahead 11–7 in the fourth quarter, but Army was marching toward our end zone. Navy called timeout and Margaret said, out of the blue, "I *so* hope we can get that apartment!"

"Right now, I don't give a *damn* about that apartment!" I replied, almost in disbelief that she was focusing on that during such a tense moment in the game. Fortunately, we got a turnover, and we beat Army 11–7. That was one of the only two games we won that year and I credited Margaret with the win! We also got the apartment the next day, so all was well. Life was good!

Our big day was January 2, 1971, which did not give us much time to prepare. However, with great help from our families, we managed to get everything organized in just two short months. One thing we had not counted on was that the rehearsal dinner was on New Year's Day, the same day as all the football bowl games. Unfortunately for us, LSU was playing in the Orange bowl, which meant that a couple of the more rabid fans opted to stay home and watch the game rather than join us for the rehearsal dinner. I could not be too upset; had I been in that situation, I might have considered the same thing.

We had a large wedding, which took place at the First Presbyterian Church. My brother-in-law, Bob Ratelle, and Dr. Frank Alexander, senior minister at First Presbyterian, officiated. My brother, William, was my best man. The moment Bob pronounced us husband and wife still stands among the happiest times of my life.

The reception followed at the Shreveport Country Club, and while the church had been full, many more friends joined us for the party. We were touched that so many had come to wish us well. By the time it was over, Margaret and I were very happy, and we thought everything was perfect and would not have changed a thing!

*Our wedding on January 2, 1971.*

For our honeymoon, we drove to the Grand Hotel near Mobile in Point Clear, Alabama, a beautiful, luxurious hotel overlooking Mobile Bay. It was not easy on my bank account, but I wanted to spare no expense. By chance, George Wallace, the segregationist four-term governor of Alabama, was honeymooning there with his second wife. It was interesting to see him there on his honeymoon at the same time.

We had a truly wonderful honeymoon, and I wished it could have lasted longer. However, as much as we wanted to, we could not ignore the real world forever, and before long, it was time to get back to it. That did not mean that things were the same, though. Now that we had tied the knot, there would be no more living apart. We drove back to Philadelphia and moved into a new apartment near Swarthmore College, while I attended my fourth and final semester at Wharton.

On the way back to Philadelphia, I made detours for a number of interviews. I understood that school would be over before long and hoped to have the opportunity to begin work shortly after graduation. The interviews included a Houston regional investment banking firm and Wachovia Bank in Winston Salem, North Carolina, among others. Some interviews went well, others less so: in Winston Salem, I was apparently taken out of consideration because they thought I was too sleepy in the interview. Those little missteps aside, most of them went well, and as graduation inched closer, I had narrowed my selection down to two excellent options: McKinsey and Goldman Sachs.

Goldman Sachs was more relevant to my personal interests in finance and investment, but McKinsey was (and remains) a very prestigious consulting firm with an exciting opportunity. I was blessed to have received offers from both of them, and for a while, I was fence-sitting, unsure of which opportunity to take. Goldman took the initiative, and I spoke with Tommy Walker, a partner in their Dallas office where I would be working. He gave me an absolutely convincing sales pitch, and, by the time we had finished talking, he had sold me that Goldman Sachs was the right place for me to be.

Once back in Philadelphia, I took Margaret to meet my friend the Reverend Rick Lobs. I had met Rick in January 1970 after I visited his church, the Church of the Atonement in Morton, PA, where he was the rector. Later that week he left a nice note at my apartment thanking me for visiting his church, and I rendezvoused with him at the church the following week. We were about the same age and shared a number of interests, and we quickly became good friends.

Margaret had been reared a Presbyterian, and I was a Methodist, but something about that church and Rick's interpretation of our faith inspired us. We decided to go to the inquirers' class and were confirmed as Episcopalians soon thereafter. To celebrate this and say thank you, the first dinner guests we had in our new apartment were Rick and his wife, Donna. We became close friends and did a lot of things with them. Rick and Donna have been wonderful friends since then, and we would later ask Rick to be the godfather of our firstborn son.

With my new career lined up and my education at Wharton coming to an end, Margaret and I still had some time to indulge in something both of us had wanted to do for a long time. Selling her Chevy Malibu to scrape together a down payment on a new car, we took a flight to London for a vacation around Europe. We had ordered a Volvo to be picked up in London, and over the course of three weeks, traveled from London to France, Switzerland, Italy, Austria, Germany, and Sweden.

It was an incredible journey, from Buckingham Palace and the Louvre all the way to the shores of the Baltic Sea. It was not exactly the lap of luxury, though, as we were following the book *Europe on 5 Dollars a Day*. For the majority of those twenty-one days, we stuck to that budget (approximately $32.50 in today's money), proving that it was indeed possible, if you lived frugally. While we spent the occasional night bedding down in our new Volvo, we usually managed to find cheap hotels with complimentary breakfasts as we traveled Western Europe's beautiful countryside and experienced its diverse cultures. However, one time in Italy, we decided to splurge on a rosemary-filled rotisserie chicken and wine for a picnic on the Appian Way. We have called it "Appian Way Chicken" ever since!

When Margaret and I were touring in Rome, we ran into Ann and Cedric Lowry, who were very good friends of Margaret and Bob in Alexandria, LA. We were excited to see them, and our visit was immensely enjoyable. We learned that they were going to be in Florence at the same time we were, and they invited us to dinner at restaurants in both Rome and Florence. That was very thoughtful and generous of them, and it certainly beat finding cheap eateries on five dollars a day!

As the three weeks in the old world drew to a close, we drove to Sweden to turn in the car for shipment back to the states, and we headed home via London. It had been a great trip, and it was incredible to see a swath of Europe I had never experienced before, as well as not having to worry about reporting for duty aboard a submarine afterward.

Not long after getting back to the States, it was time to start the exciting adventure with Goldman Sachs. Though the position was in their Dallas office, I was first due to attend eight months of training in New York, so Margaret and I found an apartment on Staten Island. I officially started my new career on July 5, 1971. I was married, starting a new career, and ready to forge my own path forward to success.

The eight months of training Goldman Sachs gave us were intensive, but I was used to working under pressure thanks to the Naval Academy and my Navy days. Meanwhile, while I learned and grew into my new career, Margaret took a job with Oppenheimer as a "floater," someone who filled in when others were unavailable. It made sense not to get too settled into New York, since we both knew it was a temporary situation. Still, we enjoyed our time on Staten Island, and I got a kick out of commuting on the ferry every day. I guess you can take the man out of the Navy, but you can never truly take the Navy out of the man! We spent most of our weekends in Manhattan being tourists.

During my training, I met someone who would become one of my closest and dearest friends. Rex Jennings and I were in much the same boat: we were both recently married, both new to Goldman Sachs and both destined for the Dallas office once our time in New York City was finished. We stuck close together during the training program, and I was surprised how quickly we hit it off on a personal level. Our friendship swiftly graduated from mere colleagues to genuine friends, and we would spend time together outside of work with Margaret and his wife, Sue. With him by my side as my partner in crime, I knew that I had made the right choice. In the training program, I also became well acquainted with our good friend, Ralph Severson.

Even though I had been promoted to lieutenant commander in the Navy Reserve, due to the long hours and hard work of the training program at Goldman Sachs, I decided to resign my commission. That was a hard decision to make, but I had no choice, since there simply were not enough hours in the day to do everything, and I knew that I had to focus on my career. The Navy had been very good to me, and I loved the service and the wonderful experiences it had given me. I thought that was the end of my time with the Navy, but little did I know what the future had in store for me....

Despite the intensity of the training, our time in New York flew by, and in March of 1972, it was time to pack our bags and head south to the Lone Star State. It was a good thing we moved then. Margaret was now pregnant with our first child, so we were in need of a bigger, proper home. Our friends Rex and Sue moved close by, and all four us looked forward to beginning the new chapter of our lives in earnest.

I was partnered with Ed Allbritton, a co-worker with more experience at Goldman than I. His region was east Texas, and, as I was a native, I was given Louisiana as my territory. From New Orleans and Baton Rouge to Alexandria, Monroe, Lake Charles and, of course, Shreveport, I made frequent business trips up and down my home state on behalf of the firm. That worked just fine for me, because it also afforded me plenty of opportunities to drop in on family and friends. I may not have lived there anymore, but I loved the fact that Louisiana remained such a big part of my personal and professional life.

The work was tough, but rewarding. Ed Allbritton was a professional and hardworking partner who had high expectations and expected me to pull my weight. To start with, I was earning a respectable $16,000 a year, and in 1973 I became eligible for commissions. That same year, I spoke with Ed and our boss, Sam Beard, about how we would split our commissions. Previously, Ed had said he wanted me to double my income from Louisiana. That was going to be a challenge, but I believed it was doable. In return, I expected an even 50/50 split of our commissions. Our supervisor, Sam Beard, agreed with this equitable arrangement, and Ed and I continued to work well together.

Our arrival in Dallas coincided with the region acquiring its own baseball team: the Texas Rangers (formerly the Washington Senators). That meant we were lucky enough to attend their opening game against the Milwaukee Brewers. Coming from a business trip in Louisiana, I met Margaret, Rex, and Sue at Love Field Airport and went straight to the game, which the Rangers won. That was the first of many Ranger games we attended, as Goldman Sachs covered part of the costs for season tickets. Not only that, the seats were absolutely terrific: three rows back and close to home plate, between it and the on-deck circle. Rex and I went to Rangers games whenever we could. I was in Hog Heaven!

On July 6, 1972, the big day finally arrived. Margaret had a long and difficult labor, and I was with her for most of the time to lend whatever support I could, but I could not go into the operating room. Close to midnight, she finally delivered a baby boy. Relieved that the ordeal was over for Margaret and overjoyed at the birth of our son, I called my mother and Margaret's parents to tell them the good news. They were similarly ecstatic to hear about their newest grandchild, and my mother asked if I had seen the baby. I told her I had not. Without a skipping a beat, she said she would see about getting over to Dallas with Margaret's mother, so they could see us and help us with our newborn.[2] We were excited to have them meet John Howard Dalton, Jr.

Sometime after speaking with our parents, the OB/GYN, Dr. Richard Martin, came to see me in the waiting room and told me that John had been born with a minor defect. I was finally allowed to see our baby. John had been born with a cleft lip, a birth defect that caused an opening running from his upper lip to the base of his nose. The doctor informed us that he was otherwise healthy, and it was something that

---

[2] My answer to my mother's question had told her more than I realized at the time. Later on, she would inform me that she immediately knew that something was wrong when I told her I had not yet seen our son, but she played it cool as she did not want to alarm me. As usual, my mother was right.

could be repaired with plastic surgery. It was well after midnight; Margaret was in the recovery room, and the doctor and I decided to wait until morning to tell her.

Shortly after I had learned about the problem, I called Rex and asked if I could come see them. He welcomed me with open arms, as always, and I spent some time with them confessing my fears and anxieties about the situation. I knew that I could not relay those concerns to Margaret; it would not have been fair to her. She had been through a lot, and I did not want to compound any fears she may have had by heaping my own on top of them. Rex and Sue's support was invaluable, and they helped pull me out of an emotional tailspin. Sue was a nurse, and she confirmed that the cleft lip could be fixed with plastic surgery. While I was still upset and worried, that did give me a level of comfort.

The next few months were tumultuous for Margaret and me. I did not think that having a baby would be a walk in the park, but, when you are expecting a child, you, of course, want everything to be perfect. When it is not, it can be hard to reconcile the facts with the expectations. Despite these challenges, Margaret and I came through it stronger than ever, thanks to leaning on our faith, family, and friends. In particular, Rex and Sue, my mother, and Margaret's mother were always there for us whenever we needed them. My sister, Margaret, also drove over to Dallas from Alexandria to spend a couple of days with us, and as always, she was loving and caring.

Our faith was also something that gave us comfort. We were visited by our minister, the Reverend Ted Nelson, and he was very helpful to us. He was the rector of the Church of the Resurrection, where I was on the vestry, a lay reader, and a chalice bearer. We knew that God, in His infinite wisdom, has a plan for all of us. Even at that time, I knew in my prayers that we would make it through to the other side. And we did. We all go through trying periods in our lives, but I can promise that those three relationships (family, friends, and faith) are worth more than their weight in gold. If you cultivate those, then they will get you through anything that life may throw at you.

It took three surgeries over the course of about three years before little John's lip was finally repaired. Margaret sagely informed the plastic surgeon that she had an issue with producing too much scar tissue and was concerned it could adversely affect the baby, too. Despite those difficult times, John was always a happy, healthy, and outgoing baby. From day one, I was proud of him, and even then, I knew he was destined for great things.

On March 1, 1974, when John was about nineteen months old, we welcomed our second son, William Christopher, to the family. After the birth of John, Jr, we were hesitant about having another child: the doctor had told us that, while the odds of a child being born with a cleft lip were about one in a thousand, the odds of subsequent children being born with the same condition as their sibling were one in fifty! However, we very much wanted a second child and wanted them to be fairly close in age. Thankfully, William Christopher beat the odds. We were ecstatic to be blessed with another healthy child; however, Margaret and I decided not to test our luck again. Even though a daughter would have been a nice addition, our two sons were an enormous blessing!

After that rocky start in 1972, we continued to live an eventful and happy few years in Dallas, where I would work for Goldman Sachs until April, 1977. In 1975, I was making a healthy annual income. Considering that I had grown up on a railroad man's salary and then earned a rather meager wage in the Navy, this was a huge deal for me. I knew this was no excuse to spend carelessly, and I did not let this newfound good fortune go to my head, but it still felt good to have risen from such humble beginnings and now not have to live as frugally as before.

I felt that I had truly found my calling in investment and finance, and despite the stagflation that came to define much of that decade in American history, I made a good go of it. I was leading a happy and fulfilling life, and for a while, I had almost let politics and public service fall by the wayside.

Little did I know, but this was soon to change, with something as innocuous as a Dallas chapter Naval Academy alumni lunch.

# CHAPTER 8

# LUNCH WITH A PEANUT FARMER

Though I had left the Navy behind me when I bid farewell to the Naval Reserve, I was still an active member of the USNA Alumni Association. After moving to Dallas, I joined the North Texas chapter, which was conveniently headquartered in the city. It felt good to be connected to so many former midshipmen, regardless of what year we had graduated. We were all united by shared bonds, both with our time in Annapolis and in our nation's great Department of the Navy, and this fostered a strong sense of brotherhood. By 1975, I had been elected to our chapter's executive committee and had a hand in organizing the various events we would hold in that part of the state.

At one of our committee meetings in late spring of that year, we were approached by another alumnus, George Goodwin, who was a classmate of Jimmy Carter. He excitedly told us that Governor Carter was coming to Dallas to speak at the Texas American Federation of Labor and Congress of Industrial Organizations (AFL-CIO). Carter had just completed his term as the seventy-sixth governor of Georgia in January and was now one of the presidential candidates in the crowded Democratic primary. He was also a 1947 graduate of the Naval Academy and a nuclear Navy veteran like I was. So, even though he wasn't a household name yet, we were glad to host a lunch for him when he came to Dallas.

We held the event in the same building, One Main Place, as the Goldman Sachs offices, literally one floor above our office, which was very convenient for me. After the typical glad-handing and back-slapping that was always a big part of those occasions, Carter spoke to the chapter. That was the first time I had heard a presidential political stump speech in person, and I was immediately inspired by Jimmy Carter. Usually, you expect self-promotion and the touting of personal achievements in those kinds of remarks, and there was certainly some of that. It was also a comprehensive, courageous, and visionary speech including covering the energy sector and what he had accomplished as the governor of Georgia. Here he was in the Lone Star State whose principal industry was oil and gas. He said that it was very important to focus on all types of energy including solar, wind, and nuclear power. I was impressed with him. However, what I remember most clearly from his speech was his candor, his sincerity, and his humility. Several sentences still ring clearly in my mind to this day:

> If I ever lie to you, don't vote for me…. If I ever make a misleading statement, don't vote for me…. I want a government as good, as open, as honest and as filled with love, as are the American people!

Needless to say, I was sold! As a member of the executive committee, I was lucky enough to sit next to Carter at lunch, and there was nothing on the other side of him but the podium. I eagerly engaged him in conversation over lunch. Before that time, I truthfully did not know much about him, but as we spoke, it was clear that we had a lot in common: we were both southerners from humble beginnings, we had both been submariners (and experienced Hyman Rickover's infamous interview!), both Naval Academy graduates, and we were both men of faith and very family-oriented.

The Democratic primary was hotly contested that election cycle, including some more famous names like Senator Lloyd Bentsen of

Texas, Governor George Wallace of Alabama, Congressman Morris Udall of Arizona, Senator Birch Bayh of Indiana, Senator Fred Harris of Oklahoma, Senator Henry "Scoop" Jackson of Washington, Senator Frank Church of Idaho, Governor Jerry Brown of California, and others. Governor Carter had less than 1 percent name identification at that time. So, understandably, I felt like I had to address the elephant in the room.

"Governor, how are you going to break out of the pack?" I asked.

Carter thought about this for a moment, and then he responded with an answer that freed me of my doubts. He explained that his advantage was the fact that he was campaigning "full time," while most others were balancing their other commitments, be they governor or a member of Congress. He planned to campaign in all ninety-nine counties of Iowa, and he understood the agriculture business, and he spoke the language of most of the voters there. Carter also expressed a calm but unshakable belief that he would win Iowa and use that momentum to win New Hampshire, and that if he beat Wallace in Florida, and he thought he could, then the nomination was as good as his. Finally, he could connect to "Joe Six-pack" in a way that was unpretentious: Carter may have had a Bachelor of Science degree, with nuclear training, but he had also famously been a peanut farmer. He was sharp as a tack, and he could speak to people plainly and empathize with their needs and worries. That was all the convincing I needed, and as lunch came to end, we exchanged contact details.

I went home later that day, and I told Margaret, "I had lunch today with the next president of the United States. Governor Carter is going to win, and I am going to help him." I was as sure of that statement as I was of my own name!

That lunch with Jimmy Carter, while brief, had utterly persuaded me that he was both worthy of the office and that he was going to win it. The first half of the 1970s was a tough time for our country. From an inglorious withdrawal from the quagmire of Vietnam to economic and moral troubles from the Watergate scandal of the Nixon administration, our country was in need of new, principled leadership.[3] I believed that Jimmy Carter could provide that leadership, and I wanted to do whatever I could to help him win the White House. Shortly after the alumni lunch, I wrote my first-ever campaign donation for fifty dollars to Carter's campaign.

Life went on as usual for a few weeks after that. While I had thoroughly enjoyed meeting Carter, I had not seen it as an opportunity to get more actively involved in politics at the time. That soon changed when I was contacted by Chip Carter, one of Governor Carter's sons. Chip told me that his father enjoyed meeting me at the lunch, and he asked me whether I wanted to get involved in helping the Carter campaign.

I was excited to do so and asked him what I could do to help. Congress had changed the law with respect to campaign finance after the Watergate debacle. Chip explained that the campaign needed to qualify for matching funds in Texas and inquired whether I would be interested in fundraising in the state for his father in order to achieve that goal. I was definitely interested; if I could help Jimmy Carter secure the nomination, I would. I signed on as a volunteer for the campaign and was later named chairman of his finance committee in Dallas County. I have been a registered Democrat ever since.

That was the first time I had been so actively involved in national politics. While I was confident that Jimmy Carter had a real shot at winning, I knew that it would be an uphill battle to secure the Democratic nomination. Senator Lloyd Bentsen had thrown his hat in the ring, which meant that most Texas Democrats were rallying around his flag. Nonetheless, the calm but quiet optimism of Carter's campaign was infectious, and I set about doing my best to help him raise funds.

---

[3] Scott Caven, a co-worker at Goldman Sachs, was a member of Nixon's Committee to Re-Elect the President (CREEP). After the Saturday Night Massacre in 1973, I bet him twenty dollars that Nixon wouldn't last another twelve months. Not only was I right, but when I won the bet, he paid me in four six-dollar Texas Rangers tickets, which was fine with me!

Our first big break came when I hosted a fundraiser at the new Dallas/Fort Worth International Airport. It had only recently opened and was considered cutting edge and modern at the time. We held the event at one of its hotels and attracted a wide range of interested people from all over the Dallas/Fort Worth area. Many of the guests donated, but the late Roger Horchow, founder and CEO of the Horchow Collection, was the biggest contributor of the day, writing a $1,000 check to the Carter campaign (almost $5,000 today). We still had a long way to go, but it was a strong start for us. We raised about $20,000 at that event, which was a significant fundraiser at that early point in the campaign.

Earlier that year, and with Senator Bentsen's encouragement, a law had been passed in the Texas Legislature. It mandated that, in order to get on the ballot in each of the thirty-one Texas senatorial districts, a candidate was required to have a petition signed by 1 percent of each district's voters who had participated in the Democratic primary in 1972. This was a shot across the bow to the other Democratic candidates campaigning in the Lone Star State, including ours, because it threatened to suppress the ability of Bentsen's competitors to compete and be represented. It was too big a hill to climb for all of the candidates except Lloyd Bentsen and George Wallace. Wallace had run for President in 1972, and, of course, Bensten had organizations in place in Texas.

We had to act quickly, or our momentum and everything we were working for could be lost. For my part, I grabbed a USNA Alumni directory and wrote a letter to every single USNA alumnus in Texas (This was long before email was available!). I was not asking for their vote, but I told them that Governor Jimmy Carter, one of our own, was running. In the spirit of representation and the democratic process, I implored them to make their voices heard so that, in turn, Carter could also be heard. In a gesture of USNA loyalty that even now warms my heart, many of them signed the petitions; Jimmy Carter would be on the ballot in all thirty-one districts. I was so proud that our alumni contributed to this, and it meant that we could keep campaigning without worrying about some roadblock undoing all of our hard work.

As the months passed and Carter's primary campaign gained traction, I was devoting more time to the campaign and less to putting in the legwork at Goldman Sachs. I knew this was unfair to my partner, Ed, especially after I had stood my ground on getting an even split on the commissions. In the spirit of fairness, I went to him and said that, because I was now dividing my time and doing a bit less at Goldman Sachs, he deserved a bigger piece of the pie. In the end, we settled on a 60/40 split in his favor.

The Democratic primary occurred on a Saturday in early June, and Carter cruised to victory with more than 100 of the 130 available delegates. On the Monday after the primary, I had a call from Jess Hay, a senior member of the Texas Democrats who previously had been working on Bentsen's campaign. He suggested that we get together to plan for the fall. We had a great meeting and attempted to unite the Democratic party behind Jimmy Carter.

Almost a year to the day after I had met Jimmy Carter, the 1976 Democratic National Convention (DNC) was held in New York City at Madison Square Garden. Thanks to the hard work of everyone on the campaign and Carter's astute and forward-thinking strategy, he had overcome all his opponents to become the presumptive nominee, including the resounding primary victory in Texas. I felt honored to have been a part of that effort.

As part of that victory, I was chosen as one of the delegates from Texas to the Democratic National Convention in July. I flew back to the Empire State with Margaret to attend the convention, arriving a few days before it was to start. We stayed at the Pierre Hotel, most notable for being Nixon's preferred place to stay when he visited the city. After a couple of days on the town with Margaret, we rendezvoused with the other Texas Democrats at the Essex House Hotel across from the southside of Central Park and attended the convention the next day. We especially enjoyed going to events with Jess and Betty Jo Hay.

That was the first time I had gone to a political convention since I had wandered into the Goldwater nomination more than ten years prior; at least this time I was on the list, and I had the proper credentials. It was a terrific four-day event. The real standout moments, however, other than Carter's acceptance speech, were the keynote speakers: Senator John Glenn and Congresswoman Barbara Jordan. John Glenn, the famous astronaut, spoke first, then it was Barbara Jordan's turn. The Congresswoman from Texas' Eighteenth District was the first-ever African American woman to be a keynote speaker at a convention, Republican or Democrat, and she made the most of the opportunity.

> There is something different about tonight, there is something special about tonight.... What is different? What is special? I, Barbara Jordan, am a keynote speaker! My presence here is one additional bit of evidence that the American Dream need not forever be deferred... we are attempting to fulfill our national purpose to create and sustain a society in which all of us are equal...we believe in equality for all and privileges for none...we are an inclusive rather than exclusive party, let everybody come!

Her speech brought down the house, and the crowd erupted into wave after wave of applause as she spoke. It brought to mind the brutal realities and moral bankruptcy of Jim Crow when I was growing up. I had long ago seen the truth of that, thanks in part to my attendance at the nonsegregated Naval Academy more than twenty years before. Jordan's powerful words were a reminder that, while there was still plenty of work to do in combating racism and discrimination, we had come a long way both as a party and as a nation, and it reaffirmed my commitment to equality for all. There was still a lot of work to be done.

I continued to work with the campaign after Carter's nomination, but now our sights were firmly set on replacing President Gerald Ford in the White House. After returning to Texas, I was again visited by Jess Hay. We joked about my being elected to the convention instead of his wife, who had been running as a Bentsen delegate in the same district as I had. With the primary over, we both understood the importance of working together. Jess was a very prominent man, and, with his help, I was chosen as the business and professional coordinator for Texas in the general election for the Carter campaign.

With the election only a few months away, there was no time to lose. Jess and I worked closely together, and along with our colleagues Charles Kirbo, Bert Lance, and Frank Moore, we set about drumming up support for Carter and trying to get as many endorsements and donations as possible. Our greatest success came when we secured the endorsement of two major newspapers: the *Dallas Times Herald* and the *San Antonio Express-News*. All four of us met with the editorial board of the *Dallas Times Herald*, and Frank Moore and I met with the *San Antonio Express-News*. These papers were more centrist or liberal leaning, but having them in our corner was a genuine windfall for us.

In November, with the election looming only a day away, Margaret and I joined Carter's youngest son, Jeff and his wife, Annette, and flew to five different cities in central Texas in a final effort to turn out the vote. We had a good reception wherever we went, giving us hope that Texas would vote our way. On election day, Margaret and I voted early and then traveled to the headquarters of the campaign in Atlanta. We wanted to be on the ground floor when the results came in. When Governor Carter arrived at the hotel, I met with him again. We only spoke briefly, but he thanked me for all my hard work and asked whether we would win Texas. Despite our former Governor John Connally's declaration on the national news that Texas would go for Ford, I told Carter that the weather had been great all over the state, we would have an excellent turnout, and I was confident that we would win it.

With Margaret by my side, we watched the election results trickle in over the course of that November 2 evening. As the late night drew to a close, it was clear Jimmy Carter had triumphed, carrying both the popular vote and the electoral college by fifty-seven votes. I felt a surge of joy when Texas was called for Carter; all of our hard work had paid off!

It felt amazing to have been a part of the campaign, and I made sure to congratulate Carter on his well-deserved victory. He thanked me, and a couple months later, I was asked whether I would consider becoming a part of his administration.

Carter would not be sworn in until January 20, 1977, and Margaret and I attended the inauguration. It was our first such ceremony and the last inauguration to be held on the eastern side of the Capitol Building. In the first words of his inaugural address, he said, "For myself and for our nation, I want to thank my predecessor for all he has done to heal our land."

In his last sentence he quoted from the Bible, Micah 6:8:

*O man, what doth the Lord require of thee, but to do justly, and to love mercy and to walk humbly with thy God?*

This is a short Scripture, but I think it is very telling of who he is. It spoke both to his faith and his good character. The American people had chosen a good man to lead them.

I was soon nominated to be president of the Government National Mortgage Association, also known as Ginnie Mae, which was part of the Department of Housing and Urban Development (HUD). Later, I would learn that Carter had asked Chief of Staff, Hamilton Jordan, to call HUD Secretary Patricia Harris and encourage her to select me. Sometimes, that is just how things are done in Washington, and I was honored to be chosen. The opportunity, as well as my work on the campaign, reminded me of the value of public service. While it was not the armed forces, a chance to work in government for the betterment of the American people was something that greatly appealed to me.

However, just because I had been nominated, did not mean the position was mine right away. Like so many other presidential appointments in the federal government, the nominee had to be confirmed by the US Senate. In my case, the overseeing body of Ginnie Mae was the Senate Committee on Banking, Housing and Urban Affairs (more commonly known as the Senate Banking Committee). Without their approval, my aspirations of serving in government would be over before they had begun. Before I went to Washington for my confirmation hearing, I paid a visit to a client of ours at Goldman Sachs, Peter O'Donnell. Mr. O'Donnell had served as the executive assistant to the deputy secretary of defense in the Pentagon, Bill Clements from Texas, during the Ford administration. So, as someone with DC experience, it was my hope that he could give me some advice and guidance.

Mr. O'Donnell congratulated me on my nomination and was confident that I would be confirmed to head Ginnie Mae. His guidance on how to comport myself when I took office was not what I expected, but it proved to be some of the most valuable advice that I have ever received.

He told me that I should not limit myself to my official duties at Ginnie Mae. Of course, I should do everything in my power to make my tenure a success, but he also stressed the importance of looking for other opportunities, even if they were not part of my primary responsibility. The key, Mr. O'Donnell said, was to make myself important to President Carter. In other words, find something that was significant to the president that was going to be hard to achieve and do everything possible to help him achieve it. If I did this, it would show my value to the administration, and they would consider me for more senior positions and more important tasks.

I believe this advice can be generalized to most workplace situations, regardless of whether it is in the public or the private sector. One should look for opportunities, take the initiative, and be ambitious. Saying that, it is important not to let personal pride cloud one's judgment, as everyone is working together to achieve something greater than himself. If one can achieve this, he will accomplish great things and be respected for his efforts. Peter O'Donnell's guidance has served me well for decades.

At any rate, it was time for me to head to Washington for my confirmation hearing. I drove to Washington in my MGB with our English bulldog, Winston. After I arrived, I went out of my way to speak to the various senators (or their staffs) on the Senate Banking Committee who would be deciding my fate. As I made the rounds, the reception I received was generally warm, and I felt optimistic that I would sail through the hearing. That was until I spoke to the staff director of Bill Proxmire, a senator from Wisconsin and the Chairman of the Senate Banking Committee. Even though he was a Democrat, he was skeptical of my nomination, and his staff director certainly did not mince words.

"You've had a good record at the Naval Academy, the Navy, and Goldman Sachs, but we don't see any mortgage experience in your background. The chairman is concerned about your qualifications for the job," he said.

As much as I hated to admit it, he had a good point. My experience thus far did not directly relate to what my duties at Ginnie Mae would be. In fact, my only involvement with mortgages was that I had a mortgage! However, I knew I could learn on the job, so I did not see it as a major impediment to my ability to serve. Thankfully, despite Proxmire's vote against me, I was confirmed, but it was a clear example of the "spoils system" at work. The "spoils system" is defined as the practice of a successful politician giving a public office to one of his supporters. I decided not to dwell on the negatives, because I was now officially part of the Carter administration. With my wonderful family by my side, I left Dallas and Goldman Sachs, ready to begin my new life in public office in May 1977.

Even though my position was a minor one compared to cabinet officials like the Secretaries of Defense, State, Justice, HUD, and others, there was still plenty of work to be done. In line with Carter's broader economic policies at the time, I set about advancing and implementing modest deregulation of the mortgage market. It was not a simple endeavor; trying to cut red tape in the market required navigating the complex web of government bureaucracy first. There was a lot of trekking up to Capitol Hill, paperwork, and public relations trying to convince many skeptics of our good intentions. I also spent a great deal of time traveling around the country, trying to encourage various state

*John taking the Oath of Office with Secretary Patricia Harris, Margaret, John, and Chris in 1977.*

or regional mortgage companies/associations to invest in Ginnie Mae certificates.

We celebrated the $50 billion mark in Ginnie Mae securities outstanding when I was in office. It was a lot of hard work, but we were making a difference and implementing part of Carter's economic program one step at a time. However, even though I was focused on making Ginnie Mae as much a success as I possibly could, I had not forgotten Peter O'Donnell's advice. I kept an eye peeled for events happening outside of my office, looking for an opportunity to help the administration achieve something important.

That opportunity came in early 1978 with the signing of the Panama Canal Treaties. In September 1977, Carter had signed two treaties with the then-leader of Panama, Omar Torrijos, the second (and more important) of which pledged to transfer control of the canal to the

Panamanians by 1999. America had owned the canal since we started building it in 1904, but there was an increasing opinion in both countries that it should be deeded to the Panamanians, because it was in their country.

However, Carter did not have the executive authority to simply sanction the handover himself. Like any major international treaty, the agreement had to be ratified by the Senate. Such a treaty needed sixty-seven votes to pass, and, while many senators were in favor of this treaty, it soon became clear that he did not yet have the numbers to push it through. The vote on the second treaty was due to be held on April 18, 1978, and as it inched closer, there was a flurry of activity to secure every vote possible.

In this political difficulty, I saw my opportunity to stand out from the pack and make a difference. With Margaret's help, I laid out my battle plans and identified two senators I could try to convince: Lloyd Bentsen from Texas and Russell Long from Louisiana. I was acquainted with Senator Bentsen from my days in Texas and working on the campaign, and as a fellow Louisianan, I knew just how to approach Russell Long. Alongside other members of the administration like Hamilton Jordan, Dan Tate, and Frank Moore, I went to work.

My strategy had two main parts. The first was the usual lobbying that is so pervasive in Washington. I would visit with Russell Long and Lloyd Bentsen at their Senate offices or converse with their staffs. Both senators were fence-sitters who were conflicted over which way to vote. I did my best to tell them that I understood their concerns, while also trying to convince them of the benefits of ratifying the treaty.

I found out who their major supporters were and lobbied them, also. If their supporters became convinced that the treaty should be ratified, I asked them to weigh in with the senator.

It took a while, but with time and persistence, it seemed my efforts were starting to get through to them, especially in the case of Russell Long. That said, I knew we did not have their votes in the bag yet. That brought me to the second part of my plan, which was finding a way to pressure them. Being in elected office, it would be unwise for them not to consider public sentiment in their respective states. So, I reached out to friends, acquaintances and former business associates in Louisiana and Texas. I asked for their help in encouraging the public to favor ratification. I even managed to get two newspapers, the *Shreveport Journal* and the *Dallas Times Herald*, to publish editorials in favor of the treaties. It was my hope that the extra push would be enough to secure their votes for Carter. Twisting people's arms was part of the process.

April 18 arrived almost too quickly. I was confident that I had successfully secured Russell Long's vote, but I was less certain about Bentsen's. On the day of the vote, I went to the Capitol and took my place in the Senate Gallery, excited to watch the vote unfold. The vote on the first, less controversial treaty, had happened a month before, and that had only barely passed. Would our hard work pay off a second time?

After closing statements were made by the majority leader and the minority leader, Senators Robert Byrd and Howard Baker, all of the other senators cast their votes. The wait was interminable, but at last the final tally came in: sixty-eight votes in favor, thirty-two against; the treaty had been ratified by one vote! The vote defied party lines, with both Democrats and Republicans voting for and against, but it still represented a great achievement for us. We had accomplished one of Carter's primary foreign policy goals, and my efforts in seeing it over the finish line had not gone unnoticed. President Carter was deeply thankful that I had helped deliver Long's and Bentsen's votes.[4] Without them, and the other votes that people like Dan Tate and Frank Moore had lobbied for, it would not have been possible. It was a team effort, and I was privileged to have been a part of it. Additionally, because I had gone out of my way to help them realize that important policy

---

[4] Senator Bentsen and I remained friends until his death in 2006. At a dinner many years after the ratification, he confided in me that it was the hardest vote he had ever had to cast, and he got a lot of grief for that vote from the voters in the Lone Star State! (See letter in the appendix.)

objective, it had put me on their radar, and I was now part of the White House team.

I continued to serve at Ginnie Mae until the Spring 1979, when the White House reached out to me. Carter was already laying the foundations for his reelection campaign, and they were interested to know if I wanted to be a part of it. I was open to the possibility, but I was not interested if my position was going to be the same as last time. Thankfully, this was not the case at all, and they offered me the position of treasurer for the national campaign. Well, that was certainly a step up from being the business and professional coordinator for Texas.

In September of that year, we were invited to a state dinner at the White House, which was celebrating the signing of the peace treaties between Israel and Egypt (maybe as a thank you for helping with the Panama Canal treaty and the successful vote). This was the first time we had attended such a function, but it was a fantastic soiree. President Carter was there, along with President Anwar Sadat of Egypt and Prime Minister Menachem Begin of Israel, so I was certainly a small fish in a big pond at that occasion. I had no part in the Camp David Accords, but it represented a huge leap forward, both in American foreign policy and for stability in the Middle East, which still remains today. It was a gamble, but it turned out to be one of Carter's greatest successes, one which deserves more recognition than it receives.

The campaign kept me busy, but unlike the 1976 election, I did not feel that same energy and momentum. I spent long periods away from home, and it was the second time I had taken a pay cut in five years. While I liked the work at Ginnie Mae, the salary was significantly lower than my income at Goldman Sachs, and as treasurer of the campaign, the income was lower still. The reelection campaign was also facing problems, including a serious primary challenge from Senator Ted Kennedy and lingering economic issues.

By the fall of 1979, I found that being treasurer of the Carter/Mondale Campaign was more than a full-time job. I had two small children at home, and this job was twenty-four hours a day, seven days a week.

On top of that, I had also become aware of a new opportunity in the administration that seemed to be calling my name: an opening on the Federal Home Loan Bank Board (FHLBB). I had a meeting with Chief of Staff Hamilton Jordan and expressed to him my misgivings about my tenure at the campaign, while making it clear that I felt my skills (not to mention my bank account) would be better suited at the FHLBB. Hamilton was a real stand-up guy and said that while he was sorry I wanted to leave the campaign, he would ask President Carter about nominating me for that position.

Unlike Ginnie Mae, the FHLBB was independent. But, just like Ginnie Mae, this required that I would again have to go through the confirmation by the Senate Banking Committee. At least it was easier the second time around: by this time, I was a known quantity and had a good track record at Ginnie Mae. The confirmation hearing was therefore more of a formality, but it differed from the last time in one significant way. Bill Proxmire, the chairman, who had voted against me the first time, was now one of my strongest advocates. He said that my tenure at Ginnie Mae had shown that he had been wrong to doubt me, and that I would be an excellent addition to the FHLBB. Needless to say, I was touched. It is not very often that a United States senator says he was wrong to vote the way he had.

My work on the Federal Home Loan Bank Board began in February 1980 and shared a number of similarities with my time at Ginnie Mae. Again, we often found ourselves in Congress, trying to cajole wary senators or congressmen into supporting a cautious deregulation agenda and trying to convince them that we were not in the pockets of banks or mortgage companies. That position also involved a lot of traveling. There were twelve Federal Home Loan Banks around the country, and they met six to eight times a year in regular conferences, taking turns hosting the event. There were only three of us on the board: Chairman Jay Janis, who had been the Under Secretary of HUD when I was at Ginnie Mae, Andrew DiPrete, and I, so there was never a shortage of work. President Carter had named Andrew to the FHLBB in order to get the vote of Senator John Chaffee for the Panama Canal treaties. Despite this example of political backscratching, Andrew was a shrewd and capable member of the board.

That was the status quo until November, when the election took place. My work with the FHLBB took up most of my time, so I was not nearly as active in the campaign as I had been in 1976. That did not mean I was oblivious to how hard fought it was, and I knew Carter was facing a difficult election. Even after he defeated the primary challenge from Senator Ted Kennedy, he had to contend with his Republican rival, the charismatic former governor of California, Ronald Reagan.

There also was only one presidential debate. I believe Carter generally had the stronger arguments, but Reagan came across as more personable, and he used his Hollywood charm to great effect. When Carter used facts and figures to back himself up, Reagan managed to paint him as bookish and out of touch: "There you go again," he would say. Sadly, I think most people who watched were more taken with Reagan's style, instead of Carter's substance. Also, regardless of all of Carter's achievements, the economy was still only slowly recovering, and stagflation remained a stubborn thorn in our sides.

Perhaps, Carter's biggest problem was contending with the fallout of the 1979 Iranian Revolution and the subsequent hostage crisis, where many foreign service officials at the embassy in Tehran had been taken hostage a year before. Though President Carter had been broadly successful with the rest of his foreign policy, it was the Iran Crisis that everyone remembers and that overshadows his other accomplishments to this day. The failure of the mission to rescue the hostages only made a bad situation worse. It was a handicap for the remainder of the campaign and something his opponents kept attacking him on. I believe the final nail in the coffin came the weekend before the election, when the news channels and newspapers ran documentaries and articles on the one-year anniversary of the Iranian Hostage Crisis. That tipped a lot of undecided voters onto the Republican bandwagon.

I remember that the Friday night before the Tuesday election, on the PBS program *Washington Week in Review*, the moderator, Paul Duke, said they had been covering this campaign all year long and it was now time to declare, "Who is going to win the election?" Two of the commentators picked Carter, two picked Reagan, and Paul Duke said, "I am going to use the prerogative of the moderator and say that it is too close to call." I am convinced that the one-year anniversary of the hostages being taken and all of the news coverage that it got made the difference. People were throwing their hands up and saying, I don't know what we are getting, but I think we need a change.

The election results, when they came were hard to swallow: Reagan had won in a landslide. It was a dark day for all of us: I truly believed Carter had so much more to offer the American people and deserved a second term, but the voters had spoken. Not only did we lose the White House, the Senate also flipped to the Republican party.

Jay Janis stepped down shortly after the election, leaving me as the chairman of the Federal Home Loan Bank Board. When the new administration took over, they would, of course, nominate their own people to the departments and agencies. It would be only a matter of time before I was replaced as chairman.

I knew that soon I would go back to being a member and no longer the chairman of the board. I began looking for other opportunities and was soon contacted by the executive search firm of Heidrick & Struggles. They knew that I was looking for greener pastures, and, with my experience, they thought I would be a great fit as president of the real estate division of Gill Savings in San Antonio.

I did not expect that I would be going back to Texas after my time in Washington. A part of me was disappointed that I would be leaving so soon, because I had hoped to spend at least two presidential terms there. However, things do not always go according to plan, and the ability to adapt to changes is important. It had been a privilege to serve in the Carter administration, and in its own way, heading back to Texas felt as if the family and I were coming full circle.

I said goodbye to DC and the FHLBB in July 1981, about six months after Reagan had been sworn in. I knew my role was not coterminous with the Carter administration, and I was pleased to have remained Chairman for that long after the transition. Although my term on the board lasted until June 1982, it was not as much fun being a member as serving as the chairman. President Reagan named Richard Pratt from Utah to be chairman, and he took over in June of 1981. We packed our things for the long journey back to Texas, and before we left, I decided to telephone President Carter. I thanked him again for everything he had done for me and our country and told him I was heading to San Antonio to start a new career. Carter, who was in his hometown of Plains, invited us to stop by his home in Georgia on the way.

I looked forward to seeing him again and readily accepted, but the only time we could successfully coordinate was an early morning meeting. So, when the day came, I woke my family at the crack of dawn, and we took the 158-mile drive south from Atlanta to Plains. Even though it was a major detour for us, it was still terrific to see the president again, especially in a more relaxed setting.

"John, have you and the family had breakfast?" President Carter asked.

I told him we had not, and he offered two or three different breakfast options, each one of which involved peaches. Now, maybe it was because he was hungry, or perhaps he was cranky from being awakened so early, or perhaps he was just feeling a little surly from all the recent travel (or all three), whatever the reason, our younger son, Chris, said, "I don't like peaches!"

Here we were, in the president's home, in the Peach State! Carter took it in stride with good humor, but I was quite embarrassed.

Finally, after what felt like a marathon journey, we made it to San Antonio. It had been an exciting, fulfilling few years in politics and government. Even though I wish it had not ended the way it did, I would not trade the experience for anything. I felt privileged to have served in the federal government in appointed offices. It was hard work, but gratifying, and it meant a great deal because I knew I was working for the American people. I hope that, in my own way, I made a positive difference in the lives of everyone touched by the mortgage industry. I had made some wonderful friends and learned many things, and it reaffirmed to me the value of public service in all of its forms.

But now, the time had come to become a private citizen again and stretch my entrepreneurial wings in the private sector once more. Gill Savings was an exciting opportunity, and I was eager to see where this new chapter in my life would take me.

# CHAPTER 9

# THE ALAMO CITY

Having arrived in San Antonio in July, 1981, we would live there for more than a decade. Thinking back, I have truly come to appreciate what a formative time that was for us as a family. While this part of my life may have lacked the pomp and circumstance of my time in the Navy or in our nation's capital, it came to encompass some of our most cherished memories.

We moved into a lovely house in the Castle Hills Estates on the northwest side of the city. I had almost forgotten how much cheaper real estate was in that part of the country, and our new home was palatial compared to our former Washington residence. I had fallen in love with the house when the agent, a lovely woman by the name of Jane Bane, had first given us a tour. In a remarkable coincidence, Jane's husband also worked at Gill Savings, in the same area as I did, but he did not report to me. I took this as a good sign, but before I signed any check or contract, I decided to make a deal with her.

"Look, Jane," I said, "I like this place, but if we buy this house, you have to agree to be Margaret's friend, because we don't know anyone here."

Jane was surprised, and who could blame her? It was certainly a request out of left field. However, I had a feeling that they would get along very well, and it would mean that Margaret would not be coming into San Antonio cold. Jane smiled, agreed, and we shook hands. I bought the house soon after, and Margaret and Jane became good friends, much closer than I had expected!

The move went smoothly, but there was still plenty on the to-do list. Getting to know the city, finding good schools for the boys, and choosing the right church for us were just a few of the tasks needed to turn our house into a home. All of these would take time, but Margaret and I were determined to make the most of our new life in the "Alamo City!" I started my tenure as president of the real estate division the same month we moved to San Antonio, and I did not want to waste any time. Thanks to the people at Heidrick & Struggles, I had signed with a generous benefits package, including memberships in the Oak Hills Country Club and Club Giraud, a lovely dining club, as well as a percentage of my division's annual profits.

I was also blessed to meet again with former Vice President Mondale and the new mayor of San Antonio, Henry Cisneros. Even though the VP had been to our home for dinner in Washington, DC, I did not know Mondale as well as I knew President Carter. It was still good to see him again, and I was pleased to visit with Cisneros, too. As a mayor, he was business friendly and went out of his way to form strong relationships with the private sector. He was the first mayor in San Antonio history to bring the Hispanic community and the private sector together. It was important to his leadership in the community for him to be able to accomplish that goal. I was fortunate to have those connections and to foster and maintain those friendships. Cisneros and I have remained friends to this day, and Chris Gill was clearly impressed by my network of acquaintances, especially when Mondale spoke well of me.

As far as my faith was concerned, it was as strong as ever, though it took us longer than I thought it would to find the church that was right for us. In the months following our move, we visited several different churches. They were pleasant places, filled with good people, but none of them felt like the right fit for us. It was about more than just finding a place of worship. Each church and its congregation are a community, with its own history, values, style, and identity. When you find the right one, it is like discovering a new extended family.

This search finally came to an end when we found Christ Episcopal Church. The rector, John MacNaughton, was a man of great faith and integrity, and he welcomed us warmly. After our first Sunday service at the church, I knew we had finally found our spiritual home in San Antonio. At different times, Margaret and I would each be elected to the vestry, the governing body of the church. I was even chosen to be chairman of the search committee to find a new rector when John MacNaughton left to become the Bishop of the Diocese of West Texas, though that was some years later.[5]

During a season of Lent several years after we joined Christ Church, the Reverend John R. Claypool, a Southern Baptist minister, was invited to speak during the week for several weeks in a row. He was an outstanding speaker and indicated that he loved the Episcopal church liturgy. One of the senior laymen said to him that he was sure it would be possible for him to become an Episcopal priest, if he were so inclined. He eventually did just that and was assigned to Christ Church by the bishop while he attended seminary in Austin to make the transition. He taught a Sunday school class, and Margaret and I became good friends with him and his wife, Ann. He remained at Christ Church for a while once he completed the process of becoming an Episcopal priest, and we became even closer friends.

Even though my mother lived over four hundred miles away from our new home, she was still a huge part of our lives. She would drive down to visit us on occasion, and I always looked forward to spending time with her in Shreveport. She had married Bill Winterrowd about seven years after my father passed away. Like my father, Bill had also

---

[5] MacNaughton's successor certainly had some big shoes to fill, and it was a long, taxing process to find someone worthy of taking on his mantle. Eventually, we found just the man in Ted Schroder from Jacksonville, Florida.

been a railroad man and had known my dad back in those days. Clearly, my mother liked railroad men. It took a little time to get used to the fact that I had a stepfather. That being said, he was a good man, and they made each other happy. It was easy for me to tacitly bless their relationship.

At any rate, in the fall of 1981, it happened to be our turn to host Thanksgiving. It was the perfect opportunity to show my siblings and cousin, Jean Hoffman, and her husband Henry, our new life in San Antonio. We still were not all that familiar with the place ourselves, so we organized a tour of the city led by a good friend who was a fellow parishioner at Christ Church. Among other places, it included the most famous landmark in the city, the Alamo. It was terrific to explore the city as a big extended family, and that Thanksgiving was made even more memorable because we had two turkeys, one of which was a smoked wild turkey that I had killed!

Sadly, 1981 would turn out to be one of my mother's last Thanksgivings. In late 1982, she phoned my siblings and me separately and asked us to come to Shreveport. When we arrived, she informed us that she had been diagnosed with late-stage breast cancer. It was not her first brush with the disease: after exhaustive treatment and painful surgery she had managed to fight through it the first time.

However, now it was back, and she did not want to go through all of that again. She was calm in explaining her decision, and we all understood what that meant.

"I have been diagnosed with breast cancer, and I have made the decision not to go through all that process another time," she told us. My mother chose to live her last months to the fullest, spending as much time as she could with her family. We have photos of her last Christmas with us, happily doting on her grandchildren and opening gifts. It is a bittersweet memory, but I would not trade it for the world. She passed away on January 6, 1983, to the profound regret of her family she loved and who loved her. Unlike with my father, I was able to be with her, as

*Mother with me outside the Oval Office at the White House.*

was Margaret. I can still recall some of her words when I was last with her, kneeling down by the side of her bed and hearing her pray:

"Father, I am ready to come home."

I could not have asked for a better mother. She was a kind, fun-loving, generous, and selfless woman who always went out of her way to help her family and those she cared about, and she had a huge influence on me. I know in my heart that she has reunited with my father in heaven and that they are happy.

After my mother's death we remained close with our extended family. Margaret's brother Bucky was part of a group that rented a house on Inks Lake near Burnet, Texas. We were fortunate to become part of the group and enjoyed many family weekends there with friends fishing, swimming, water skiing, and watching the great blanket of stars light up the clear Texas nights.

To the northwest of San Antonio near Hunt, Texas, there is a summer camp, Camp Stewart for Boys. We found the place almost by accident. I had a friend who lived in Hunt, and one day we went to see him with Chris and John Jr. My friend knew the owners of the camp and offered to take us on a tour of the place. John and Chris loved it and practically begged me to let them go. They started attending the next summer, with John going for five years and Chris for eight. Chris was even a counselor for several years. Both would end up reaching the rank of chief (Camp Stewart's version of an Eagle Scout), and while they were campers, I would sometimes visit to give talks to the campers at chapel services on Sunday. I was very pleased that they were both such big fans of the outdoors, and I believe that those experiences very much helped them grow into talented and sociable young men.

We learned too late the high schools in the city did not have a stellar academic reputation and, eventually, we agreed to consider boarding school, but only if the boys wanted to go. Chris was not taken with the idea and wanted to stay home and attend public school. John, on the other hand, took the proposal and ran with it. With the help of a consultant, we chose the Asheville School in western North Carolina. Midway through his freshman year Chris changed his mind and asked if he could go to Asheville as well. It turned out to be an outstanding experience for both.

Our lives in San Antonio were full. Compared with our time in Dallas and Washington, we had time to travel abroad more often. Such trips had been few and far between since our honeymoon, and I had cultivated an interest in foreign lands since my trip to the far east during my academy days. As I remember, we had three major trips outside the country while we lived in San Antonio.

The first happened almost by accident. In December 1982, we had a call from a friend of Margaret's brother Staman. Apparently, Staman's friend and his wife had won a trip to Switzerland for a road rally, and as part of the prize, they were allowed to bring two other people along. We would be driving around the Swiss Alps in Mercedes cars, staying in cities like Basel and Zurich, all while taking part in a "treasure hunt": visiting various landmarks and collecting a specific memento at each one. Margaret and I had a terrific time with our new friends, and driving through Switzerland in comfort and style was a real treat.

The second of these vacations was in 1986, when I took the family to London. Since the tennis tournament at the Byrd High School reunion some years before, I had become more interested and active in tennis. By the time I was living in San Antonio, it had become the sport I played most, and I never turned down an opportunity to visit the courts if I had the time. By 1986, I wanted to see one of the grand slams in person, and what better tennis tournament is there than Wimbledon? So, in late June of that year, we headed for England. It was the first major international trip for the boys, and we spent a fantastic week in and around London, seeing everything from Shakespeare's Globe Theatre in Stratford to Buckingham Palace. It also included two days at Wimbledon: I knew the tennis would be incredible, but seeing it in person was breathtaking; television did not, could not, do it justice. To this day, it remains the greatest tennis I have ever had the privilege of watching firsthand. Boris Becker won the tournament, and we had the thrill of seeing him win a match on Center Court. I can still remember Chris cheering him on and saying, "Come on, Boris!"

The third major foreign trip during that time was completely different from those before. In late 1991, I had a call from my good friend Rick Lobs. Rick had been the rector of the church we attended when I studied at Wharton. He asked if I would be interested in traveling with him and some of his congregation to the Holy Land early in 1992.

I had never been to Israel or the Middle East before, so I did not hesitate to say yes. My faith was, and is, one of the most important parts of my life, and I had long toyed with the idea of going on a pilgrimage to the holiest sites in Christendom. Now, I had the chance to go with a dear friend, and there was no way I was going to turn down the invitation. The high dome of the Church of the Holy Sepulcher, the sweeping view from the Mount of Olives, the solemnness of Golgotha where Christ was crucified were all very special sights to me. We even spent a night in the desert with Bedouins, climbed Mount Sinai and floated in the Dead Sea. I can still remember it as if it were yesterday. I have never once wavered in my belief or commitment to God, yet that journey breathed new life and understanding into my faith. I have made several more trips to Jerusalem since, but that first pilgrimage will always be something I will never forget.

The Carter Center was founded 1982, and in March of 1984 President Carter came to San Antonio to raise money for it. I hosted both a fundraiser breakfast and lunch where he spoke promoting the Center. The president stayed at our home, and prior to the breakfast, the president and I and Secret Service protection jogged in the neighborhood. Amazing how many neighbors were out at dawn that morning to make sure they got a glimpse of the former president! Our fourth-grade son, Chris, went to the breakfast with us, which made him late for school. President Carter wrote an excuse note to his teacher: "Ms. Taylor, I'm

*President Jimmy Carter with our family in San Antonio.*

afraid I made Chris late. Please excuse him. Jimmy Carter." She called the *San Antonio Light* and reported that President Carter had written an excuse note for one of her students. A reporter came to our home to talk to Chris and take pictures. The article and picture soon appeared on the front page of the *Light*. In addition to the breakfast and lunch, President Carter spoke that evening at Trinity University and left having had a successful visit to San Antonio. The Carter Center in Atlanta was dedicated in 1986. President Ronald Reagan was the speaker, and Margaret and I were pleased to be in attendance.

The 1980s were a very busy time for me and our family. With the obvious exception of my mother's passing, it was a happy time, and there was rarely a dull moment.[6] During the first several years in San Antonio, my work with Gill Savings was going well, the real estate division I headed was going strong and the future looked bright.

In late 1983, a series of events began that would change my life forever. I was approached by three men, who came to me with an offer. They were not employees of Gill Savings, nor were they clients, but I agreed to visit with them. As it turned out, they were not interested in Gill Savings but in me specifically. They were planning to acquire a small savings-and-loan company in the town of Seguin, a little under forty miles east of San Antonio. They were looking for another person to help them do so and asked if I wanted to be part of the deal.

I was perplexed: why me, specifically? They responded that they wanted someone with experience in the S&L industry, and I would be the CEO of the new company if I joined them. That offer was tempting enough, but they followed up by not so subtly reminding me that the CEO of Gill Savings, which was a private company, was younger than I

---

[6] When God closes a door, he opens another. A friend I had hunted with had a black Labrador retriever, who had puppies. Knowing my fondness for sporting dogs, he asked if we wanted one of the puppies. The litter was born on the same day my mother died, and when they were old enough, we were given the sweetest little puppy, whom we named Pepper, which our son John recommended. She lived to be sixteen and a half years old when we finally had to put her to sleep.

and not likely to retire anytime soon. Ergo, further career advancement there was unlikely. That was a chance for me run a business of my own. Even though I was happy where I was, I cannot deny that the prospect intrigued me.

However, I knew they were not offering me that chance purely out of the goodness of their hearts. It was time to get down to brass tacks: what did they want from me? The answer, of course, was my investment. They needed me, along with themselves, to invest money into the project in order to acquire the company. How much? $1 million.

I balked at that number. I was certainly not a poor man; I was making a good income and had some respectable assets, including stocks and real estate. Saying that, I did not have a million dollars to spare. In total, I was worth less than half that amount. If I were going to invest that kind of money, I was going to have to take out a substantial loan. That was not a trivial decision, and I knew that I would be taking a significant risk if I joined them in the venture.

Looking back, I perhaps should have declined their offer. Knowing what I know now, it would have spared me a great deal of stress and many sleepless nights. However, that's the nature of hindsight. While I would have greatly preferred to have avoided what was coming, at least I can say that I learned some important, but painful, lessons from that experience.

As things were presented, I decided it was worth the gamble, and we shook hands on our future success. It was not easy, but after some serious number-crunching and meetings with the bank, I successfully scraped together the money I needed to live up to my end of the bargain. We now had a total of $4 million invested in the venture, and we still needed another million dollars. I reached out to a few others with capital to meet the purchase price. Not everyone saw the potential we did, but my salesmanship managed to win over another six investors, who each invested $270,000.

With our finances raised, we moved to acquire the business. Thankfully, it was straight forward, and it did not take long before the Seguin

S&L was in our ambitious hands. In 1984, after we formed a holding company called the Freedom Capital Corporation, we were officially in business. I may have only spent a couple of years with Gill Savings, but I had enjoyed my time there, and my departure was amicable. I would have happily worked there for more years had this prospective venture not landed in my lap. I always answer the door when opportunity knocks, and I had high hopes for our venture.

For a while, those hopes were not misplaced. During our first couple of years in operation, the business grew steadily, and we made a healthy profit. The American economy was riding high that decade, and, now that I was the captain of my own ship, I helped steer us on the rising tide. That is not to say things were easy; nothing worth doing ever is, and I was keenly aware of the responsibilities I carried on my shoulders. My partners, our employees, and our clients were all heavily invested in our success, and I was determined to do my best. I had to set an example for our staff, listen to good advice, and lead decisively. Our hard work was reaping dividends, and for about two years, the Freedom Capital Corporation prospered.

There is a line by Ernest Hemingway about financial collapse: It happens "two ways. Gradually, then suddenly." For me, I can certainly pinpoint where things started to go wrong: the 1986 oil price collapse. After a low in the 1970s, the price of oil had climbed considerably to around forty dollars a barrel by the middle of the 1980s. Considering how big oil was in Texas, this was great news for the state, and we were making our own tidy profit as a result. Furthermore, an economist with Fortune magazine predicted that it would rise to seventy dollars a barrel by the end of 1986. It would be painful for people at the gas pumps, but the future looked bright for businesses like ours.

However, in 1986, the exact opposite occurred. I do not pretend to know all the complicated minutia surrounding oil and global politics, but in that year, a huge glut of petroleum was dumped onto the market. That surge in supply caused oil prices to plummet to ten dollars a barrel and threw our business model into chaos. We were expecting it to climb, but instead it was now a quarter of its original value. That put a great deal of pressure on us, and together with the developers and investors, I scrambled to right the ship and get us back on track.

The collapse in oil prices was bad enough and, had it been an isolated event, we may have survived. Unfortunately for us, we were dealt another blow when new legislation was passed in Congress that had the effect of devaluing commercial real estate, a key component of our portfolio. That one-two punch crippled the company, and even though we did not see it then, it marked the beginning of the end for Freedom Capital Corporation.

That put a tremendous amount of pressure on me. Margaret was worried about me and suggested that I go see Dr. Don Anderson, who was the head of a charitable counseling firm where I served on the board. I went to see him and told him the story of my savings and loan, and he said, "OK, what is the worst thing that could happen?"

I said, "Don, I could have to declare bankruptcy!"

He said, "OK, let's assume that turns out to be the case. The streets of Texas are lined with those who've had to declare bankruptcy, including Clint Murchison, who owned the Dallas Cowboys, former Governor and Secretary of the Treasury John Connally, and Dr. Michael DeBakey, the noted heart transplant surgeon." He said, "You can start over! You have a degree from the US Naval Academy, an MBA from the University of Pennsylvania, a wonderful wife, and two great sons. Many people have had this kind of reversal and have begun their careers all over." That was not what I wanted to hear, but it was comforting to know anyway.

I pulled out all the stops to save the business. I sought out new investors to inject capital into the company, tried to diversify our portfolio, and when that failed, even approached other savings-and-loan companies with the hope of a merger. Sadly, no matter what I did or how hard I tried, I could not make anything happen. Over the next couple years, I watched, feeling helpless, as the company drifted from treading water, to life support, to circling the drain. As 1988 came to an end, I could no longer ignore the handwriting on the wall. The business was going to fail. The ax finally fell that December, just after our Christmas vacation. I called the association to catch up on what I had missed while I was away. I was greeted by an unfamiliar voice on the other end of the line and immediately felt a sinking feeling in the pit of my stomach. I asked what was going on, and that's when they told me the Federal Home Loan Bank Board had made the decision to take over our S&L association.

Having the business go under was bad enough, but I felt terrible about those who had trusted in me and invested their money. Despite my best efforts, their money was gone, and there was no way I could make them whole. What made the situation even more dire was that I had put such a big part of my own finances on the line to make it succeed. It was all in vain, and now I had a huge debt looming over my head, over twice what I was worth. There was the real danger that I would have to declare bankruptcy. With no options left to me, I sheepishly sat down with the bank to negotiate my fate. I sold every liquid asset I owned and paid it to the bank where I had the loan. I paid the rest of it over time.

The settlement was about as fair as it could have been, but that did not make it any easier to swallow. The business would be merged into other savings and loans as part of the Federal Home Loan Bank Board's Southwest Plan. There was some relief in that: I no longer had to deal with the stress of trying to save a dying company. I managed to avoid personal bankruptcy but made a number of other concessions. I had staved off complete financial ruin, but when was all said and done, I barely had a penny to my name.

It is hard to describe what a painful, sobering experience that ordeal was. I had almost lost everything, and it was the lowest point in my life. When the dust settled, I was unemployed, cash-strapped, and humbled. Indeed, I was a hurting puppy!

The night before the news of the closure of the Freedom Capital Corporation went public, I gathered my family together. I wanted them to hear it from me first. I sat down with them and explained, the best I could, what had happened and what the situation was now. The future was uncertain, and we would have to live more frugally for the foreseeable future, but at least we still had the house, and I had made sure that school and camp for John and Chris were paid for that year. The atmosphere was somber, but I did not want them to worry. I needed them to be strong, just as they needed me to be. As the conversation came to an end, I quoted from Romans 8:28: "And we know that in all things God works for the good of those who love him, who have been called according to his purpose."

That verse from the Bible gave us hope: We were down but not out. As with all trials in life, God rarely puts something before us that we cannot endure. The Lord loves His children, and as dark as things were then, we had faith that somehow, some way, He would see us through. My friend the Reverend John Claypool told me over and over again, "Miracles still happen!"

As I have said before, there are three things in life that are vitally important, and which you should do all in your power to nurture: Your family, your friends, and your faith. If you do, then there is no obstacle you cannot overcome, and no hardship you cannot endure, for they will steer you through the hardest times. Those next few months were bleak and difficult. Things did not get better overnight, and, for a while, it was a struggle to make ends meet. However, we pulled together as a family, put our faith in God, and were supported by true friends during our struggle. My sister and brother, Margaret and William, were very helpful to me and supportive, as was my father-in-law, Buck. I had a good friend and classmate, Waddy Garrett, who offered to make me a loan. His offer was deeply appreciated, but I declined, not knowing how I would pay it back. Sadly, Waddy died on April 2, 2018, and I miss him greatly.

After I was no longer with Seguin Savings, I got a license to sell life insurance. Business was hit and miss, but it meant that I had some income. After a few months of this, I got a call from Margaret's brother Bucky. He told me there was an opportunity open at Mason Best

Company, a private equity firm in Dallas, where he was employed. The position was similar to the one I had had at Goldman Sachs, and he offered to recommend me to his boss. I saw that as proof of my principles: the Lord worked through Bucky, who was both family and friend, to deliver us from our crisis. I took Bucky up on his offer, and not long after, I was starting a new career with a new company. I opened an office for Mason Best Company in San Antonio.

The job lacked some of the benefits I had had at Gill Savings, but I was earning almost as much as I had as president of the Freedom Capital Corporation (when everything was going well). It was a good job with a good income, and I was back doing something I enjoyed. About a year after I had joined, Elvis Mason and Randy Best, the founders of the company, ended their partnership, and I went with Randy as part of Best Associates, where I would stay until 1991.

Now that the worst of my financial troubles were over, I could refocus on other things in my life that gave me joy, namely my family, my hobbies, and some charities. Unlike Dallas, San Antonio did not have an active USNA alumni chapter. That was a shame, but at least there was a loosely affiliated community of Army and Navy veterans. We would get together for the annual Army-Navy football game, and it was always fun to rib each other over a couple of drinks as we cheered our boys, hopefully, on to victory. Despite the lack of a Naval Academy Chapter, I continued my commitment to attending our class reunion every five years. From 1969 to the present day, we have never missed one. It is always great to see so many familiar faces, catch up on what they are doing with their lives, and reminisce about the good old days. I think I am one of the few classmates who has made it to every single five-year reunion!

In 1991, I decided to go back into the investment banking business with Stephens, Inc. One of the founders of the firm was Jack Stephens, a Naval Academy classmate of Jimmy Carter. It was one of the most successful investment banking firms outside of New York City. Tom Beard, who was a good friend and had worked in the Carter White

House had joined Stephens, Inc., in 1981. He recommended me to Warren Stephens, who was the CEO of the firm in 1991. I had a series of interviews and joined the firm that year and opened an office for Stephens, Inc., in San Antonio. I was involved in corporate finance, public finance, and sales. It was a great job, which I enjoyed very much and was glad to remain in that historic city.

As far as sports went, I was enjoying hunting and tennis, but my true favorites continued to remain baseball and football. Much to my disappointment, San Antonio did not have a major league baseball or football team. I continued to be a devout Texas Rangers fan, but now that I was out of Dallas, I rarely had the chance to see them live. To compensate for that deficit, we threw our weight behind the San Antonio Spurs, the NBA basketball team. It did not captivate me in quite the same way as my favorite spectator sports did, but basketball managed to fill the void for us, and Margaret and I turned into strong Spurs fans. On one occasion we even had David Robinson, a Naval Academy graduate and NBA MVP, and RADM Tom Lynch, a fellow classmate of mine, who was then the Superintendent of the Naval Academy and in town, join us at our home for dinner. David was a joy to dine with, and I relished talking with "The Admiral" about basketball and his military experience. So did our sons!

For better or worse, there was a never a dull moment for me and my family during our life in San Antonio. It certainly had its challenges, the death of my mother and my brush with bankruptcy chief among them. When all was said and done, however, there were far more highs than lows, and life was looking a lot brighter than it had for the last couple of years. I had my family, my health, good friends, and a stable job. For that I was thankful, because they were the most important things to me. There would still be some challenges on the job front, but none of it compared to what had come before with the collapse of my business. Of course, I wish that had never happened, but the situation could have been much worse. I learned some valuable lessons from it, and I walked away a wiser, humbler man.

By the second half of 1991, things were steady, and the future looked promising. Since my arrival in 1981, I had stayed in touch with Henry Cisneros and followed local as well as national politics. As we transitioned from the eighties to the nineties, I became more actively involved in politics once again, albeit in the background. Unbeknownst to me, that would send me down a path that eventually would catapult me back into appointed office, into the position that I would be most remembered for, overseeing the institution I cared so much about.

# CHAPTER 10

# THE BEST JOB IN GOVERNMENT

"Well, what about you?" Cisneros asked.

Henry was on the transition team for the 1992 Clinton campaign. It was still three weeks before the nation went to the polls, and there was confidence for a Clinton victory. Fueled by this confidence, the team was already putting names together for the hundreds of appointed positions in the federal government. Cisneros would not have asked me to come to his office just to get a list of names; we could have done that over the phone. I had a feeling this question was coming, but I was not sure how to answer it. Was I indeed ready to commit to public service again?

This question marked the inflection point of an unusual road for me. For all of my time in San Antonio, I remained connected to the Democratic party, former Carter administration colleagues and local, state, and national politics, but it was certainly not my main focus at the time. My interest in politics never faded. I just did not have any intention of going back into public service myself. I saw it as mostly something to remain connected with.

However, I did not abandon the arena entirely. Politics, whether you love it or hate it, is important, and I was not going to be a passive observer. My political engagement in San Antonio, at least during the

1980s, was defined by three factors. First, I played a part in helping in Mark White's election as governor of Texas in 1983. Though the Lone Star State was becoming more and more red as the years went on, we still managed to score an important victory here and there.

Second, I joined the Democratic Leadership Council (DLC) when it was formed in 1985. It represented the moderate wing of the Democratic Party. Like many others at the time, I felt the party was shifting too far to the left, and it needed to realign itself on a more moderate, forward-thinking agenda if we were going to win the presidency again. It took some years for the DLC to successfully change the platform and the trajectory of the party, and I was glad to have been part of that mission.

Our efforts did not bear fruit in time to save us from defeat in the 1988 election. I supported and did some advocacy work in the primaries for Dick Gephardt, a fellow DLC member, even going to Iowa for him. Unfortunately, he lost to Michael Dukakis, who in turn was defeated by Vice President George H. W. Bush. At least that loss was a wakeup call, and the DLC began to gain significant traction in the aftermath of that setback.

The third factor was not an event, but rather my connections to people in the party. On the local level, that was Henry Cisneros. As I mentioned before, I met him soon after I moved to San Antonio, and we remained in touch after that. He was an excellent mayor and deservedly won several consecutive terms by wide margins. I gladly made donations to his campaigns, and we soon became friends. At the state level, my main relationship was with Senator Lloyd Bentsen. We did not visit with each other as often as we had when we had lived in Washington, but we remained close nonetheless, and it was fascinating to hear firsthand what was going on in the Senate. I also helped his reelection efforts in 1982 and 1988. And then, of course, there was President Carter. As with Bentsen, we did not talk as frequently as we used to, but he remained a friend. I was always very interested to learn about what was happening with the newly established Carter Center.

This was largely the extent of my political activity from 1983–1990. I was focused on my family and my career, and that level of engagement was plenty for me. There was nothing to suggest that I would find myself heading back to our nation's capital. However, as the final decade of the twentieth century dawned, more political prospects presented themselves. Freed from the stresses of the Freedom Capital Corporation, I had more time to engage with these opportunities which, without my intention, would ultimately sweep me back toward the corridors of power.

It started simply enough. In early December 1989, Ann Richards, who was running for Governor of Texas, called me to say that she would be in San Antonio on Saturday and would like to visit with me. Ann was a well-known quantity in Texas—smart, hardworking, and with a great sense of humor. I had met her previously when she was treasurer of Texas under both Mark White and Bill Clements. I told her that I was on the board of KLRN, the local public television station, and unfortunately, I would be working there fundraising all that day. Without missing a beat, Ann said, "OK, I'll come there to see you." I was pleased to agree.

I asked Margaret if she would like to join me, but to my surprise, she was not enthusiastic about meeting with Ann. At the time, she thought Ann was too liberal. I urged her to join me, telling her it would mean a lot to me, that Ann may be the next governor and we should hear what she had to say. She reluctantly agreed. The day arrived, and by the time Ann finished telling us her plans for the state if she prevailed in the election, Margaret had had a complete change of heart. In fact, after I had said I would support her campaign and help with fundraisers and other events in San Antonio, Margaret was onboard and even offered to host a fundraiser in our home at the end of January.

Wow, what a turnaround! Margaret explained that she was having surgery after Christmas and that was the earliest time possible. Ann understood completely. Margaret had that surgery, and when she returned to her room, she was greeted by two dozen yellow roses with a card attached wishing her a speedy recovery and signed, "Love, Ann." Needless to say, after a kind gesture like that, Ann would always be a good friend. She went on to win the election, and with staff work like that, who could be surprised?

She was now the forty-fifth governor of Texas. We attended her inauguration on January 15, 1991, and soon after, now-Governor Richards appointed me as a trustee of the Texas Growth Fund. I was surprised by this selection, but very pleased. Memories of the closure of my company were still fresh in my mind, and I wanted to help any aspiring, responsible entrepreneurs prosper in their own ventures.

Thanks to Ann Richards, in May of 1991, Texas was blessed with the unusual but great honor of hosting Queen Elizabeth II of England as part of the itinerary of her royal trip. She was the first British monarch to visit Texas, and Margaret and I had the privilege of meeting the queen at the Governor's Mansion in Austin, courtesy of a gracious invitation from Ann.

It was a great treat to meet the queen! As part of the occasion, we had the opportunity to have a picture taken with her, so we eagerly lined up along with the other guests. My turn came, I stepped forward, and my photo was snapped. Margaret had less luck. (Remember that we were having pictures taken before the days of digital cameras, which meant rolls of film were still being used.) When Margaret stepped forward, the photographer had to change the roll in his camera, and she realized her picture had not been taken. What a disappointment!

She never received a picture of herself standing with Queen Elizabeth. This was obviously a frustrating experience, but as the years have gone by, it has slowly turned into a joke that I like to tease her about.

"Are you sure you met the Queen, Margaret? I just can't remember your being there and there's no picture of you...." She always shoots daggers at me when I say that, but it never fails to make me laugh!

At any rate, things remained more or less the same until the late summer of 1991. We were hosting a DLC event in San Antonio at a bar called the 50/50, owned by our good friend Lukin Gilliland.

*Meeting Queen Elizabeth II and Prince Philip with Governor Ann Richards at the Governor's Mansion.*

The principal speaker was the one-and-only Governor Bill Clinton, chairman of the DLC. I had first met Clinton years before, when I was treasurer of the Carter-Mondale presidential campaign, but it was when we were both part of the DLC that we really got to know each other well. He already had the reputation as an ambitious rising star within the party, cemented by his tenure as fortieth and forty-second governor of Arkansas. With the "New Democrats" (as they later came to be known) gaining influence in the party, Clinton was already being seen as a potential candidate in the upcoming election. I was one of those who held that opinion, and when I introduced him to speak, I introduced him as "The next president of the United States." Clinton had not officially thrown his hat in the ring yet, but he seemed to appreciate my introduction.

When Clinton did declare his candidacy in October, I was not surprised at all. He already had my vote, but I was not expecting any serious involvement in his campaign, beyond perhaps some help through the DLC. I was blindsided when I got a call in late November from Rahm Emanuel, the director of finance for Clinton's campaign. We had met before, though I did not know him well. After the usual pleasantries, he asked if I would serve as chairman of a fundraiser for Clinton in January.

Hosting a fundraiser was definitely within my wheelhouse; I had done it plenty of times before from Carter to Gephardt to Richards, and I was pretty good at it. Still, I saw two hurdles with this request. The first was that it was short notice: not an insurmountable obstacle, but it would impact what venue to choose and how many people we could get to attend. The second issue was more important.

"How much money do you want me to raise?" I asked.

"Twenty-five thousand dollars," Rahm replied.

"Well, I'll pencil that in, but if you want to raise big dollars in Texas, we would be better off hosting the fundraiser in Dallas or Houston, not San Antonio."

Rahm waved off my comments, "Look, I know Texas, and I'm sure you can get it done."

It was going to be a challenge, but I did not want to turn him down, so I accepted. There was a lot to do and only a little time to get it done, so I immediately set to work planning how to squeeze $25,000 out of San Antonio by January. I knew I could not do this on my own, so I created a committee of about six people to organize and execute the event. We chose Club Giraud, the private dining club where I had a membership, as the venue, and to our relief we found a lot of people who were interested in attending the event.

However, the fundraiser we were organizing deviated from the norm in one key respect. It was usual to get the amount a person was going to pledge when they signed up, and then collect the check from them at the event itself. We made sure to get the donations as soon as they agreed to attend. That way, we had a more reliable tabulation of the proceeds, and it encouraged people to come to the event, since they had already paid up front.

This tactic turned out to be prescient for another reason that none of us could have predicted. The day before the fundraiser, the Genni-fer Flowers scandal broke on national news. Ms. Flowers was a media personality, and she claimed that she had been involved in a twelve-year affair with Bill Clinton. This news was definitely a black eye for the campaign.

Under normal circumstances, we would have expected our fund-raiser to take a real hit. However, because we had already gotten the money, we came out largely unscathed. There was a lot of gossip about the affair at the event itself, but most of the guests attended, and we did not lose a dime in donations. At the end of the day, we raised over $30,000 from that event, well above what I expected or what Rahm had as a goal. Mission accomplished!

Despite the Gennifer Flowers scandal, Clinton held his own and sailed through the Democratic primaries. As with the Carter campaign sixteen years before, I was invited to the attend the Democratic National Convention, once again held in New York City. I cheered along with everyone else when Clinton was officially nominated, since I knew he had the skills to be a great president. I respected the incumbent, George H. W. Bush, a great deal as well, but it was time for a change, and to get a Democrat back in the Oval Office after twelve years was critically important.

I continued to be active in the Clinton general election campaign. This included another bigger fundraiser held at the Hyatt Regency Hotel on the banks of the San Antonio River. The speakers included me, who introduced Senator Lloyd Bentsen, and he then introduced Governor Clinton. We could all feel the energy and momentum of the Clinton campaign.

Our enthusiasm was not misplaced, especially after Clinton's strong performance at a televised town hall debate. We had all been surprised that Bush had even agreed to that format, since it was definitely Clinton's preferred ground. When, from the heart, he answered an African American woman about her experiences and sympathized with her financial difficulties, saying "I feel your pain," we knew the election was his.

Which brings us back to the meeting in Cisneros's office, three weeks before the election.

"Well, what about you?"

I hesitated for a moment. "I don't think that now is the best time for me to go back into government service." I did not explicitly mention my financial difficulties from a few years ago, but we both knew it was implied.

"It would have to be something really meaningful," I replied.

"I don't know what you mean by really meaningful?" Cisneros pressed, leaning forward in his chair. "All the cabinet positions are spoken for; we have three or four people for each spot. Is there anything else you would consider?"

I knew the answer to that question immediately. If I could not have a cabinet position, then there was only one other job in the whole federal government that I wanted.

"I would like to be considered to serve as Secretary of the Navy."

Cisneros smiled. He knew about my time at the Naval Academy and in the Navy. "John, I think you would be a great choice for Secretary of the Navy. Get me your resume, and I will deliver it to Warren Christopher when I see him in Little Rock in the next few days." Christopher was chairman of the transition committee.

I walked out of the room in a daze. Had I just put myself forward for SECNAV? It was exciting, but I almost could not believe it. While the Secretary of the Navy was not a cabinet position, it was still one of the oldest and most prestigious offices in government, going back to our nation's earliest days. Many great men had filled that role, including

131

two other USNA graduates. The prestige and pedigree of the office were certainly appealing, but that was not the main reason I wanted it. I might have been out of the Navy for over two decades, but it was still a part of me, and it was an institution that I held very near to my heart. It would be the greatest honor for me to lead it.

I was getting carried away: we still had to win the election first, and then I had to actually make it through consideration to be nominated! The election, however, went just the way we expected. We flew to Little Rock for election night, where we stayed with my Aunt Coy and Uncle Elmer.[7] We all celebrated when Clinton won with an overwhelming 370 Electoral College votes and a margin of five million in the popular vote. No matter what happened next, I was grateful to have been a part of the effort to retake the highest office in the land.

Still, I felt my excitement grow when Cisneros phoned me a couple of days later. He told me that Warren Christopher was happy to officially consider me. However, now that I was officially in contention, I had to do the legwork to make sure my name stood out from the pack. I agreed with him when he recommended that a good first step would be to get the backing of both the governor and senior senator from Texas. Their recommendations would lend credibility to my bid. Luckily for me, they happened to be two good friends of mine: Ann Richards and Lloyd Bentsen.

I visited with Ann first. As we shot the breeze and talked about the election, I told her that I was being considered to be SECNAV, and I asked for her support.

"Does that mean you'll be wearing a uniform?" She asked.

"No, ma'am!" I laughed "It's a civilian appointment."

Ann readily gave me her support, no questions asked. Next was Bentsen. Like me, he was also hoping to be in the Clinton administration. He had his eyes firmly set on the cabinet as Secretary of the

---

[7] Aunt Coy was one of my late father's sisters and twenty years his junior. I did not get the chance to see her very often, so it was terrific to catch up with her during that time. She and Uncle Elmer were thrilled that their governor had been elected president of the United States!

Treasury. Still, he said he gladly would support my nomination and, like Cisneros, offered to put in a good word for me the next time he was in Little Rock. With references like that, I dared hope that I might have the edge over the other SECNAV hopefuls, even if I did not know who or how many there were!

What I did not expect was to receive a call from Bentsen on the Friday after Thanksgiving. He was a man who was very protective of his private and personal time, so the fact he reached out to me then meant it must have been serious. At first, I feared it could be bad news, but it turned out to be the opposite. Not only were his chances of becoming Secretary of the Treasury looking good, but he told me that the president-elect was also giving me serious consideration. Senator Bentsen told me that the president-elect had not even been aware that I had been to the Naval Academy and served in submarines. SECNAV was not mine yet, but this was still terrific news.

Not much else happened until January 20, 1993, when I flew to DC with Margaret to attend Clinton's inauguration. By chance, during the festivities, I bumped into Rahm Emanuel. He was soon to become one of the president's senior advisers, and, because of the campaign, he was already close to Clinton. Seeing an opportunity, I quickly pulled him aside and explained my aspiration, asking for his support.

"The sun will not set before I talk to the president-elect on your behalf," he said. Rahm was a hard worker and well respected; having an endorsement from him would definitely help my cause.

During the inauguration, we attended a party at the home of Ethel Kennedy. While there, I ran into Sonny Montgomery, the venerable congressman for Meridian, Mississippi, where my brother had previously lived. Sonny was more of an acquaintance than a friend. During our conversation, he mentioned that he was trying to help former Mississippi Governor Ray Mabus get the nomination to be the Secretary of the Navy. I smiled, took a conspicuous sip from my drink and decided not to bring up my own hope for the nomination. After a few more minutes, I politely excused myself and went to rub shoulders somewhere else. I knew I would not be getting his support, and I did not want to tip off Ray Mabus that I was hoping to get the job as well.

Thankfully, I had more success elsewhere. In particular, I caught a couple lucky breaks when I met with Larry Smith, a senior staffer for the Chairman of the House Armed Services Committee, Les Aspin, who went on to be Clinton's first Secretary of Defense, and Bruce Lindsey, who was senior in Clinton's campaign and was the Deputy White House Counsel. They were both important voices. In 1992, I had attended an event at the LBJ Ranch in Stonewall, Texas. A number of prominent Democratic senators were there, so I approached Senator Jeff Bingaman of New Mexico; Senator Byron Dorgan of North Dakota and Senator Chuck Robb of Virginia. They all agreed to vouch for my candidacy. Whether they could help me directly or not, their support was greatly appreciated, because it showed that people trusted in my ability to do the job.

As the months ticked by, I was still waiting for an answer from the administration, but I was optimistic about my chances. That was until I saw an article in the Washington Wire, a section in the Friday edition of the *Wall Street Journal*. It was basically a loudspeaker for the rumor mill in Washington, and, apparently, some people were saying that President Clinton already had someone in mind for his SECNAV nominee, and that someone was not me. According to the Washington Wire, Ray Mabus was the favorite. It made sense: Mabus and Clinton were both governors of their states at the same time, and they were friends, but it was not the news I wanted to hear! I was definitely despondent; had I gone through all of that effort for nothing? It was then that the White House Chief of Staff Mack McLarty, managed to get a message to me:

*"Don't believe everything you read."*

It was a ray of hope. I did not hold my breath, but I trusted him.

Sometime in April, I finally received a call from the White House. I was in Houston on business at the time, but as soon I learned that they had reached out, I called them back. I got in touch with a woman by the name of Antonella Pianalto, who worked in the White House presidential personnel office. She gave the happy news to me: I was officially President Clinton's nominee for SECNAV! I almost could not believe it; it seemed too good to be true. She congratulated me, gave me some information, and told me that I should prepare for the confirmation hearings just as I had for the Ginnie Mae and FHLBB hearings.

Later that week, I also received an interesting report. I learned that the Pentagon inspector general's report on Tailhook was going to be released very soon. We had to get ahead of the story, so I called Antonella back and told her that it was important I speak with President Clinton before his next press conference. I explained that it was necessary because of the Tailhook scandal. (This issue I will discuss more later.)

Thankfully, Antonella relayed the message dutifully, and later that week I picked up the phone to hear a staffer tell me that President Clinton would be on the line. Even though we had some important issues to talk about, I knew that first things came first. I began by thanking him for his faith in me and for choosing me to be his SECNAV nominee.

"John, I have had more people ask me to appoint them SECNAV than for any other post in my administration." He stated, "I chose you because you're a good man, you understand the culture of the Navy and Marine Corps, and I know you are right for it. I look forward to working with you."

The first part of that comment surprised me: SECNAV was certainly a respected posting, but I did not think it would have the largest field of applicants. At any rate, I was thrilled that, out of that entire pack, I was the one to be nominated. I was set on doing the best job possible, and that would begin right then. Tailhook might have happened almost two years before, but with that IG report soon to be released, it was about to enter the national spotlight.

I spoke about it with the president, giving him some context on the Navy and the current situation as I understood it. He would soon be my boss, and we had to be on the same page so we could formulate a coherent strategy and report to the press. President Clinton quickly grasped what I told him and thanked me for my take on the situation. Sure enough, at the press conference later that week, the first question he was asked was about Tailhook. In his answer he demonstrated that he understood everything I had said and explained to the reporter that he was and would be working closely with the Pentagon to resolve the debacle. I was very impressed by how he handled it, and I knew we had taken a good first step.

I spent some time in Washington during my confirmation hearings, which I sailed through,[8] and my swearing in occurred on July 22, 1993. This gave us just enough time to find a new house and move from San Antonio to Washington for my new government job. It was a hectic time: once again I was uprooting my family from Texas to DC, while trying to be as prepared as possible for my new duties. The long to-do list was made shorter when our good friend Bruce Smiley said that he would look after selling our house. It was a truly generous offer for him to make, and it took a lot of pressure off us, so I gratefully accepted. I stayed with our friends Frank and Nancy Moore for a couple weeks and then moved to the Navy Yard P quarters, guest lodging for flag officers, before we closed on our new home.

As I was making the final preparations, I had a call from Colonel Wayman Bishop. He had served as the military assistant to the previous Secretary of the Navy (and would serve as mine for six months after I took the job). He had a comprehensive understanding of both the department I would soon be leading and the current situation it was in. He offered to fly down to San Antonio, and we would drive back to the nation's capital together. Such a long car ride surely would give us plenty of time to go over a lot of information.

---

[8] Obviously, the topic of my savings-and-loan failure came up. I was ready for the line of questioning, answering honestly and handing over any requested documents. It was not an asset to my confirmation hearing. However, they concluded that it had not come down to any malpractice or improper behavior on my part, so that hurdle was overcome. Their questions were covered in a private hearing, rather than in public, which I would have preferred.

*Confirmation hearing before the Senate Armed Services Committee to become Secretary of the Navy.*

Finally, the day came to leave San Antonio. Despite the highs and lows, it had been a terrific twelve years, and that city will always be special to me. I picked up Colonel Bishop at his hotel and began the long, 1,600-mile drive northeast. After the Carter administration, I thought my days of working for our country were over. And yet, here I was heading back to Washington to serve our nation once again. But this time, it was going to be in the best job in government!

# CHAPTER 11

# THE BURNING BUNK

August 14, 1993, was a bright, sweltering day when I rose to be sworn in as the seventieth Secretary of the Navy. In truth, I had already officially taken the oath of office on July 22, so I could go to work at my job. Steve Honigman, the Department of the Navy's General Counsel, was the swearing-in official. That was a quick and simple affair in my new office. This ceremony, which I chose to host in front of Bancroft Hall in Tecumseh Court at the US Naval Academy, was ceremonial, yet it symbolized my new position. My brother-in-law, the Reverend Bob Ratelle gave the invocation, my old friend the Reverend Rick Lobs offered the benediction, and Admiral Arleigh "30-Knot" Burke, who had been Chief of Naval Operations (CNO) and had sworn me in as a midshipman in 1960, swore me in while Margaret held my mother's Bible.

I invited all my family, in-laws, and friends, many of whom made the long journey to Annapolis to be with us. Returning to my alma mater to preside over the institution that I love so much felt right. Rear Admiral Tom Lynch, a classmate from the great class of 1964, was the Superintendent, and he rolled out the red carpet! He arranged for me to review a dress parade of the plebe class, hosted a lovely lunch for all my family, and had a beautiful reception at Alumni Hall after the

*Swearing-in ceremony at the Naval Academy by Admiral Arleigh Burke.*

swearing-in ceremony. Many of my friends, classmates, some former shipmates, and senior staff from the Navy and Marine Corps attended. Deputy Secretary of Defense Bill Perry was the principal speaker and did a fine job. (My remarks are in the appendix.)

My appointment as SECNAV did not come at an auspicious time for that great institution. The Navy was mired in crisis and scandal and was perhaps in its worst peacetime condition in living memory. I recall a headline in the *Navy Times* saying, "Navy Morale at All-Time Low," and it certainly showed: the organization was in the throes of both structural reorganization and a culture shock, which it certainly was not handling well. "The bunk was on fire when I got in it" was a line from my speech.[9] This was not going to be some easy appointment I could coast through for a few years with minimal effort. Yet I loved every day

---

[9] This was a reference to a tale of a sailor who was being punished for being intoxicated and disorderly and setting his bed on fire. As the story goes, when asked to explain himself, the sailor had said "Sir, I plead guilty to being drunk, but the bunk was on fire when I got in it." Needless to say, I felt it was an apt metaphor for the state of affairs I found myself in!

of it! It did not matter that the problems besetting my beloved Navy were not of my making, I was going to do everything in my power to improve the Navy and Marine Corps services and make it the best department it could possibly be.

From my days at school and running my own business, I was no stranger to leading, but SECNAV was a larger and more important leadership position than any I had assumed before. In one way or another, my decisions would impact the lives of hundreds of thousands of people. I felt the responsibility keenly, and I knew this would be the greatest test of my life.

A month before, however, I had received a letter from a minister in California. It was a package of congratulations with a nicely framed document titled *The Timeless Traits of Leadership*. They were eight simple principles that someone in charge should embrace if they are to be successful:

*A Leader...*
1. *Is Trusted.*
2. *Takes the Initiative.*
3. *Uses Good Judgment.*
4. *Speaks with Authority.*
5. *Strengthens Others.*
6. *Is Optimistic and Enthusiastic.*
7. *Never Compromises Absolutes.*
8. *Leads by Example.*

I believe any good leader naturally embodies most of these traits, and I certainly learned from them over the years. Still, seeing them presented all in one place and in such a succinct manner was profound. It carried even more resonance with me when I realized that these principles came from chapter 27 of the book of Acts in the New Testament and the life of Saint Paul the Apostle, in particular, when he saved the lives of his Roman captors during a shipwreck. To this day, I firmly believe that these values will aid anyone who finds himself or herself in a position of leadership, and they certainly guided me through all the ups and downs of my tenure as SECNAV.

In my confirmation hearing before the Senate Armed Services Committee, Chairman Sam Nunn asked me my approach to leadership. I told him that my approach was something that I had to memorize as a plebe at the Naval Academy. It was said by the Father of the Navy, Captain John Paul Jones:

*"It is by no means enough that an officer of the Navy should be a capable mariner. He must be that, of course, but also a great deal more. He should be as well a gentleman of liberal education, refined manners, punctilious courtesy and the nicest sense of personal honor. He should be the soul of tact, patience, justice, firmness and charity."*

There was a lot on my plate from day one, so I needed to hit the ground running. I had never been in charge of a large organization of almost a million people with so many working parts before, and much of my first weeks was spent learning the ropes and meeting those who reported directly to me. Arguably, the most important offices under my authority were the presidential appointees of the Navy Secretariat, the Chief of Naval Operations, and the Commandant of the Marine Corps, who were the highest-ranking officers of their respective branches (The Department of the Navy is the only organization that has two military branches under its jurisdiction, which meant twice the responsibility for me).

The Commandant of the Marine Corps was General Carl E. Mundy, who had held the office for two years prior to my arrival. Mundy was a Vietnam veteran and a man of considerable skills. During our first meeting, I agreed with him that I should visit the Marine Corps's main facility on the West Coast at Camp Pendleton near San Diego, California, to meet the Marines who were serving there. I walked away from our first meeting impressed.

I flew out to the West Coast at the first opportunity and was greeted with great warmth and respect. Even though I would not be working directly with them, these people were my responsibility, and it was just as important for them to see me as it was for me to see them. It was a great but exhausting trip, not least because I had to fly back to Washington to attend an important dinner at the White House with President Clinton and senior military leaders and then back out to San Diego to continue my work!

*At the White House with President Bill Clinton and First Lady Hillary Clinton.*

The other important working relationship within the Department of the Navy was with the Chief of Naval Operations. That position was held by Admiral Frank Kelso, who had been acting SECNAV from January to July prior to my appointment. In many ways he was an impressive man. He had a long and distinguished career in the Navy and had earned the Defense Distinguished Service Medal. He had also been a submariner like I had, so I immediately felt a connection with him through our shared experiences. However, not all was as it appeared with Admiral Kelso, as I realized when I was presented with the first major challenge of my secretarial career: Tailhook.

The Tailhook scandal was an event that had occurred in September 1991 at the Las Vegas Hilton. It was an annual event hosted by the Tailhook Association, a fraternal group of naval aviators, but it was this one that would live in infamy. Held in the wake of the Navy success in the Desert Storm operation with many officers feeling their oats, this Tailhook convention was defined by virulent and disgusting displays of sexism perpetrated by naval aviation officers. Naval aviation is a stressful, highly technical occupation, and now, there was growing talk of integrating women in the military into combat roles (more on this later), which inevitably would mean fiercer competition for missions and a challenge to their traditions. It was a combustible situation, and in 1991 it finally exploded.

On the notorious third floor of the hotel, female sailors and other women who were present were physically and psychologically degraded by many of their male counterparts. At Tailhook 1991, men wore shirts which read *Women Are Property* and made misogynistic comments like "never in my Navy!" to the speakers and panels, whenever the subject of women pilots was mentioned. Drunken squadron parties were held in rooms with strippers, prostitutes, and random women they had cajoled to join them. It all came to an ugly head with the "Gauntlet," a despicable game where women were harassed, verbally abused, and often groped when they were forced to walk through it. It was an absolutely disgraceful, shameful chapter in the naval history of our great country.

As a controversy, it did not erupt all at once, but instead slowly escalated as allegations surfaced. The first to come forward was Lt. Paula Coughlin, a rescue helicopter pilot who had been thrust through the Gauntlet against her will, and she took her case all the way up to the inspector general of the Department of Defense. It made national headlines, and more than one investigation was conducted. By the time I entered office, things were at a boiling point. Many of the previous senior civilians who had been in the department when it had occurred had either been replaced by new political appointees or had left office, so now it was the job for my team and me to clean up the mess.[10]

When I read the IG report on what had happened, I was absolutely appalled. Such treatment of fellow sailors went against everything the Navy stood for. It was a total failure of ethical and moral character. I was resolute to get to the bottom of what happened, but it also inspired me to implement my Courage of Character strategy: in other words, to get the Navy Department back on track by living up to its principles, as well as trying to encourage a stronger sense of ethics and moral integrity. Everyone, male or female, black or white, admiral or janitor, should be treated with dignity and respect. Those who failed in this would be held accountable, and that would begin with those who were culpable at Tailhook.

My first step was to draw up a plan of action with my team. I did this with the Department of the Navy's General Counsel Steve Honigman, his deputy Carol DiBattiste, my executive assistant, Captain Bill Schmidt, and my military assistant, Colonel Wayman Bishop. I valued their advice and kept the team tight so we could make decisions easily. Together, Steve and I decided to reinterview all the flag officers who had

---

[10] However, I must give credit to my predecessor, the sixty-ninth SECNAV, Sean O'Keefe. Before he left office, he significantly modified an agency within the Navy Department, the Naval Criminal Investigative Service (NCIS), and, as a result, it reported directly to the civilian secretariat rather than the Chief of Naval Operations. This meant it was more impartial, and it was a vital tool in our efforts. The NIS (informally known as "the Admirals' Gestapo") was renamed NCIS.

attended the Tailhook convention. A number of them seemed remorseful for their actions. From there, Honigman created a matrix. In it, we sorted people by their level of authority and their knowledge/involvement in what had happened. That way, we hoped to separate those who were guilty from those who were not and respond accordingly.

The Inspector General of the Department of Defense asked the sailors who attended Tailhook which admirals they had seen on the third floor of the hotel. I was alarmed by the worrying trend emerging; over thirty of the sailors said that they had seen the Chief of Naval Operations, Admiral Kelso, on the third floor of the hotel at Tailhook. This revelation was deeply distressing for three reasons. First, it suggested that the fallout extended to the highest military office in the Navy. Second, it explained why Kelso's response to the scandal when he was acting secretary seemed slow and more concerned about protecting the Navy instead of ferreting out those responsible. Finally, it meant that Kelso appeared to have misled me when he told me that he had never been on the third floor of the hotel.

Needless to say, this undermined the confidence I had in him, and when you cannot wholly trust one of your most important subordinates, the situation soon becomes untenable. By late September, I made the decision to ask for his resignation, but my idea did not go according to plan. On September 30, 1993, my memo to Secretary of Defense Les Aspin, which outlined my intent and request to replace Kelso, was leaked to the press.

I found out about the leak late afternoon on September 30, and on my drive home, I listened to the news reported on the radio. Over the weekend, I understand that other DoD officials were hounded for comment by the media. That news coverage certainly was not what I wanted. On Monday, I was visited by Deputy Secretary of Defense, Bill Perry, who informed me that, in the wake of the media headache, Secretary Aspin had decided to overrule my decision and keep Kelso on as the Chief of Naval Operations. Secretary Perry informed me also that it was important to him and to Secretary Aspin that I remain in my job. Apparently, President Clinton had told Secretary Aspin that the decision was his to make. I found the decision hard to fathom: in my opinion, he was clearly guilty and a liability to the reputation of the Navy if he remained where he was.

A week or so later, I was at the White House for a ceremony, and former President Jimmy Carter was also there. He saw me and came up to tell me that I had made the right decision on Admiral Kelso. I believe he is one of the most highly respected presidents in the history of our country for his honesty and integrity, and his opinion was very important to me. I will be forever grateful to him for seeking me out to tell me his belief.

Kelso was planning to retire in June 1994, but my hope was to replace him earlier. Aspin's decision went against my crusade of accountability, but to my great chagrin, my hands were tied. For a while, things were awkward, to say the least. I continued using the power of my office to deal with the fallout of Tailhook, with some success. However, Kelso obviously knew of my attempt to push for his removal, so our relationship was frosty. My decision on Kelso was vindicated some months later when a Navy judge, Capt. William T. Vest, Jr., in a related Tailhook case, agreed with me publicly. He may not have been among the worst of the perpetrators, but Kelso was complicit, and he had to go. Thankfully, Secretary Perry and President Clinton agreed as well, which meant Kelso did not have anyone to protect him. At any rate, even though he had survived my first attempt to replace him, Kelso was getting grilled in the court of public opinion over his role in Tailhook. In April 1994, Kelso accepted the facts and retired early. (A *New York Times* lead editorial on this issue is in the appendix.)

I took no satisfaction in this: his career in the Navy was long and deserving of respect, so it was sad to see him leave under this pall of controversy. Part of his motivation was clearly to protect the Navy, which I could understand, even if I did not agree with it. As a final act of respect for his service as a whole, Secretary Perry and I came to his defense when a large group of senators, who deemed his recent conduct unsatisfactory, tried to rescind some of the retirement benefits he was entitled to as a four-star admiral. We were successful in preserving those, because he had previously served well in another four-star job as Commander-in-Chief of the Atlantic fleet. He was replaced as CNO by Admiral Jeremy "Mike" Boorda on April 23, 1994. Now I had someone who had my full confidence residing in that important office, and it was also an important symbolic victory, both for me and for the victims of Tailhook. It showed that no matter how important you were, all were going to be held accountable.

There were many other naval officers implicated in the controversy, so I wanted to take a firm stand and show that kind of tawdry behavior would not be tolerated. The problem was, I was trying to clean up a system that was often determined to defend its own. Additionally, it was extremely bureaucratic. Finally, some people were certainly more guilty than others, and some members on my team urged a more merciful approach to those less involved. I was sailing into a headwind, and the process was slow going.

In the end, no one was criminally charged, though I believe there were a few who certainly deserved it. Forty of the Navy and Marine officers who were involved in the scandal received nonjudicial punishments (in other words, reprimands that did not have to go through a drawn-out legal process). That was mainly in the form of formal letters of reprimand or censure, which would permanently be attached to their service records and would adversely affect their careers. Others were demoted, and three officers, whose actions I viewed as especially deplorable, were subject to court-martials.

The system had stymied some of my efforts to fully prosecute those involved and see justice done; however, there were other options. The first was used with those whose culpability was either unclear or their involvement was less direct. For those men, we created two new types of documents, which we called letters of guidance and letters of instruction. Unlike reprimands, these were not officially punitive and served more as a caution for their future decisions. Secondly, as SECNAV, I had the authority to influence promotions. In an organization where promotion was vital to career advancement, that was very important. People had to be held accountable for their actions!

The Tailhook scandal was the first major challenge of my tenure as SECNAV. While I wish the system had allowed me to take more decisive action, I did what I could to see justice done. I made it clear that I would not stand for that kind of thing and that I was hellbent on getting the institution heading back in the right direction. The core values of the Navy and Marine Corps are honor, courage, and commitment. Not only was I going to reaffirm those principles, but also I was determined to make sure dignity and respect for everyone became firm aspects of the culture.

That was precisely what I set about doing. As awful as Tailhook had been, it was just a manifestation of a deeper problem in both the Navy and the Marine Corps. The military, I would argue, is in many ways an inherently conservative institution. It does not like to change, and, when it must, it is often a slow and reluctant process. In the early 1990s, it was going through two seismic shifts. The first of these was around the push for equality in general and for the integration of women into combat roles in particular.

For a number of years, there had been much discussion about if and when to allow women to be in combat. They had already been serving in noncombat roles and support units for decades: in the case of the Navy, this had started in 1917 when they had been allowed to join the Naval Reserve. When the Clinton administration came in, we decided to push forward with our agenda of integrating women into combat roles. Personally, I was fully on board with that, and as previously said, I believe that anyone who is willing and able to serve our great nation should be allowed to do so. Preventing someone on grounds of their sex felt dated and arbitrary to me.

Unfortunately, not everyone felt the same as we did. The sentiment had clearly been bubbling under the surface for quite some time, even before we took office. Tailhook was perhaps the highest-profile and ugliest example of that. Ironically, opponents of change shot themselves in the foot with that display of misogyny, because it gave us the justification we needed to push forward with our plan. Until then, there was still uncertainty among the public about whether to allow women into combat roles. After Tailhook, public opinion swung firmly in our favor. The military was understandably criticized for the scandal, but it gave us all the reason we needed to move ahead with integration and to implement a wide-sweeping cultural reformation.

Secretary of Defense Les Aspin made the announcement in late 1993 while we were still deeply mired in the fallout from Tailhook. However, it would not be until 1994 that we began to take steps to implement it. Even so, the integration was not implemented universally, or without some protest. Most notably, as the result of Department of Defense policy that came into effect in 1994, women were still banned from serving in direct combat roles in the Army. That did not apply to me, though; I was Secretary of the Navy, not the Army, and I was going to go full steam ahead!

My approach to integrating the Navy (and to a lesser extent, the Marine Corps) was related, yet distinct, from how I handled Tailhook. In the case of the latter, I was trying to buffer the fallout from something that had already happened, but with the former I was trying to engender a broader paradigm shift within the Department of the Navy going forward. That would require a patient, diligent approach, with a focus on the long term. If there was one good thing that came out of Tailhook, it was that it gave me the clout to push for cultural rejuvenation that I believed the Navy needed. Broadly speaking, this took two forms: implementing legislation and winning hearts and minds.

Implementing legislation was actually quite straightforward, at least on paper. It was now the law of the land that women should have greater access to combat roles. As far as the Navy was concerned, that largely took the form of allowing women to compete for combat roles in naval aviation and allowing women to serve on virtually any ship, from destroyers to aircraft carriers. It was my job to facilitate this as smoothly and as quickly as possible, so I went out of my way to make sure female sailors were represented. Men would always be the majority; there were simply more of them serving than women. Yet, by getting as many women on the decks and in the air as quickly as possible, we would be ensuring the door would remain firmly open for future generations.

In general, I got little formal pushback on this. The Navy knew it was the law, so there was not much they could do to stop it in an official capacity. I also think that many welcomed the change and were happy to see their female counterparts granted those long-overdue rights. However, there was certainly a sizable minority of officers who resented the culture shift; Tailhook did not happen in a vacuum, after all. A hostile work environment would discourage bright and patriotic women from serving, and that simply could not be tolerated. All of our hard work would have been worthless if we did not pull out the weed of sexism by its roots.

That is where winning hearts and minds came in, and it was without a doubt the harder of the two efforts. I knew that, in the same way that Rome was not built in a day, changing the culture of an old, vast institution like the Navy would not happen overnight. Still, I sometimes found myself fretting about how and what I could do. It dawned on me that, now that I was carrying the issue of equality forward, there was an opportunity to embody another two of those timeless traits of leadership: leading by example and being optimistic and enthusiastic.

I wagered that these principles would be the most constructive and morale boosting. By enthusiastically leading by example, I hoped to show everyone that we were going in the right direction. For my part, I made sure that two of the five assistant SECNAVs were women. Smart, talented, and hardworking, Nora Slatkin and Deborah Christie were true assets to my team and completed, to the highest standard, whatever job I tasked them. On a larger scale, for a time, I prioritized female sailors and naval aviators wherever I could. Getting them represented in those newly integrated roles swiftly was an imperative. The majority of them served the Navy terrifically, and in tandem with my secretarial

*John at his desk with the first Secretariat. Left to right: Robin Pirie, Deborah Christie, Steve Honigman, Richard Danzig, Nora Slatkin, and Fred Pang.*

appointments, they helped discredit the notion that the Navy was not a place for women. As for enthusiasm, I always spoke highly of our servicewomen in public and in department correspondence. If people saw that they had my full and vocal support, they would have less reason to doubt the changes we were making.

I will not claim that it was an unbridled success. Fostering this kind of lasting change takes years, if not decades, and it was still an ongoing process after I left the job. We also got off to a rocky start when the first woman who wanted to fly combat missions failed her qualifications. Obviously, this was not a good look for what we were trying to achieve, and I suspected foul play might have been involved, so I visited with the Grey Eagle, the most senior aviator in the Navy, to review her application. After a great deal of consideration, he agreed with the decision, stating that she would be a risk to her fellow pilots if she were pushed through. However, she was welcome to practice and try again. Begrudgingly, I accepted his verdict. In spite of that failure, however, we began to see a steady trickle of female recruits qualify as the years went by. We may have lost the first battle, but it looked like we were winning the war.

There were also still cases of sexism, but nothing approaching the level of Tailhook. We dealt with such transgressions swiftly and decisively, and as time went on, fewer and fewer incidents were reported. That being said, because we were changing the spirit of the culture of the Navy, there were inevitably going to be other forms of friction. For example, a fifty-year-old admiral could have a completely different outlook and approach compared with his new, young female aide. Things were not perfect when I left, but we had come a long way in just a few years, and I can say with pride that the Navy was on course to answer all bells.

I would be reminded of all this hard work years later, from an unexpectedly close source. Both our sons had served our country: John, Jr., in the Navy and Chris in the Marine Corps. During his time in the Marine Corps, Chris had become a helicopter pilot, and during his training he met a woman named Kelly Singleton who was also a helicopter pilot. They connected again some years later and began dating in 2007. Early in their relationship, Kelly learned I was Chris's father, and in May of that year she sent me a long handwritten letter. Chris had told her about some of the challenges I faced while I was serving at the Pentagon. The entire letter was incredibly heartfelt, but the following extracts stood out:

*As difficult as it is for an organization to change a policy or a rule, it is clearly exponentially more difficult to go about changing a culture—especially when the culture defines itself by the very traditions you're trying to change. I can't imagine how professionally and personally taxing it must have been to make the difficult decisions you made…*

*I wanted to say a personal thank you for those decisions. For me, the culture of naval aviation was not just a physically safe place to be, it was a place where I was able to succeed and excel to the very limits of my ambition, intellect and talent…when I was 6 years old, I told*

*my parents that I wanted "to fly planes off the big ship like dad"...*
*thank you so much for being a big part of the reason why it turned*
*out that I could.*

Never in my life did I expect to receive a letter like that, let alone
one that was written over ten years after my efforts and from someone as close as my son's girlfriend! It is hard to put into words how
much it means to me, even to this day. To hear from someone who had
been able to chase her dreams, and to do so without the fear of harassment thanks to me and my team, was beyond vindicating. It was proof
that all our tireless work had made an impact. I was proud of what we
had managed to accomplish and glad the door was no longer closed to
women like Kelly.[11]

While the push to fully integrate women was our main focus on promoting equality in the Navy, it was not our only effort. We also tried
to make the Navy and Marine Corps more accessible to the LGBTQ
community. Sadly, on this front, we were less successful. There was a
general consensus within the Clinton administration that, if a gay person wanted to serve, they should be able to do so without fear of reprisal.
Ideally, they would have been able to serve openly, but this was seen as a
bridge too far by many politicians and even the public as a whole.

Attitudes toward the LGBTQ community have shifted seismically
since the early 1990s. Gay marriage was only federally recognized in
2015, which was a milestone, but this occurred two decades after what
we were trying to accomplish. In other words, we were trying to push a
policy forward before the military or the country was ready to accept it.

In December of 1993, we were forced to compromise with Congress,
resulting in the controversial "Don't Ask, Don't Tell" policy (DADT).
In short, it allowed gay servicemen and women to serve, but only if

---

[11] I would meet Kelly soon after she had sent me the letter, and she was just as impressive
in person as her letter suggested. About fifteen months later, Chris and Kelly were married,
and I am honored to have someone as wonderful as she is as my daughter-in-law. (Her
entire letter is in the appendix.)

they remained closeted, and barred those who were openly homosexual from serving at all. We were not permitted to ask about someone's sexuality, and they were not supposed to disclose it or they would be forced to leave the service. Our intentions were good, as we wanted to make the military accessible to all, but it was obvious that compromise was discriminatory. No one should have to hide who they are for fear of abuse or losing a job.

Laws are laws, and it was my duty to see that it was implemented across the Navy and the Marine Corps. I do not recall any specific instance where I received notice on my desk of an openly LGBTQ individual being forced out, but that does not mean that it did not happen at lower levels. In 2011, the Obama administration repealed DADT, and the LGBTQ personnel were finally allowed to serve without worrying about hiding who they truly were. Had we been more successful earlier, we could have avoided that unfair compromise.

I left the Navy and Marine Corps a fairer, more integrated and equal place than I found them. I believe that those attempts were the exception and not the norm. To paraphrase Kelly: "It is difficult to change the culture of an organization like the Navy, especially when the culture is defined by the traditions we were changing." Today, the Navy has the second-highest number and percentage of servicewomen in the US military, making up 20 percent of enlisted and 19 percent of officers as of July 2020, with the Air Force ahead by only the smallest of margins. To know that I played a role in that is humbling, and I am honored to have helped achieve such a positive result.

However, as important as changing the culture of the Department of the Navy was, it would not be the only thing that would define my legacy as SECNAV. The Navy was undergoing sweeping structural and organizational changes, which I had to shepherd it through. Not only that, but I would have to deal with yet another scandal before my term was up, one which came from an institution very important to me.

# CHAPTER 12

# ACCOUNTABILITY AND RESPONSIBILITY

The legacy of Tailhook would, in one way or another, persist throughout my tenure as SECNAV, improving over time but never completely fading away like some lingering illness. Whenever anyone who had attended the Tailhook convention was on the promotion list, I had to personally approve the promotion before it went to the US Senate. What had transpired could never be forgotten, but I did my upmost to bind the wounds it had caused and tried to ensure that those officers who had been implicated in the scandal were held accountable in some way.

Yet, it was not the only problem my team inherited when I took office in the middle of 1993. Before I was going through the SECNAV confirmation process, I was informed of another issue that would soon be on my desk. It had recently come to the attention of the Department of the Navy that a number of midshipmen at the Naval Academy were suspected of having cheated academically, specifically on the electrical engineering (EE) exam in 1992. That was the first I had heard about it, and it troubled me deeply. This was my alma mater, an institution that I held in immeasurable esteem. It was almost impossible for me to fathom that such a thing could happen there, beyond the rare individual midshipman.

155

Whatever was going on at the academy, it was a fairly new and developing situation. I was told there had been an internal investigation, the NCIS was looking into the matter already, and a report from the Navy IG was forthcoming. It was not front-page news at the time like Tailhook was, and there was a desire within the Navy to keep it that way; they did not want the headache of two public scandals swirling around at once. Still, since I was the nominee for SECNAV and hoping to be confirmed, there was a consensus that I should be informed of this.

There was so much on my plate in those early days, and so much to learn about my responsibilities and authorities, that I did not dedicate much time to that at first. However, it would be unwise to let this issue fester, and I knew we had to take action sooner rather than later. After I was confirmed, I sat down with some of my team, determined to get a better understanding of both what had happened and about the investigation.

I knew that civilian oversight of the Navy, which I embodied as SECNAV, would be critical. History has shown time and time again that, when a group is left to oversee itself, it is usually more inclined to sweep any problems under the rug rather than try to actually correct them. We had to do everything we could to settle these problems at their source, even if this took structural reforms or risked making enemies. As Tailhook was the dominant issue at the time, I decided to focus my efforts on that. Meanwhile, I asked several members of my team—Assistant Secretary Fred Pang, Assistant General Counsel for Manpower Joe Lynch, Steve Honigman, and Vice Admiral Richard Charles "Sweetpea" Allen, who was recommended to me by Admiral Kelso, to pick up where the NCIS investigation had left off.

Our investigation would be cutting it close: the class of 1994, the class implicated in the cheating scandal, would soon be graduating. The results I got back were problematic. Vice Admiral Allen had been tasked with the initial analysis of the issue, and it appeared the investigation had not had a consistent framework. He had clearly put in a great deal of work, but the results were not as precise or conclusive as I had hoped they would be. That being said, one thing stood out clearly. It was his opinion that a number of athletes were involved. His research convinced him that some of them were unquestionably complicit in what had happened.

Reading this, I felt a cold, sinking feeling in the pit of my stomach. That was not because I felt they should be above reproach, but because I had always held them in such high regard. Being an athlete was prestigious but required extra time and effort not normally demanded of other mids. Training and traveling around the country for competitions took up a great deal of time, meaning fewer opportunities for study. I could appreciate that this meant more academic stress for them, but that was not an excuse for fraudulent behavior. They knew the extra responsibilities that would be involved. Cheating on an exam was just as bad as cheating in sports, a violation of principles that could not go unaddressed.

While this news and what it implied were troubling, we still needed to get to the truth. After speaking with Fred Pang, I asked for a thorough review of 106 cases. That was no small feat, but we had to get it right. We were dealing with the fate of so many young men and women, and I was cognizant that what we decided would fundamentally impact their lives.

The Naval Academy, like the rest of our nation's great Navy and Marine Corps, adheres to our core values of honor, courage, and commitment. They all fundamentally revolve around personal integrity, honesty, and high ethical standards. Cheating, by its definition, is a betrayal of all those principles. It is fraud and a violation of one's solemn word.

Some midshipmen were unquestionably guilty of knowingly and willfully cheating, but the cases of the majority of the midshipmen occupied a moral grey area. What do we do with those who cheated accidently and were too afraid to come forward, or who did not cheat personally but would not bilge their classmates and friends? It was those cases that kept me up at night. The punishment had to fit the crime, and I was wary of putting a permanent, damning strike on someone's record unless I felt sure they deserved it.

The Bible, among its many lessons and wise verses, encourages us to love mercy and forgiveness.

**Micah 6:8**—*Do justly, and love mercy and walk humbly with your God.*

**1 John 1:9**—*If we confess our sins, he is faithful and just to forgive us our sins and to cleanse us from all unrighteousness.*

In hindsight, I think those verses may have subconsciously influenced my decision-making process as we went through the cases one by one. I wanted to show mercy where I could, especially to those midshipmen who had not lied or been a direct part of the conspiracy.

However, the honor concept was also deeply important to me, and I felt it was vital that it be upheld. All the midshipmen needed to know that actions had consequences and cheaters should never win, whether they were directly involved or not. I do not deny that it was a fine line to tread, but it was the duty of my team and me to satisfy both requirements as well as we were able.

In April of 1994, over a year after the cheating scandal had transpired, we reached our final conclusions. All in all, I agreed that twenty-nine midshipmen be expelled from the class of 1994. An additional forty-two were spared from expulsion but received lesser punishments. For the rest, the evidence was either unreliable or their exposure to the scandal was minimal, so we opted to exonerate them. From expulsion to forgiveness, it was rarely an easy decision to make, and sometimes it came down to the smallest of details. However, at the end of the day, I think we made the right calls. We had preserved the honor concept and punished the most guilty but shown that there was room for appropriate leniency for others.

Despite all of our meticulous efforts, there were those who disagreed with our verdict. The mids we decided to expel did not take it quietly or with grace, far from it! Many of them complained bitterly, bringing in their families (some of whom hired lawyers), petitioning the Department of the Navy, and even lobbying their members of Congress, all in an effort to get their expulsion overturned. Sometimes, the flak we received from them was intense, but I knew we had to stand by our decisions. If we blinked on one case and overturned it, that would open the floodgates and risk making the entire investigation pointless. Not only that, but it would have set a terrible precedent: one can lie and cheat and get away with it.

While Tailhook and further integrating women into combat roles were more consequential to the Department of the Navy, for me the cheating scandal at the Naval Academy hit closer to home. It felt more personal because it involved my alma mater and people who were friends. While the present crisis had been resolved, I wanted to ensure that it would never happen again.

In that regard, after seeking the advice of the retired and highly venerated Vice Admiral James Stockdale, I also founded the USNA Ethics Center, now known as the Stockdale Ethics Center in his honor. It remains my enduring hope that this center helps to remind the midshipmen of the importance of integrity. Indeed, as of the time I am writing this book, there has been only one instance of cheating at the Academy that has remotely approached the scale of what happened in 1992.

The most prominent engagement I had with the Naval Academy while SECNAV was in 1995, when I gave the commencement address at graduation. The class had been the one after those who had cheated, and I had no doubt that it was still fresh in their minds. I wanted to strike a hopeful and optimistic tone, not dwell on past issues of others. As far as I was concerned, the cheating scandal was now in the past, and I looked forward to a brighter future for all graduates to come.

My speech focused on leadership, and I used the eight timeless traits of leadership with an example of a Naval Academy graduate who personified each trait. I also quoted Rear Admiral Charles C. Kirkpatrick,

*John with Vice Admiral James Stockdale receiving advice on the Ethics Center named after him.*

who had been the Superintendent of the Naval Academy when I was a midshipman, "You can do anything you set your mind to do, and don't you forget it." I also said,

> There is a long line of Naval heroes before you...men and women tried by history. Your turn has come...in character and in deed, you will always be the ones to set the example. This institution is unique because its mission is to ensure that in your hearts you are unique... that foremost and everywhere the defense of American liberty will remain your task...whether in the Naval Service or elsewhere....
>
> When you shake hands with me as you receive your diploma, let's regard it as a pact—a bond between two graduates of this extraordinary institution—to be as worthy as we can possibly be of

160

*those who have gone before us…of those who march with us today…
and of those who will follow us. In a few moments, your diploma and
our handshake will seal that bond. And then, the real challenge will
begin!* (The entire speech is in the appendix.)

I was happy to end that turbulent chapter of USNA history on
a high note. It was a difficult time for everyone involved, but we had
gotten through it. I would, for a while, still have to deal with some of
the outraged families of expelled students, but after that died down,
it finally seemed to be the end of that major hurdle. I could then keep
my attention focused on other matters. From Tailhook to the cheating
scandal, when those are front and center, it is sometimes easy to forget
about events grinding along in the background.

Those were just as substantial and important to the Department
of the Navy but did not generate the publicity or headlines that other,
more acute problems did. The Base Realignment and Closure Commission (BRAC) was one such example.

BRAC was a response to the end of the of the Cold War. For
decades, the US military had been spending colossal amounts of money
and built countless installations across both the country and the world.
While much of this was necessary, some of it was, without a doubt,
superfluous as we were drawing down in size after the end of the cold
war. At the time, there was the mentality of spending all of the budget
the government gave you to ensure you would receive the same or more
the next year combined with a "better to have it and not need it than
need it and not have it" mentality.

With the collapse of the Berlin Wall in 1989 and the official disso-
lution of the Soviet Union in 1991 came a reassessment by politicians.
With the end of the evil empire came a desire to curb what was increasingly seen as wasteful spending by the military. That was where BRAC
came in: reign in the budgets by closing facilities that were no longer
relevant. That sounds simple enough, right? The reality was anything
but. Of course, there were elements in the military who did not want

to see their base closed or their staff potentially eliminated, but by and large, they accepted the change with good grace. When it got complicated, which it often did, it was usually because of the politicians.

Politicians, from mayors and governors to congressman and senators, usually fought as hard as they could to stop military facilities from being closed in their jurisdictions. That was because those facilities, even if they were not being used effectively, were a great source of jobs. Having an airfield, a shipyard, a base, or other kind of station close would mean that the local economy would take a hit and unemployment would rise. And when that happens, not only do the people suffer, but reelection becomes that much harder.

There were other dimensions to the BRAC process. Once a base had been approved for closure, it would typically cease operations within a two- to three-year period. That gave time to complete any unfinished business and to organize the transfer of personnel or useful equipment. After that time, the base would be dismantled, the site cleaned, and then it would be marketed to private-sector buyers. That was its own arduously long and complex part of the process, due to the 1969 National Environmental Policy Act and statutory frameworks around the disposal of federal property. I was not involved in that part of the procedure, so I cannot comment much further on it, but I can at least say that the majority of those former Navy sites have since been put to great use.

The base closures and realignments also had effects within the Navy and the Marine Corps themselves. Primarily, what to do with all the sailors and Marines it affected? I must give credit to both the Navy and the Marines. They did a terrific job in ensuring that as few people as possible were discharged early. Some voluntarily retired or left the service for civilian life as their service commitments expired, but the majority were successfully reassigned.

While my main responsibility was to oversee the realignments and closures of the 1993 cycle, there was another BRAC round that I would supervise directly. The last major session of BRAC was in 1995.

It would not cut as deeply as the 1991 or 1993 closures had, but we were still expected to trim any excess fat from the Navy and the Marine Corps. The Department of the Navy already had the Base Structure Executive Committee in place, which had overseen the bulk of our previous BRAC work. It consisted of two Marine commanders, two Navy admirals and two senior civilian staff, including Assistant Secretary for Installations and Environment, Robert Pirie. They had done a great job previously, so I was comfortable letting them get to work without micromanagement.

With the aid of teams on the ground and knowledgeable, experienced personnel like my friend and neighbor Deputy Assistant Secretary for Installations Bill Cassidy, they soon delivered to me a dense report on their findings and conclusions. As with the previous BRAC studies, their investigation was multifaceted and complex but was premised on one simple equation: the reduction in excess capacity versus the reduction in military value. As long as the reduction in excess capacity was greater than the value lost, then we were doing the right thing.

This round in 1995 was the final round of BRAC that the Navy, Marine Corps, and military at large had to endure and smaller than previous rounds. Though I had not overseen the first two rounds, it was sad to see so many of these bases closed—and not just because I had a personal attachment to some of them. However, I had to remind myself that this downsizing did not equate to the Navy being in decline. Quite the opposite, we were preparing it to function the best we possibly could in a new world. These closures also saved the Department somewhere between $5 billion–$6 billion annually of taxpayers' money in wasteful spending, which we reinvested in ships, sites, initiatives, or research and development. In total, the closures and realignments had been sweeping, with dozens of bases and support installations slated to be closed, downsized, or moved. We may not have gotten everything right, but overall, I think we did a good job.

Those were not the only things that happened while I was SECNAV. There were countless other smaller challenges, events and ceremonies that filled my calendar, a number of which deserve mention. After all, there was more to my time as the seventieth Secretary of the Navy than dealing with problems!

# CHAPTER 13

# LITTLE THINGS ADD UP

I was Secretary of the Navy from July of 1993 to November of 1998, and during that time there was rarely a dull moment, for better or for worse. Beyond the major headlines of my tenure that I have already covered, there were countless other experiences that rarely made headlines. It would be impossible to list them all; not only would it take too long, but reading about some of the more bureaucratic workings of a government department would be about as interesting as watching paint dry! Still, there are a number of memories that I do think are worth discussing, even some of the more "mundane" events of my time as SECNAV and some of the most interesting of my life to date.

As I mentioned in the preface, 1994 commemorated the fifty-year anniversary of a number of the major conflicts of WWII. D-Day was one of those solemn ceremonies. The multiday observance of Operations Trident and Overlord were filled with pomp and circumstance, due heavily to the British skill at planning and ceremony, as well as that of Lieutenant General Mick Kicklighter, US Army (retired), who oversaw the Pentagon's plans. I was fortunate and honored to attend as Secretary of the Navy. The United States sent quite a delegation. In addition to me, it included President Clinton, First Lady Hillary

Clinton, the Secretaries of Defense, State, Treasury, Veterans Affairs, Army, Air Force, and many D-Day veterans.

Margaret and I arrived June 2 and stayed with Admiral Bill Crowe, ambassador to the Court of St. James. Earlier that day he had presented his credentials to Queen Elizabeth II. We had been invited to several events prior to going to Normandy. They began with a grand ceremony at Grosvenor Square, former site of the US Embassy. Not only did President Clinton speak but so did luminaries from other allied nations, including the son of Winston Churchill. Even Bob Hope spoke, and his wife Dolores sang.

Later, there was a dinner where there were even more dignitaries than at the Grosvenor Square ceremony, including government officials from Canada and France, and Queen Elizabeth II, of course. The next day there was a Beat Retreat, a parade hosted by Princess Margaret. Seeing the British guards in full ceremonial regalia marching up and down the parade ground was unforgettable.

After such an amazing time in London, it was time to focus on the D-Day ceremonies themselves. On June 5, I traveled down to Portsmouth and from there out to the USS *George Washington*, a new and mighty Nimitz-class aircraft carrier where my classmate Rear Admiral Al Krekich was the battle group commander. President Clinton was to speak to the crew later that day. David Gergen, one of his senior advisers, came aboard about an hour before the president. I visited with him, and, at one point, he asked me whether there was any news from the Navy that the president should know. I thought about it for a moment and gave him several facts, including that morale was low due to the expected slower promotion rates: however, this year's promotion rates were better than last year's, and next year's were anticipated to be better than this year and, within two years, they would be back to normal levels. Sure enough, President Clinton later arrived on the captain's barge along with the First Lady, and all the sailors were on the hanger deck waiting for his remarks. Gergen pulled me aside and asked me to tell the president the same thing I had told him earlier. Clinton acknowledged with a quick nod and took his place, waiting patiently for Captain Robert Sprigg, the commanding officer of the USS *George Washington*, to introduce him.

A couple minutes later, the president stepped forward to address the crew with his prepared comments. He was as smooth and charismatic as always, speaking about the Navy, the USS *George Washington*, and the fiftieth anniversary of D-Day. It was a short speech but an excellent one. As he was concluding, he seamlessly worked in the news I had shared.

> *As I conclude my remarks, let me say congratulations to those who are re-enlisting. I know this has been a difficult time for many young people who wanted to commit their careers to our armed forces because of the downsizing that inevitably came [after the end of the Cold War]. I want you to know that number one: we're more than halfway through. Number two: it'll be over in two years. Number three: there will be more advancements this year than last year, [and] more advancements next year than this year.*
>
> *We still need you; we need your devotion, we need your talent and the military of the United States is still going to be an important and good place to make a career because it's still defending the security of the greatest nation in the history of the world.*

The crowd exploded into deafening cheers! I clapped with a big smile on my face and shaking my head in wonder. President Clinton had so seamlessly added my information to his speech at the end and had done so with such eloquence and virtually no preparation time. At the end of the day, I know it meant more to the sailors coming from our commander-in-chief than it would have from me, though I was glad to have played a role in raising their spirits.

In 1994, almost a year to the day after I had been sworn in as the seventieth SECNAV, I woke up one morning in New Orleans (where the Navy was christening a new ship) to find a less-than-flattering article about me in the *New York Times*, and on the front page, no less!

The journalist, Jeff Gerth, had written a piece slamming my confirmation process the year before. In essence, he had apparently dug up some information related to the hard assets I had during my brush with bankruptcy. Ostensibly, said assets had not been mentioned during the public confirmation hearing, and therefore, Mr. Gerth was implying my confirmation process was not up to standard. Unfortunately, that was covered in the private hearing, which Mr. Gerth was not aware of.

A few weeks before, one of my mentors, Bob Strauss, had told me that Jeff Gerth had called him and was working on a story about me. That revelation blindsided me. Granted, almost going bankrupt was far from the proudest moment of my life, but I never tried to conceal anything about it during my confirmation hearing. I would not call his article a smear campaign; he was doing his job as a journalist and had no ax to grind. It was, nonetheless, an attack on my reputation and my legitimacy as SECNAV. Unsure of how to proceed, I called my friend, Jim Lehrer. He was the anchor of the *PBS Newshour* in those days, so, as a journalist, I figured he would have a better idea than most how to respond. His answer was welcomed but not what I expected.

"Just give him everything negative about you related to your confirmation, John." He said, "Show him that you're willing to cooperate and that you have nothing to hide. If he sees that you were not trying to hide any wrongdoing, he should back off."

What Jim said made a lot of sense, but I was reluctant to do it. Sending the press every detail relating to one of the most painful experiences in my life was a hard step to take. Still, I dug up everything in my own records that I could find and had my public affairs officer call Gerth at the *New York Times* and give the information to him. The next day, I was given a copy of the newspaper in which a related article was on page 7. Just as Jim had predicted, once I had divulged all the information to him and proved that there was no foul play, he was no longer calling my confirmation into question. That had been a close call, but thanks to Jim's advice, I came out of it well.

To my chagrin, the Tailhook scandal was still casting a long shadow over the Department of the Navy. Hardly a week went by when I did not have to deal with something related to it, but upon reflection, there are two issues that still stand out in my mind to this day: Darlene Simmons and Bob Stumpf.

The first story was not directly connected to Tailhook, but was a result of the crusade of accountability I conducted in its aftermath. There was a lawyer within the Department of the Navy, Darlene Simmons, who had been sexually harassed by her superior officer. When she tried to report it, he denied it and had the gall to force her to take a psychological evaluation. Not only was this sexual harassment, which would not be tolerated, it was also a gross abuse of his authority. I asked my incredible principal Deputy General Counsel Carol DiBattiste, to investigate.

She corroborated that Simmons had indeed been sexually harassed but could not substantiate retaliatory action by the officer. Still, this was enough for me to act. I relieved the guilty officer of his duties, reprimanded an additional two officers who were involved, and cleared Simmons's record of the criticisms he had asserted. I also took the opportunity to visit with Ms. Simmons. I apologized to her on behalf of the Navy; she never should have been subjected to that kind of treatment, and, on top of everything we had done, I offered to extend her contract an additional two years.

Regarding Commander Bob Stumpf, his was arguably the most high-profile case in terms of promotions relating to the fallout from Tailhook. Commander Stumpf was a decorated veteran and commanding officer of the legendary Blue Angels squadron of Naval aviators. He was something of a maverick. However, beyond hearing his name, I did not know much about him. One day, when we were considering the next crop of names to be sent to congress for promotion from commander to captain, the list included Commander Bob Stumpf. However, the file that I was presented did not say that he had been at Tailhook.

While Commander Stumpf was being considered, it was revealed that he attended that event. He had flown to an airstrip near Las Vegas in a Navy plane (something that was explicitly against orders), and it was purported that he had been in one of the rooms on the notorious third floor with his squadron mates where unseemly activity had taken place. There was no evidence Stumpf had taken part himself, but even so, as the commanding officer, he should have stopped such unacceptable conduct. Another concern was that that information had not been in his file when I had put his name forward. Had it been taken out, or had someone made sure it never got there in the first place? I interviewed him in my office and asked him about each of the issues that he had been accused of, and he emphatically denied each one.

Needless to say, when this revelation came to light, it immediately torpedoed his promotion. I thought that might be the end of it, but sometime later his name was brought forward for promotion *again*. I had a moral obligation to ascertain the truth and hold those responsible to account. One of my team, a Navy Department senior attorney named Joe Lynch, offered to take the initiative and depose Bob Stumpf before we went any further. I thought that was a good idea, so I gave him the go-ahead.

I don't think any of us could have predicted what happened next. The deposition went smoothly at first, that was until Joe Lynch asked Bob Stumpf and his lawyer about his presence at Tailhook. He was under oath, so he was wise not to perjure himself, but rather than speak openly about what had transpired, he failed to answer questions. We were dumfounded: this was unprecedented, especially in regard to what amounted to a background check for a promotion. Joe Lynch pressed him on the issue from other angles, trying to get an answer, but Stumpf refused. Finally, Stumpf stormed out of the hearing. Soon after, he tendered his resignation from the Navy. I accepted his request and opted not to pursue further action against him. What was done was done, and we had avoided promoting an allegedly guilty party. There were some who seethed about this, both in the Navy and on the Hill, but I believe that things turned out the right way.

That being said, that would not be the last time the Navy heard from Bob Stumpf. Sometime in the early 2000s, I received a call from the then-SECNAV Gordon England. He informed me that Commander Stumpf had reached out and was asking to be retroactively promoted to the rank of captain that had long eluded him. While he was no longer serving, if he received the promotion, it would increase his retirement pay. I informed Secretary England that it was his decision to make. In the end, Secretary England approved his retroactive promotion, which was disappointing for me, but at least I did my part in making sure that did not happen on my watch or during my tenure.

A tragedy occurred with the untimely passing of Admiral Mike Boorda. He was the first enlisted man to reach the senior position of Chief of Naval Operations (CNO). As I stated before, Admiral Boorda became the new CNO after Frank Kelso retired. I liked Mike Boorda: he was smart, hardworking, and responsive both to me and the needs of the Navy. He also worked hand in hand with the Commandant of the Marine Corps (first Mundy and then Krulak), especially in regard to budgeting issues. I can still remember vividly a day in May 1996, as if it were yesterday. CNO Boorda and Commandant Krulak came into my office and told me they had reached an agreement with regard to dividing the budget between the two services; they even high-fived in front of my desk!

It was the day after the high-fiving that Chief of Information Rear Admiral Kendell Pease visited with me. We discussed a number of different issues, and as we were finishing, he mentioned to me that a *Newsweek* reporter was asking about Boorda's Combat V, an allegedly unmerited ribbon he had been wearing on his uniform. I remember the next day so well. I was sitting in my office visiting with another officer when Commandant Krulak came barging into my office, which was highly unusual, and said that the CNO had been shot, and the Marines had surrounded the Navy Yard and were trying to find the perpetrator.

I immediately went to the hospital where he had been taken. Later that afternoon, we learned that Mike Boorda had taken his own life.

Sadly, Boorda was a troubled soul, though I did not realize how troubled he was until it was too late. Being CNO was a complex job in the best of times, and I was aware that he had a somewhat stressful home life. Nonetheless, I fear all that pressure may have been getting to him, and the media issue with the ribbon was the straw that broke the camel's back. Before his suicide, he wrote letters to his family and the Navy, the latter apologetic for what he saw as his mistakes and praising all the sailors he had served with.

His death came completely out of left field for me, and I was left in a state of complete shock. Margaret and I tried to reach out to his widow, offering to be there for her during that dark time, but she wanted nothing to do with it. Perhaps she needed space. News spread quickly, and in the days following his death, President Clinton visited Boorda's family. He was loving and empathetic, doing all he could do to console Boorda's wife and children. That did not make the news, but to this day, I believe that was one of the president's finest moments. When the time came, both of us spoke at Boorda's funeral at the National Cathedral, extolling his virtues and honoring his memory. His death was the first time I had experienced a suicide among my close circle of friends, family or colleagues, and I pray that he is at peace. Admiral Jay Johnson, who had been serving as the Vice Chief of Naval Operations, soon replaced Boorda as CNO.

After that somber recollection, I think it is a good time to focus on a happier story, and one that makes me particularly gratified: Margaret's role in improving the Navy and Marine Corps's quality of life. It began early in my tenure with a trip to Hawaii. Not long after I was confirmed, Margaret was asked by some members of my staff what kind of first lady of the Navy Department she wanted to be: did she just want to attend the parties, receptions, and formal events, or did she want to be proactive? Clearly, they did not know the type of woman Margaret is!

Without hesitation, she said, "Be active, and I want to be helpful where I can." She decided that she preferred to focus on quality-of-life issues. This covered a variety of issues, including housing, childcare, education, and medical care. We both knew that this was no small task, though we did not expect it to come to the fore so early in my tenure. One of my first trips was to the Pearl Harbor Navy Base. Margaret almost always joined me on my trips, and this early venture was no exception. As we landed and I was whisked away by Navy and Marine officials to begin my busy schedule, Margaret went with the wives to begin her own tour.

They visited Air Force housing first, which was clean and modern, with extensive amenities. She was impressed, clearly the Air Force took good care of its service men and women. Next on the list was the Navy and Marine housing, which involved their doubling back toward the airport. "Is it close to that slum we drove past?" Margaret inquired.

No. It *was* the slum.

The Navy and Marine housing was a pale shadow of its Air Force counterpart. Most of it had been built around the time of the Second World War, and it was clearly showing its age. Bad extensions that left gaps in the roof, gardens that were sea weeds and trash, and rampant termite and water damage; the list went on. Margaret was absolutely appalled by what she saw; how could our great sailor and Marine families be made to live in such deplorable conditions? When we met again to change clothes for the evening official dinner we were attending, I asked her how her day went. It was a casual question from me, and I expected a similar answer, so imagine my surprise when Margaret began to tear up. She told me everything she had seen and how upsetting it had been. I had no idea the housing situation was so dire but now that I knew, I would not let that stand.[12] I promised Margaret that

---

[12] There is an old joke in the military: when the USAF builds a base, they build an officers' club, nice housing, a gym, and then if there's any money left over, they build a runway. When the Navy builds a base, they build a dock, piers, and ships, and then, if there's money left over, they build housing. It seems it had a kernel of truth!

I would arrange a meeting with the head of naval housing when we got back to Washington, and I wanted her to be there.

I managed to schedule the meeting soon after we got home, and Margaret eagerly attended it with me. The woman in charge told us that was the first time in her twenty-plus years of holding that job that she had ever met a Secretary of the Navy and that she had certainly not given one a briefing before. She was excited that we were taking an interest in that quality-of-life issue. It was supposed to be a thirty-minute meeting, but it went on for over an hour, and I had to leave before it finished. Margaret stayed, asking insightful questions and taking copious notes, which she relayed to me along with her own thoughts. I was truly pleased how committed and invested she was and determined not to let her, or our sailors and Marines, down.

After that meeting, I scheduled a meeting with Secretary of Defense Perry. I told him that I had done my homework on the issue of housing, and the Air Force was in first place financially, the Army was second, the Navy was third, and the Marine Corps was fourth. I told him we must do something about Navy Department housing, and I asked for extra funding for the Navy Department for the purpose of improving housing. He did not give me an answer right away, and I left him with some of the material we had covered. I had a call before the close of business that day from Deputy SECDEF John Deutch. "Secretary Perry has agreed to your request, the DoD will budget your department with an extra $100 million over the next two years. But I have to ask you, John, are you sure you want to spend all of that on housing?"

"Yes, sir, every penny!"

And so we did. Thanks, in large part, to Margaret's compassion and her tireless efforts, we made a real effort to improve the housing units in Navy and Marine Corps bases across the world. It was not enough money to fix every problem with regard to quality of life, but it made a big difference, and Margaret went above and beyond in trying to improve the quality of life for those under our care.

By and large, this was well received and went well, though there was one major exception to this rule. At one point, we traveled to Italy, and, while we were there, I decided to open bidding for the housing contracts for our base. Unbeknownst to us, the company who currently held the contract (whose work could be described as subpar at best, which was the reason we opened the contract) was connected to the Mafia. The owner of the company was clearly incensed, and reached out to his "patrons" for help. Soon after, I received a letter from what I can only assume was that infamous criminal syndicate. Actually, it was less of a letter and more of an ultimatum: demanding that we hand the contract back to the contractor, and threatening dire consequences if we did not.

I have never been someone who responds to threats, and I disregarded the correspondence and pushed forward. A new, better contractor was chosen, and I was prepared to move on. Weeks later, before a function at our new Navy base in King's Bay, Georgia, I got another letter from the same source. It threatened to kill me, murder Margaret or one of our sons; it even knew where they were living! I will not deny that made my blood run cold. In the days before 9/11, most senior government defense officials were not escorted everywhere they went by a coterie of security guards. However, this threat was deemed credible enough that we should receive protection for a while. Margaret had no idea what was happening until she noticed NCIS agents at the King's Bay function. When I told her that we now had a security detail and why, she processed the information with a remarkably level head and agreed that was best. Above all, we had to remain alert but calm.

We received round-the-clock protection for two or three months before the "all clear" was sounded. I want to thank those outstanding NCIS officials who protected us during that time, especially a woman named Ronnie who attended Margaret. Never in my life did I think that I would cross paths with the Mafia!

I mentioned that the Mafia knew where our sons were stationed, but what does that mean? Simply put, both John and Chris had decided to join our country's Navy and Marine Corps, respectively. Frankly, I do not think they had any plans to serve until I became SECNAV. However, during my work, one or both of them would sometimes join me for meetings or a trip. They were both deeply impressed by the caliber

*Joseph Rosenthal with a painting of his Pulitzer Prize-winning photograph of the flag raising on Iwo Jima.*

of men and women who served, and after college, they independently made the decision to head to their local recruiting stations to volunteer for officer candidate school. John became a surface warfare officer in the Navy and served seven years, while Chris became a helicopter pilot in the Marine Corps and served nine years.

As I am sure anyone with family in the armed forces can understand, Margaret and I were both very proud of their decisions to serve, but also a little nervous for their safety. In hindsight, we need not have worried: apart from a hand injury that John received during a boarding action, both our sons served honorably and got out in one piece. This was a big relief for us, especially as Chris participated in Operation Iraqi Freedom in 2003. Even though they joined while I was serving as Secretary, I appreciate that they did not receive any special treatment, either good or bad. However, Chris did experience one funny interaction. One of his drill sergeants discovered that I was his father and asked him to recite the chain of command. Chris did, and referred to me as the Honorable John H. Dalton, Secretary of the Navy (which was the correct thing to do). Then, the sergeant stopped him.

"And what do you call the Secretary?"

"I call him Dad, sir!"

When Chris told us this hilarious story from his Marine training, which he did not think was funny at all, Margaret and I laughed so hard that we almost cried! At any rate, I am very pleased that they chose to serve our country. They both learned a great deal, and I was delighted to see the tradition of service in our family continue.

As SECNAV, there was always something that required attention or a decision. That meant that, for a number of years, many of my previous hobbies fell by the wayside. However, there was a major exception to this rule, and that was the Army-Navy football game. If anything, being SECNAV was almost an excuse to indulge that love of mine, and I attended each and every annual game during that time and still do to this day. We used to take the highly decorated Army-Navy special train

*Chris holding the Army Navy football game trophy. Navy won 39 to 7!*

to Philadelphia or New York for the game, and we invited friends and family to join us. It was great fun!

I sometimes spoke to the team before or after games I managed to attend, doing my best to inspire them and to let them know that we were rooting for them. One year, I came up with the idea to sing a song for the team, but when I broached the topic to Margaret, she blanched, especially when I drafted her into singing it with me. Undaunted, I pushed forward with writing it, and together we sang it to the team. Contrary to the doubters (which included Margaret and our daughter-in-law Kelly) it was well received and immensely enjoyed by the players. Still, Margaret all but forbade me from pulling another stunt like that again!

I also had a friendly rivalry going with Secretary of the Army Togo West, at these games. We would wind each other up, but always with the best of humor. Despite the multiple defeats, attending those games was special. As Secretary of the Navy, it felt different than it had before; I was even more invested in the outcome. When we lost an Army-Navy game, I somehow felt like it was my fault! The train ride home was always fun, partying in the club car and singing old Navy fight songs. We may have lost the game, but we always won the party!

Serving as Secretary of the Navy made it my responsibility and privilege to travel extensively worldwide. Luckily, Margaret was always able to travel with me. I obviously traveled less than President Clinton or the Secretary of State, but I was blessed to journey to many places both foreign and domestic. I was especially excited for the international trips, which included the UK, Italy, Israel, Ecuador, Egypt, Singapore, Australia, UAE, Oman, Korea, Portugal, the Philippines, Diego Garcia, Thailand, Hong Kong, and many other places I might never have otherwise visited. Going to Russia in 1996 to celebrate the three hundredth anniversary of their Navy was a unique and rare treat. Who could have ever imagined, just five years before, our nations were Cold War rivals? Whenever such a journey was scheduled, I requested to visit the head of state.

Not all of these asks were accepted, but over the almost five and half years I was in office, I had the great honor to meet with more than ten of the world's leaders including Pope John Paul II, Prime Minister John Howard of Australia (we had a laugh about how our names were so similar), Prime Minister Yitzhak Rabin of Israel, President Rafael Caldera of Venezuela, Emir (later King) Hamad bin Isa bin Salman Al Khalifa of Bahrain, President Fidel Ramos of the Philippines, President Alberto Fujimori of Peru, President Abdalá Bucaram of Ecuador, President Carlos Saúl Menem Akil of Argentina, and I met with John Bruton and Bertie Ahern, two prime ministers (Taoiseachs) of Ireland in the 1990s.

If I did not meet the head of state, I was usually introduced to whoever my counterpart was, or their secretary of state or defense equivalent. When meeting with government officials of other nations, I was as much an unofficial ambassador as I was the Secretary of the Navy, which was a humbling honor. I was responsible for facilitating positive relations with these countries and took this very seriously. The Secretary of the Navy has historically served a diplomatic role for this country.

Those engagements extended to American soil, also. While I was SECNAV, I became good friends with the Australian ambassador to the United States, Andrew Peacock, after a joint naval exercise we had with Australia. We had a lot of shared interests, in particular a mutual love for tennis. We spoke at length of our fascination with the grand slam tournaments and who our favorite players were. One day, I had Ambassador Peacock over for lunch in the Pentagon, and he told me that he had a grass tennis court at his residence, the only one in the Washington-Baltimore area. Due to a longstanding elbow injury, he was unable to take advantage of it, but he extended me an open invitation to play there whenever I wanted.

"Be careful what you offer, Mr. Ambassador!" I said.

Still, he insisted that it was mine to use whenever I wanted, and I took full advantage of his offer. I went there on the weekends, often taking friends, colleagues, or other government officials or people from Capitol Hill with whom I was trying to establish a closer relationship. It became not only a great place to blow off steam but one of the greatest perks at my disposal.

There was one international trip that was not strictly business but out of personal connection and principle. In 1997, I went out of my way to travel to Diego Garcia, a tiny island in the middle of the Indian Ocean, thousands of miles from anywhere. Now, why did I feel it was important to travel to the middle of nowhere and to a British overseas territory, no less? Well, the story dates back many years. Ken Fusch, one of my best friends at the Naval Academy, was stationed there on a one-year unaccompanied tour, at a base on land we rented from the British.

I had done what I could to help him while he was there, including going to his daughter's wedding as her godfather when he could not get back for it. While that had been a long time ago, the reasoning behind my trip was simple: I wanted to show our men and women stationed there that they were appreciated and that while that beautiful but distant corner of the world felt lonely, they were not forgotten. As usual, Margaret went with me, and we spent a couple days in that tropical paradise with our great sailors. Everyone was welcoming, including the locals, and when it came time to leave, they ladened us with gifts, including pith helmets and a painted wooden Diego Garcia sign that I still have hanging in my office at home. In the grand scheme of my SECNAV career, I know that that trip was a blip, yet it meant a lot to me, and I believe it meant a lot to our sailors stationed there, as well.

# CHAPTER 14

# ALL GOOD THINGS MUST COME TO AN END

Whether it was making hard decisions that affected the lives of hundreds of thousands of sailors, Marines and civilians, or traveling the world to meet with world leaders, Secretary of the Navy was a great job but also very demanding. However, I was shocked when 1997 came around: the last four years had just flown by! Still, there was always more to do, and this was just the way I liked it, but I still could not believe that time passed so quickly.

I mention 1997 specifically, because that was the year I was awarded my highest accolade. It was a day much like any other, meeting with Navy and USMC officials, reading policy briefs, listening to the advice of my assistants, and making decisions accordingly. This flow was interrupted when a member of my staff told me that the office had just received a call from Capitol Hill. Apparently, I had been chosen to receive the International Security Leadership Award.

It is always an honor to be recognized, and I quickly learned that this was an annual award given by the National Security Caucus in the Congress to someone they decided had made great contributions to our nation's security on the world stage. It was usually awarded to presidents, secretaries of defense and, occasionally, a member of the House or Senate. Previous award winners include: former Presidents George

*Receiving the International Security Leadership Award, the first service secretary to be given the award.*

H. W. Bush and Ronald Reagan; former Secretaries of Defense William Perry and Caspar Weinberger; and former Senators John Stennis, John Tower, Henry Jackson, and Sam Nunn. I was the first secretary of any military department to receive this award. It took a moment for that to sink in, but to this day, I am deeply humbled, honored, and grateful for this recognition.

I visited with Dick Gephardt, the leader of the House Democratic Caucus, and asked him if he would speak at the ceremony, which he kindly agreed to do. The award itself was presented at a lunchtime gathering in a hall near the capitol. When the time came for me to accept the award, I approached the podium to the sound of applause. As I took the award in my hand, I felt a deep sense of fulfillment. I had never expected that kind of honor, but I am deeply grateful to those who deemed me worthy of that recognition. It goes to show that, if you work hard and diligently at something you love, the impact you make will be recognized and respected by your peers.

I had plenty of dealings with the federal legislature in one way or another. However, it was not always business, at least not in the conventional sense. As SECNAV, I always had to look out for the interests of the Department of the Navy on the Hill and in DC, more generally. Not long into my tenure, it dawned on me that there were other ways of engaging with important officials and their families and building relationships beyond office meetings alone.

As SECNAV I had two "soft power" methods to do just that, and Margaret played an important role in both. The first option available to us were events known as embarks. Every few months or so, one of our aircraft carriers that was home-ported in Norfolk, Virginia, became available. Knowing that, we would schedule at-sea embarks, tours of those active aircraft carriers for congressional spouses. Margaret would be the group leader, and by the time I left office, she had become a consummate expert.

She would escort the eager group from Washington, DC, down to Norfolk, where they would tour a local surface ship or submarine that was in port. Then they would go to the airfield on the base, don cranial helmets and life vests, and fly about fifty to one hundred miles out to the cruising aircraft carrier off the coast, where it was handling carrier qualifications for the aviators. The typical aircraft the group used was a C-2 carrier-onboard-delivery (COD). They would land in style using the famous "tailhook" arresting cable for which the infamous event had been named. Disembarking onto the mighty vessel, they would then go on a day-long tour of the carrier, witnessing catapult takeoffs and landings, seeing many of its inner workings, and learning its unique history. They also had the chance to speak to the sailors, both officer and enlisted, and Margaret would tell me that this was the part of the trip many found to be the most interesting. Finding out why they were serving and seeing the pride they took in their jobs tended to have a lasting impact.

Before dusk approached, it was time to depart, and Margaret led the group back onto the aircraft. The trip ended with a flourish as the plane conducted a catapult takeoff, hurtling into the air on its way back to Norfolk. As fun as they were, these embarks served a very practical purpose: they inspired awe and hammered home the importance of a well-funded Navy. These congressional spouses would, in turn, sing our praises and encourage their spouses to vote in a way that was favorable to us whenever there was a budgetary motion on the floor of the House or Senate that involved our department. Overall, I would say these embarks were a real boon for us. In addition, along with government officials I was also able to arrange embarks for some of my friends and relatives when I was at the Pentagon. They all became great ambassadors for the Navy! I have hosted embarks every year since 2002, except for the pandemic years, with business leaders and persons of influence. Recently, we toured the USS *Mason* (DDG-87) and the USS *Washington* (SSN-787) alongside the pier and flew out to the USS *George HW Bush* (CVN-77).

Our second strategy was also, fittingly, boat related. The CNO had exclusive use of a barge that was available to me as SECNAV whenever I wanted. The barge was seized in a drug raid in the 1980s and turned over to the Navy for its use. Calling it a barge is a misnomer: if anything, it was a three-bedroom yacht. It was not as colossal or ornate as those owned by the very wealthy, but it was, without a doubt, a fine vessel, complete with crew, galley, and able to accommodate about a dozen passengers for dinner.

Margaret and I enjoyed a wonderful cruise the first time we went aboard, but we both realized we could use it for more than just an escape from work. We could invite government officials, even foreign luminaries and a couple good friends for a wonderful night's sailing up and down the Potomac, gazing at the sparkling lights of our nation's capital. We wined and dined them on tables with white tablecloths, silver, and crystal, and even today decades later, I can still remember some of the sumptuous dishes the Navy catering team served. Margaret and I would also engage entertainment for those cruises. It did not take us long to settle on a favorite act: a terrifically talented pair, Chief Wayne Taylor and Petty Officer Pat White, who were part of the Navy's Sea Chanters and sang country songs.

We enjoyed all of those cruises, as did our guests. How could they not? On one occasion, as we docked after another wonderful evening, the wife of Senator Howell Heflin, Mike, remarked that it was the most fun she had ever had in their twelve years in Washington. High praise indeed! Not only did we have a lot of fun, but we also made many friends and political allies that way. Who says that you cannot combine work and pleasure? We did not make excessive use of the barge cruises, as we were aware it could give the misleading impression of too much leisure and not enough work at the taxpayers' expense. Still, those were wonderful times, and it is one of the major perks of being SECNAV that I really miss.

Speaking of ships, another part of my job involved naming them, choosing their sponsors, and attending many christening and commissioning ceremonies. Sometimes I used this for diplomatic effect, like naming a new guided missile destroyer (DDG-81) after Winston Churchill as a nod to our British allies. President Clinton was going to be addressing the House of Commons and the House of Lords in November 1995, about a year and a half after the fiftieth anniversary of D-Day. It was during his speech that the president decided to reveal a gift that we had for the British people. The president loved the idea of announcing it to the UK by speaking to their Parliament. The Brits were touched that we were naming a ship after one of their greatest prime ministers, and the applause was loud and long. Later that day, I received a call from Nicholas Soames, a member of Parliament and Winston Churchill's grandson, who said, "Secretary Dalton, please come to London. There is a very nervous fatted calf awaiting your arrival!" I enjoyed his joke, as he had a way with words, just like his grandfather. I am honored to still count him as a friend in London.

In other cases, audiences were domestic. Republicans pressured me to name an aircraft carrier after President Reagan, and the Democrats did the same for President Truman. I decided to satisfy both sides by publicly announcing on the same day that a new aircraft carrier would be named after President Truman and another after President Reagan, thereby gratifying both sides and not playing favorites.

I remember other such stories with great fondness, and considering my naval service, most of them involve submarines. The first was the USS *Columbia*: Its name was chosen before I came into office, but as its christening neared, I named our nation's First Lady Hillary Clinton as its sponsor. I thought it was appropriate as there is a Columbia, Illinois (her home state), and, of course, the Columbia statue, which stands tall and majestic atop the dome of the capitol building. Hillary was clearly surprised to be named sponsor but graciously accepted, and we all went to the *Columbia*'s christening in September 1994. After the traditional pomp and ceremony, Hillary took the champagne bottle in her hands and spoke the words,

"I christen thee, USS *Columbia!*" She then swung the bottle.

The bottle collided with the hull with a metallic clang, but it did not break. Recovering quickly, the First Lady wound her arms back and swung a second time. Again, it failed to break, and a tense silence filled the area. Hillary swung a third time, and to everyone's great relief, the bottle finally shattered. The place exploded into applause, and I leaned forward from behind her and said,

"Hillary, every baseball player who has ever been in the major leagues would love to have a lifetime batting average of .333!" Hillary looked at me and laughed heartily.

After the christening, the submarine slid down the 1,300-foot wooden ramp into the water of the Thames River, a process known as "going down the ways." For generations, that had been the traditional way for a ship to leave the christening area. However, this submarine

*Hillary Clinton reception at the White House for the USS Columbia crew, the first crew to be so honored.*

would be the last-ever vessel in the US Navy to do so.[13] This christening marked the end of era for the Navy, and I admit it left me feeling a little melancholic. Still, if it had to end, it did so on a high note, and I am glad it was with our country's First Lady as the sponsor.

Sometime after the commissioning, Hillary Clinton invited me and the entire crew to the White House for a reception. This was the first time something like that had ever occurred. The sailors and their families were awed and humbled to have been invited, and the First Lady was a wonderful host. President Clinton himself was away on other business and could not attend, so this was Hillary's reception. It was her night and the night for the crew of the USS *Columbia*. I doubt anyone has forgotten the event in the years since. I certainly have not.

Speaking of submarines, it was during that time that I received word about one of the vessels on which I served. I previously mentioned that the USS *Blueback* is now an exhibit at Oregon Museum of Science and

---

[13] One of the nicknames of the USS *Columbia* is "The Last Slider," which is more than a fitting homage.

Industry in Portland, Oregon, and I played a role in guaranteeing its graceful retirement. The *Blueback* had officially been decommissioned in 1990, with plans to be scrapped. During my first year in office, I received a call from Senator Mark Hatfield of Oregon who told me that the *Blueback* was in mothballs, awaiting her ignominious fate. He then said it could be saved and made into an exhibit at the museum: all I had to do was sign the order.

Senator Hatfield knew about my service on the *Blueback* and saw a perfect opportunity to pitch to a sympathetic audience who could do something. Needless to say, I needed little convincing and gladly signed the paperwork. Later, I, along with four other officers who served on her with me, including Ray Jones, Dudley Carlson, Bob McGee, and Peter Graef, attended the ceremony where the Blueback was commemorated as part of the museum. It was an emotional affair and a terrific reunion, and I am so happy to have saved her for future generations to appreciate.

I was amazed that five of the eight officers that served together on that submarine attended the dedication ceremony in Portland!

Another ship story worth sharing is that of the USS *Seawolf*, a mighty nuclear-powered fast-attack submarine and the lead ship in her class. Designed during the Cold War, there had been plans for twenty of them to be commissioned. However, when that long geopolitical conflict finally came to end, so did those plans, and only three were constructed. Still, it was a marvel of technology and engineering, and I knew just the person I wanted to name as the sponsor. The third *Seawolf* submarine had been a political battle, particularly since the House and Senate flipped in 1994 and were controlled by the Republicans, and building the third submarine of that class was already an issue in the 1992 presidential race. Phil Gramm, a Republican Senator with whom I was acquainted, put it in blunt terms: "You can forget about the third *Seawolf*."

I was not going to give up so easily. President Clinton and I both wanted to see it built, and it would also go a long way to preserving jobs and talent in our Navy shipyards. Together with the senators from Connecticut and Rhode Island, where it would be built, we lobbied other senators persistently, and steadily, we began to win them over. Eventually, the proposal for the third *Seawolf* came to a floor vote, and we won handily with seventy-five votes. It was a terrific team effort by all those involved and a real win for the Navy Department. Rear Admiral Bob Natter, Chief of Legislative Affairs at that time, did a great job. He later became a four-star admiral.

I wanted this announcement of the *Seawolf*'s sponsor to be a surprise, so I waited until a formal dinner in New London, CT, where the submarine base was located. When the time came, I rose to give my remarks, and as that formality came to a conclusion, I named Margaret as the ship's sponsor. She stared at me, wide-eyed, unsure if she had heard me right. I flashed her a big smile as the whole room looked in her direction and began to applaud. It only took a moment for her to regain her composure, and with her usual grace and modesty, she humbly accepted her service as the sponsor.

Though it had come as a complete surprise, Margaret was thrilled to have her name attached to such a fine boat. However, while it was primarily an honor, being the sponsor of a vessel did carry some responsibilities. Margaret took said responsibilities seriously, and between being named sponsor and the christening and commissioning of the *Seawolf*, she went above and beyond to meet the crew, including joining them in Groton for a picnic. She also learned about her duties at the ceremonies and beyond.

When the time came for the christening, Margaret was nervous. In order to face the crowd, she would have to swing left-handed. After the speeches were made, Margaret climbed the steps to the platform and inched forward until, finally, it was time. She took the bottle in her hands, and said,

"I christen thee, USS *Seawolf!*"

Margaret pulled back the bottle and gave an almighty swing. The bottle should have broken and champagne should have sprayed

*Christening of the USS* Seawolf *(SSN-21).*

everywhere, but that did not happen. Somehow, Margaret managed to miss the submarine sail entirely! What made it worse was it was a big event, and the media was out in force with all their cameras and recording equipment. You could have cut the atmosphere with a knife, even though it only lasted a moment. Her mother, who served as the matron of honor and was standing behind her, said to swing again. Not needing to be told twice, Margaret did so, and this time the bottle made contact with steel and the champagne flowed over the sail of the submarine. I could tell Margaret was embarrassed, but the ceremony was still a great success!

There was a larger press corps attending that event than normal, because it had been such a political football in the presidential election in 1992. Margaret said to me after the ceremony, "You don't think the press will cover the fact that I missed the sail of the ship when I swung, do you?"

I replied, "Of course they will. It's a classic case of man bites dog!" *CBS Evening News* led with that story, and the *Washington Post* covered it Sunday morning.

I had a meeting with the CNO and the senior staff of the Navy first thing every Monday morning. We covered the highlights that happened during the weekend. At the end of the meeting on the Monday after the *Seawolf* christening, I reminded them that I had told them it was very important that the Seawolf class of submarine be extremely stealthy. I complimented them on doing such a great job with the stealth of the USS *Seawolf* that Margaret could not even see it!

Margaret was teased constantly by friends, family, and even strangers over the coming months. The entire thing had been caught on tape, and people would ask her, amazed, about how she could have missed the submarine. Credit where it is due, Margaret did an incredible job of keeping her cool during that time, though I could tell it was beginning to get to her. However, as the months elapsed, the public slowly forgot the mishap, her three seconds of infamy passed, and Margaret could focus on her other duties as a sponsor.

The commissioning is the last ceremony before the ship officially becomes a part of the US Navy. Bill Middendorf, former Secretary of the Navy in the Nixon administration, had written the Seawolf March and wanted Margaret to conduct the band as they played at the ceremony. Before the ceremony, she asked the bandleader, "When do I stop directing?"

His response was simple and direct: "When the band stops playing!"

Every ship sponsor is invited to join the Society of Sponsors, an organization of about three hundred women dedicated to each representing her respective vessel and supporting it any way she can. Margaret was now a part of that exclusive club, and she took to her duties with gusto. It did not take many years for her to be named president of the society, a position she held for two years, and she has served in a number of other roles since then. One of her duties as president of the society, to which she was elected after I left office, was to be present at every christening and commissioning of a new ship. I would sometimes join her on these events, and Margaret joked that I had descended from head of the Navy to handling her bags! At any rate, she carried out her duties with her

*John with his son in hard hats in drydock under the USS* Constitution.

usual diligence, and despite some frustrating aspects to the job, Margaret excelled in every mission, large and small.

As a sidebar, before the commissioning of the *Seawolf*, John, Jr., went with me on a trip to New England in 1995, where we visited the USS *Constitution* in drydock. On its old wooden hull is a brass commemorative plate. At the direction of the commanding officer, we were asked to sign our names on it, and in doing so we indelibly tied ourselves to one of the living, breathing manifestations of our country's great history, a moving and humbling experience.

In 1997, for the first time in 116 years, the USS *Constitution* would sail under its own power. The Navy's oldest ship, launched back in 1797, she still, technically, is in active service. "Old Ironsides" holds a special place in the heart of the Navy and the nation as a whole; it was such an historic occasion. A number of our family joined us to commission the *Seawolf* and for the historic sailing of this key vessel. The voyage itself lasted a couple hours, as we sailed around the bay and harbor, which was terrific! Seeing and feeling the USS *Constitution* actually sail near Marblehead, Massachusetts, instead of being towed, was unlike anything I have experienced before or since. We were not the only guests aboard. We were joined by some of our country's most respected people, including Senators Ted Kennedy and John Kerry, the rest of the Massachusetts delegation, and Walter Cronkite. I spent a great deal of time with all of them.

The voyage was not flawless. The ship is old, and it should not be surprising that she has some structural integrity problems. Water leaked in and the hull and masts creaked distressingly as she sailed through the water. While nothing to worry about, we were not in any danger, we were reminded why she was kept in port most of the time. But even if she was far from watertight, I focused on the voyage itself, and I was transported not only physically, but mentally and emotionally, as well. To top it all off, the USS *Constitution* received a twenty-one-gun salute and also a flyover by the Blue Angels. What an afternoon!

I decided in late 1997 to name the third Seawolf submarine the USS *Jimmy Carter*, after the only president in history who served in the submarine force. We had a naming ceremony outside in the interior courtyard of the Pentagon. President Carter told me that other than marrying Rosalynn and being elected president of the United States, that was the nicest honor he had ever received. I asked Rosalynn to be the sponsor, and she happily agreed. The christening and the commissioning of the ship happened after I left office, but Margaret and I attended the commissioning ceremony. Stansfield Turner, who was the CIA director during the Carter administration and a USNA classmate of his, was the principal speaker. It was a great ceremony.

Our efforts to promote diversity, representation, and equality did not stop with women. In 1994, I sat down with my right-hand man Under Secretary Richard Danzig to discuss representation in the Department of the Navy with regard to race. We compared the number of minorities in uniform to national demographics and made some important observations, especially with regard to our Navy and Marine Corps.

Even in 1994, we could foresee that America was destined to become a much more diverse country over the coming decades. The enlisted ranks of the Navy and Marine Corps were already diverse, with representation of many races, but the officer corps was overwhelmingly Caucasian. Danzig and I agreed that this should be corrected. If the officers did not fairly reflect the changing face of our country, it could lead to a disconnect between the groups. At best, enlisted sailors and Marines could be disheartened by a lack of role models. At worst, the disparity could fuel racial resentment, opening the door for all the problems that stem from that. We could not wait to enact reforms that reflected the demographic change.

We knew that we should all act to implement a remedy then in order to prevent it from becoming a problem later. I asked Danzig to work with our two services to devise a strategy, and he began making calls right away. He correctly pointed out that their perspective on the matter would be essential, and he opted for a light touch in his discussions with various officials. We knew that they were obligated to enforce any program we gave them, but it was crucial that they saw the merit of our arguments, too. If not, any reform would be half-heartedly implemented, and they would begrudge being strong-armed. We would succeed if they became convinced that this was in the best interests of the Navy and Marine Corps.

During these discussions, we found them receptive to our concerns. They acknowledged that that disparity, if not addressed, could lead to problems going forward. They agreed that greater representation of minority groups in the officer corps was a good idea in principle. We settled on some changes to recruiting advertisements to appeal to minority groups, but they warned against implementing any kind of quota. They argued that it would be counterproductive and said it risked diluting the quality of officer candidates.

We had expected that kind of response, but Danzig came up with a simple yet ingenious workaround: let's not call it a quota, or a target, but an aspiration, a goal for the Navy and Marine Corps to work toward. They found that to be a good compromise and agreed to be proactive in improving minority representation. We decided that aspiration for the Officer Corps should roughly reflect the demographics of the nation at that time: 12 percent or more should be African American, 12 percent or more should be Hispanic, and 5 percent would be an umbrella for all other minorities (Asian, Native American, Pacific Islander, and so on). We soon adopted 12/12/5 as the unofficial name of our diversity drive.

Did we reach these informal milestones? Not quite. When I left office, considerable progress had been made, but the numbers of the minority officers in the Navy and Marine Corps had not yet achieved that aspiration. However, progress had certainly been made. Depending on how the statistics were analyzed, between 1994 and 1998, African American officer representation increased to 9.4 percent, Hispanics to 6.1 percent, and other minorities exceeded the goal, reaching 5.7 percent. These were modest gains, but they were absolutely a step in the right direction.

As part of the 12/12/5 aspiration, we had not set a time limit on those efforts to increase minority representation. That meant our efforts could continue for as long as we felt it necessary, and we could reassess and move the goalposts with ease as America's demographics evolved. Danzig was pivotal in spearheading our efforts on that initiative.

It is said that all good things must come to an end. My tenure as SECNAV came at the end of 1998. There had been some disagreements with a couple of elected and appointed officials and, rather than remain in a contentious atmosphere, I decided it was time to relinquish the reigns of the Navy Department. As I have said, I loved being Secretary of the Navy, but on November 16, I passed the torch to an extremely capable man who had been my deputy for four years, Richard Danzig. I knew Richard would do a great job, including keeping up efforts to promote equality in the Navy and Marine Corps. It was

*My official SECNAV Portrait.*

the greatest honor of my life to serve as the Secretary of the Navy that had molded me, and I took comfort in knowing that it was in Richard's reliable, very capable hands.

Throughout my time as SECNAV, from day one to the end, I always strove to do what I thought was in the long-term best interest of our nation's great Navy and Marine Corps. Sometimes I got it right, other times I got it wrong, but I did my best to lead us through those trying times. We had more successes than failures, and I know I helped steer the ship toward a brighter horizon, thanks in great part to the wise advice, diligent work ethic, and tireless support of my friends, colleagues, and my wife Margaret. I extend to her and all of those with whom I had the honor and privilege to serve my heartfelt thanks. I am truly grateful to you for all that you did for our country!

On the evening of November 16, my last event was a going-away ceremony held in Memorial Hall at the Naval Academy and conducted by my classmates in the great class of 1964. I told them how much I appreciated their support while I was in office. I had said in my speech when I was sworn in as the seventieth Secretary of the Navy that President Truman had said when he was in office that if you wanted to have a friend in Washington, get a dog. I said that I already had a dog, but I also had a "band of brothers" who were my classmates and my former shipmates. My shipmates were less visible since we had served together many years before, but my classmates were always there for me. I told them I had tried to leave the Department of the Navy better than I had found it and was proud of that. They formed an honor guard that escorted Margaret and me down the steps of Memorial Hall. I was and will always remain grateful for all that my classmates have meant to me since 1960.

Being SECNAV was the pinnacle of my career and achievements, but my story was far from over. I was not ready to retire, nowhere close, and I needed a break from the bureaucratic shackles of government service. Opportunities, both professional and personal, awaited me. The question was, where to go next?

# CHAPTER 15

# BASEBALL WITH "THE BOSS"

With the best job in government now in the rearview mirror, the future stretched out before me, a blank canvas full of possibility and promise. This was an exciting time, but uncertainty creates anxiety. I knew my first decisions would be vitally important to my future, so I had to plan carefully. One of my main motivations in those early days was my financial health. As terrific as it had been serving as SECNAV, it was hardly a high-paying position. My finances were stable and certainly not as dire as they had been a decade earlier, though we were anything but affluent. However, even if we had been wealthy, the idea of an early retirement held no appeal to me. I wanted to get back out there!

Thanks to my time in government, I had made a great many friends and acquaintances who I knew could point me in the direction of some meaningful private sector prospects. I got off to an early start when I met Mike Berthelot at a Forbes conference when I was in the Pentagon. He was the chairman and CEO of a company called TransTechnology, later known as Breeze-Eastern Corp. I met with Mike and the board, which went well, and I was invited to become a board member. That was quickly followed by my joining another company board, thanks to Howard Lutnick, who was the chairman and CEO of Cantor Fitzgerald. He was starting a new company called Cantor Exchange, which traded bond futures electronically. I had met Howard in New York at one of the functions on the USS *Intrepid* museum.

Around the same time, I was also introduced to another technology company, IPG Photonics, through my close friend and neighbor Bob Blair. It was an international company making their first inroads into the US. That alone was an exciting opportunity, and after meeting with their chairman and CEO, Dr. Valentin Gapontsev, and his good friend and business partner, Peter Mammen, they invited me to be on their advisory board along with Admiral Bill Crowe, Governor Doug Wilder, and some other well-known people. The company looked promising to me, and I became an active member of the advisory board. I visited their trade show in Baltimore and their headquarters in Burbach, Germany, when on another business trip. These were all high-tech-focused companies, and while I am not a tech whiz, it was clear that this sector would change the economy as we knew it and that it would be a good idea to get involved.

That being said, the fourth company whose board I joined could not have been more different. It came about from something as simple as a friendly tennis match with Marvin Bush, the youngest son of President George H. W. Bush and brother of then- Governor George W. Bush of Texas. Unlike his father and brothers, Marvin had no political ambition and had instead become a successful businessman in the private equity sector. It was after one of our tennis games that he mentioned that Fresh Del Monte Produce was looking for a new board member. This immediately piqued my interest. Marvin provided me with some information on the company and offered to introduce me to the chairman and CEO, Mohammad Abu Ghazaleh. One thing led to another, and I found myself on the board there, as well. Serving on four boards in under twelve months, things were going well.

I have always had great admiration and respect for President John F. Kennedy. I have already covered his inauguration, his funeral procession, and what he said about his service in the US Navy. After leaving the Pentagon, I decided that I would like to serve in a way that would pay tribute to him and his legacy. In a meeting with President Clinton in the Map Room of the White House, I asked if he might consider appointing me to the President's Advisory Committee of the Arts for the Kennedy Center. He agreed. Of course, that would require confirmation by the US Senate, a process with which I was very familiar. I was easily confirmed and enjoyed serving in that capacity for about two years.

After a one-year stint as CEO of a tech startup called Epcad, I began talking with IPG Photonics. The company, founded ten years earlier in Germany by a Russian scientist, Dr. Valentin Gapontsev, manufactured innovative fiber lasers. I had been on their advisory board for over a year, and now the company hoped to increase its presence and profile in the United States in a big way. They had opened an office in Sturbridge, Massachusetts, and were building a new office headquarters in nearby Oxford. In addition, they were planning an initial public offering (IPO) in the US stock market.

As a member of the advisory board and the deadline to make our IPO inched steadily closer, I found myself talking strategy with Bob Blair. It was during this conversation that Bob floated the idea of my being president of the company. I had extensive public and private sector contacts, and even if I lacked Valentin's technical expertise, I knew how to do an IPO. By offering me the presidency, they hoped to kill those two birds with one stone. The offer was not without strings attached, however. Were I to accept, I would have to work out of their Massachusetts office, sign a four-year contract, and, on the positive side, I would reap the benefits of stock options. It was a great opportunity but also a serious commitment. Still, I felt that this was just the opportunity I had been looking for, and I did not leave them waiting for long before I answered with an emphatic affirmative response.

I began work almost immediately, setting up the IPO, overseeing the construction of the new office campus from our temporary site in Sturbridge and raising the company's profile through my network of connections. I would spend four days a week there in an apartment provided by the company and three days at home in DC. This division of work and home life quickly became taxing, and I missed Margaret while I was in New England, even though she did join me on those trips about once a month. Tiresome as the commute was, we were extremely happy with the home we had, and I never considered uprooting yet again. Still, Margaret went out of her way to help turn the apartment into a home away from home, which took the edge off the stress.

It was exciting to be in a senior position at a company like IPG Photonics, especially when they were making such big moves into what was for them a new market. However, it was far from easy. There was considerable work to be done, and everyone had to pull their weight.

For about five years, internet-based companies had been enjoying almost unparalleled expansion and investment in the stock market. As a company that made products used by those companies among others, IPG prospered from this speculation, as well. After March 2000, there were hints that that this growth was slowing, and that we might be entering correction territory, but no one anticipated the market would crash the way it did. Between November 2000 and July 2002, that market lost almost 80 percent of its value and companies like Pets.com and the Enron and World.com scandals decimated the stock market. Along with the tragedy of 9/11, the bursting of the "Dot-Com Bubble," as it came to be known, helped propel the country into a recession.

Speaking of September 11, 2001, I was just arriving at work on that Tuesday morning and heard on the radio about a plane crashing into the north side of one of the World Trade Center towers. Shortly thereafter, I learned that another plane had hit the second twin tower. We only had one TV in the lab downstairs, and I went down to see what had happened. I knew then that some other government had been involved. It was the first time since the war of 1812 that the continental United States had been attacked by a foreign adversary. That was the worst day for America that I and most others had ever experienced. I was heartsick as I watched the buildings crumble and knew that so many people had been killed. At Cantor Fitzgerald, which officed a couple floors above where one of the planes hit, 658 people were lost. My friend and Cantor CEO Howard Lutnick lost his brother and would have been killed himself had he not been late for work because he was taking his son to school for his first day there. No other company lost as many employees as Cantor Fitzgerald. As a result of this attack, the leaders of our country decided to go to war. When I left Massachusetts on Thursday of that week to fly to BWI Airport near Washington, DC, on Southwest Airlines, there were only six people on the airplane!

Due to our company's connections with the internet sector and the high-tech industry, we were not spared from the backlash. The year 2001 was a difficult year for us as we struggled to make ends meet and were forced to reassess our business plan. I began to feel a deep sense of dread during this time: was this going to be the repeat of Freedom Capital Corporation? Was I going to lose my shirt once more? I could not put my family through that again.

We had to lay off dozens of employees, which is always a sad and difficult thing to do, and all the senior executives, including me, took significant salary cuts. Incorporating hard-learned lessons from my S&L days, we changed our strategy, setting smaller targets and diversifying our customer base. As difficult as these sacrifices were, they paid off, and IPG Photonics managed to weather the storm. By the end of 2003, we were growing steadily again, which was a great relief to everyone, especially me.

As tiresome as my commuting back and forth to Massachusetts could be, it turned out to be a vehicle through which I could indulge my love of baseball. Anyone who claims to love America's pastime knows that there is one rivalry above all others, the New York Yankees and the Boston Red Sox. Good tickets to these games are expensive, yet for three or four years I had a front-row seat in the Yankees box right next to their dugout at Fenway Park. For someone like me, that was a dream come true, but how did I get such exclusive access?

This came as a result of my time in the Pentagon. Sometime in 1996, I had a call from Congressman Bill Young of Florida, the ranking member of the House Defense Appropriations Committee. He told me that one his constituents was doing business with the Navy in Tampa, Florida, and wanted to speak to me. I agreed to meet with him. It was then that Congressman Young hesitated.

"Are you sure? You would be doing me a big favor, but this guy is somewhat controversial," he said.

"OK, who is it?" I asked, suddenly curious whose ire the department had managed to stoke.

"It's George Steinbrenner, owner of the New York Yankees."

I did not see that one coming! Mr. Steinbrenner was famous or infamous, depending on who you asked. At any rate, I did not want someone with such a high profile nursing a grudge against the Navy, so I agreed to meet with him. To make a long story short, after speaking with him at length, I had some of my lieutenants look into the problem, and we determined that he did indeed have a legitimate grievance. We resolved it, and Steinbrenner thanked me for our help.

I thought that was the end of it until some years later when we went to Florida in the year 2000 to visit our older son, John, in Mayport, where his ship was homeported. His naval base happened to be close to the stadium where the Yankees did their spring training and played some of their spring training games. I asked John if he wanted to go to a game while we were there, and he agreed. I contacted the Yankee ticket office, purchased three tickets and, as they requested, faxed the payment to them. I wrote on the message, "Please give my regards to Mr. George Steinbrenner."

Within a couple of days, I got a call from him. He was pleased to hear from me again, and as a thank you for my help years before, he asked whether we would join him in his suite for the game. I did not at all expect a response like that from him; my greeting was only a courtesy. Still, I was hardly going to turn down a chance for us to see the game with Mr. Steinbrenner and our son. His personality was just as large as it had been when I first met him, and we had a fantastic afternoon at the ballpark, so much so that he invited us to another game with him the next day. I checked with Margaret and John, and they were both enthusiastic about returning.

During that second day watching the Yankees play, the conversation turned, as it often did, to what I was doing now. I told him that I was going to join IPG Photonics in Massachusetts in August, and Steinbrenner cracked a joke about the Boston Red Sox. I laughed along, and then Steinbrenner said that if I ever wanted to see the Yankees-Red Sox games at Fenway Park, I had an open invitation to use the Yankees box by their dugout. It was all I could do to stop my jaw from dropping. Had he just offered me front-row seats to one the best games in baseball? That was almost too generous, but there was no way I was going to pass on that. It was such a pleasure and a privilege to watch the games from those seats, and I loved every second of it. I had come a long way from listening to the St. Louis Cardinals on the family radio back in Shreveport!

Our son John and his girlfriend, Yasmin Forlenza, visited us when Margaret was in Massachusetts for the week, and we went to Fenway Park for a Yankees game. Yasmin had been reared in Spain and had never seen a baseball game before. As I was describing the game to her, I said, "You see that guy playing shortstop for the Yankees, he is one of the all-time best shortstops ever to play the game." The very next pitch, a routine grounder to Derek Jeter went right through his legs and out into left field for an error. He has since been inducted into the Baseball Hall of Fame. Yasmin and John married on July 27, 2002, in a beautiful outdoor ceremony on Long Boat Key, Florida. She is a marvelous wife to John and has been a wonderful addition to our family. She is also an outstanding mother to their two fine sons, Antonio, born July 31, 2004, and Mateus, born February 8, 2007.

Yet there were even more baseball highlights in those years. In September 2001, a couple weeks after 9/11, I went to a Goldman Sachs reunion at the Greenbrier Resort in West Virginia for the group I had been in training with, which gave me a chance to spend quality time with my old friends Rex Jennings and Ralph Severson. We had a terrific time, and it became obvious that, even years after our days in Dallas watching the Texas Rangers, we were all still huge baseball fans. It was at that reunion that we made a commitment: the next year, we would plan a baseball trip together. We did so in 2002 and had such a good time, we decided to do one every year after that. We have been doing it for over twenty years, and this tradition is still going strong. We have been to every ballpark in major league baseball. Unfortunately, in 2020, because of the pandemic, we were unable to do our annual trip. That is the only year we missed.

Lastly, in 2002, I was honored with a request to speak at the Baseball Hall of Fame in Cooperstown, New York. Dale Petroskey was a fellow member of the Alfalfa Club, and, at that time, president of the Baseball Hall of Fame, and it was because of that relationship that I was invited to speak. Of all the sporting halls of fame, baseball's was the first and the best, and they were hosting a ceremony to honor those players who had also served in our country's armed forces in both the Second World War and the Korean War. All of the veterans who had been inducted into the Hall of Fame were invited, but only five of them were able to come: Bob Feller, Phil Rizzuto, Ralph Kiner, Bobby Doerr, and Warren Spahn. I decided to make a day of it, so I invited family, classmates, and a number of good friends to come along, as well. We all had great fun! I got to be excellent friends with Bob Feller and saw him a number of times before his death. On one of our baseball trips, we met with Bob, had breakfast, and went to see his farm in Van Meter, Iowa, and saw the barnyard where his dad taught him to pitch. The pitching rubber and home plate are still there. Unfortunately, Bob died in December 2010.

These trips and indulging my love of baseball helped keep me grounded and sane during my tenure at IPG Photonics. I diligently served my four years as president, but as my legal commitment came to an end, I made the decision not to remain in that position. It had been a challenging and rewarding experience, but I was tired of the periods spent away from home and the rigorous commute. As 2004 drew to a close, I bid IPG Photonics a fond farewell but did remain on the board of directors with the company for several more years.

That did not mean that I was retiring, however. My membership on boards kept me more than busy. On top of that, I had also agreed to be chairman for an upcoming faith-based festival on the National Mall in September, 2005, for the Luis Palau Association, so there was plenty to do. Honestly, I was quite content with my lot in life, and while I did not give any serious consideration to true "retirement," I was not looking for the next big job. However, it is precisely when you stop looking for it that the next opportunity usually comes knocking.

It was in 2004 when I had a call from my close friend, Jan Cope, who had previously been deputy director of White House personnel office under President George H. W. Bush, and even though we were on opposite sides of the political aisle, we had a wonderful friendship. Upon leaving government, she had started her own small but successful executive search firm in the capital city, and she reached out to me with an opportunity. The Housing Policy Council, part of the Financial Services Roundtable, was looking for a new president, and Jan thought it would be a perfect fit for me.

It was certainly nice to be her first pick for the post, but I replied that I was not interested. I told her that, while I appreciated the offer, I was already plenty busy with my other projects, and I did not want to pursue other opportunities that could infringe on them. Never one to meekly accept a turndown, Jan asked me if I would at least meet with the CEO of the Financial Services Roundtable, Steve Bartlett. Grudgingly, I acquiesced, believing that it would not change my mind.

Soon thereafter, I met with Steve and Jan over breakfast. I knew who Steve was, but we had never met. He had been the Mayor of Dallas between 1991 and 1995 and before that a congressman from Texas for eight years. Now he was a successful businessman in charge of the Financial Services Roundtable, a prominent trade association. We had a nice breakfast, bonding over our ties to Texas and poking fun at the DC establishment before the subject turned to the matter at hand. I told Steve the same thing I had told Jan, but he was not in the least bit discouraged.

"John, you can lead the HPC and keep all of your other commitments. This job won't take over your life, I promise you."

It took some more coaxing, but Steve finally talked me into taking the job. As far as I was concerned, this was going to be my last hurrah, at least from a career perspective, and I did not plan to do it for more than a couple of years. Well, I was right on the first count, but I did not think I would be a part of that esteemed group for over twelve years!

# CHAPTER 16

# HOPE FOR THE HOPELESS

I started my new job as head of the Housing Policy Council in January 2005, after my tenure as president of IPG Photonics had ended in December. I had barely finished enjoying Christmas with my family before I was back in another new occupation. Still, at least I no longer had to continue commuting to and from New England on a weekly basis, but I would miss the games at Fenway Park.

HPC headquarters was not entirely foreign to me. Since meeting Steve Bartlett and agreeing to take the job, I had been to their office several times to meet the people I would be working with and to introduce myself to HPC member company executives. I went out of my way to visit with as many of the members as I could before I officially started, so we would already be acquainted by the time I took over. So, while it was definitely a new environment, at least I was not coming in completely cold.

When I joined the HPC, we had fifteen members, representing a broad range of America's major banks and mortgage companies by size and region, including Wells Fargo, Bank of America, JPMorgan Chase, BB&T, and SunTrust, to name a few. They were a close-knit group, competing companies bound by a common interest in keeping the housing market healthy and prosperous. Bill Longbrake, the vice-chairman of Washington Mutual Savings Bank (WAMU) and HPC chairman when I signed on, helped me feel right at home, and in no time at all, I was settled and ready to take charge.

Frankly, things were mostly quiet for a year or so. We got good work done, but nothing that came to the public's attention. In hindsight I am thankful, because it allowed me to come to grips with the duties of my office and how the FSR/HPC were run. In particular, it was my responsibility to ensure that all the members on the Housing Policy Council were satisfied with our policy work on their behalf, or at least ensure that any concerns they had were heard. Structurally, the HPC was divided into two bodies of company representatives we worked with on mortgage policy issues. The first was the Housing Policy Executive Council (HPEC) and the second was the Housing Policy Advisory Council (HPAC).

The HPEC was the more senior group of the top mortgage executives of our members who met quarterly, and included Bill Longbrake, Rick Geisinger of American General Finance, Mike Heid of Wells Fargo, Tim Dale of BB&T, Todd Chamberlain, now of Truist (formerly SunTrust), and other official representatives of our members. They were all senior executives of their respective mortgage companies, committed to representing the interests of their organizations. They helped set the broad agenda of our organization and kept us informed of market events that they were experiencing.

The HPAC was the subordinate committee, comprised of the mid-level, business, legal, and government-relations representatives from our members that met monthly. Having less seniority, the HPAC did not have the same powers as the executive committee. Their job was mainly as a first point of contact, to share their views on potential regulations or legislation that federal regulators and Congress were considering and to report back to their companies about what policy positions we could advocate. It was with the HPAC that I conducted most of our routine work. That aspect of my job was not riveting, at least in the early days, but it was rewarding, and the people who sat on the HPAC were friendly and highly professional.

For our big annual meeting (where both councils would come together in joint session), we would escape the capital and host it somewhere else in the country.[14] The most memorable of these meetings was held in New Orleans in 2006, less than a year after Hurricane Katrina devastated the city of my birth. I wanted our members to see firsthand the destruction and difficulties the city and the Gulf Coast region continued to endure but also to see that within all of that, there was also opportunity as well. One of the speakers at that meeting was then-Lieutenant Governor Mitch Landrieu. I was impressed with his commitment to New Orleans and Louisiana then but gained even more respect for him when, in 2017, having been elected mayor, he committed to the controversial but principled decision to remove the Confederate monuments from New Orleans.

Our annual meetings included a variety of interesting outside speakers, who mostly were focused on housing issues. Given my history, I endeavored to stimulate our members with insights into national security and foreign policy. I was able to use my relationships in the Department of Defense to attract senior military officers and other defense officials to speak about the financial challenges facing young servicemembers and also give a broad overview of current national defense and international security issues.

When I first joined HPC in 2005, one member, GMAC-RFC, told us that in 2004 they had provided $20 million to start a foundation, the Homeownership Preservation Foundation, to fund assistance for customers who were behind on their mortgage and in danger of foreclosure. The foundation had grown out of a cooperative effort in Chicago with Neighborhood Housing Services, the city, and several major lenders to provide counseling and other assistance to struggling homeowners in

---

[14] As much as we cherished this tradition, we made the tough decision after 2007 to suspend hosting our annual meetings outside of Washington. The Mortgage Crisis was hitting us hard, and we had to spend our resources more frugally.

Chicago. It was a promising effort, but at that time, it was only focused on borrowers in a few markets.

I believe it was during one of our quarterly meetings in 2006 that we began seeing storm clouds brewing on the horizon. One member spoke up and, as was typical, began talking about what his company had been seeing that quarter. Most of what he said was par for the course, but all our ears perked up when he said that they had noticed a small but noticeable uptick in people falling behind or defaulting on their mortgage payments.

We formed a small working group that created the HOPE Hotline. Our logic was simple: those who fell behind on their repayments often felt embarrassed or afraid to talk to their lender about it. Many at-risk homeowners were likely to bury their heads in the sand or try and fly under the radar until they could continue their payments in full, naively hoping that their lender would not notice. Neither of these approaches was productive, but we understood their feelings. Our HOPE Hotline was intended to provide an advisory service from a trusted, unbiased third party. A nonprofit counselor could serve as a bridge or middleman who could be contacted for free advice to the homeowner on their worries about their house and their financial conundrum.

This small initiative quickly began to show its value as a steady stream of worried callers began phoning in for consultation on how to improve their tenuous situation. We were happy that the service was being used and making a difference, yet we did not fully connect the dots that this was a symptom of a huge cauldron brewing beneath the surface.

In 2007, the mortgage crisis hit the USA with the force of a runaway freight train, and HPC, too late, realized how devastatingly bad things had become. The circumstances and causes of the crisis were incredibly complex, intricate enough to make anyone not well versed in housing markets or economics scratch their heads in bewilderment. Without delving into the weeds on the details, in brief, a combustible cocktail of predatory and reckless lending practices, subprime mortgages, and a sharp deflation in housing prices brought the market to its knees. Countless thousands of people became delinquent on their loans or faced foreclosure, which crippled many lenders, especially nonbank mortgage companies with inadequate capital reserves, sending them into a tailspin toward bankruptcy. The nature of our organization—banks, nonbanks, and mortgage insurance companies—meant that our members were directly impacted by the mortgage crisis, and things went to red alert almost overnight. Several of them were in dire financial straits, and we knew we had to do something before the bottom completely fell out from beneath us.

At the FSR/HPC, we did everything in our power to help our members and to work with Congress and the regulators on their concerns about the housing market, and much of 2007 was spent trying to deal with those problems. We were in crisis mode, and the situation only worsened when the great recession slammed the United States in 2008. The mortgage crisis was the canary in the coal mine, and now the whole economy teetered on the edge of a new great depression. From Wall Street to Main Street, from coast to coast, and from banking to the automotive industry, the situation had become calamitous.

As this was all playing out, we had to focus on our own piece of the puzzle. We were not the kind of organization that could bail out our members. We were a trade association focused on public policy. What we could do was take a hard look at what had caused the crisis, as well as develop and suggest best practices to our members and work with the regulators and Congress on policy solutions. These efforts were, however, a long-term solution. People needed help now. As providence would have it, we already had one tool that could help do just that: the HOPE Hotline.

With so many people falling behind or defaulting on their mortgages and the lenders feeling the squeeze as a result, we saw an opening for the HOPE Hotline to take on a broader role beyond advisory services: mediation. As an independent and impartial third party, it could serve as a liaison between people and their mortgage company, identify the problems, and if possible, suggest a compromise such as a mortgage restructure or modification. HPC itself did not have the infrastructure or manpower to singlehandedly turn this into a huge initiative, but we were determined to press on. Even if we could only help a few people, it would be worth it. Soon enough, we began to see that the HOPE Hotline was having an effect. Dozens and then hundreds of people, beginning with customers of our members who had been directed our way, called asking for help with mortgages. We were happy to assist, and it was not long before the powers that be began to notice our efforts.

Sometime in late 2007, Henry Paulson, President Bush's last Secretary of the Treasury spoke to the executives of FSR and HPC. He asked what the industry was doing to address the growing number of delinquent mortgages. He was told about our efforts with the HOPE Hotline and was deeply impressed with our mission and wanted to discuss the HOPE Hotline further.

Secretary Paulson wanted us to expand the HOPE Hotline exponentially, so that many more thousands of people could be helped and try to curb the skyrocketing rate of foreclosures. We wanted to step up to the plate and accepted his request. Secretary Paulson understood the serious situation and offered HPC his strong support to expand the effort.

We set to work immediately to find a way to transform the HOPE Hotline from a relatively small enterprise into an expanded, well-staffed nationwide mediation machine. We even renamed it: The Hope Now Alliance. As we began to scale up, I came to the understanding that I did not have the time, nor the technical expertise, to oversee its day-to-day operations. However, I knew just the person who could fill those shoes.

Faith Schwartz was a woman with extensive experience in banking, mortgages, and the housing sector—someone who was intelligent, compassionate toward borrowers in difficulty, and thrived under pressure. We asked if Option One, an HPC core member, could loan Faith to us for a while, and we quickly drafted her into the Hope Now

Alliance full time until 2012. We may not have given Faith the chance to say no, and we were more than glad to have her aboard!

The Hope Now Alliance grew into a significant operation, helping countless households work with counselors and their lenders to modify their mortgages and find a workable compromise. The work of Hope Now became an important part of the effort to address the growing crisis. In December 2007, President George W. Bush even held a press conference to announce that representatives of Hope Now had developed a plan that would qualify more than 1.2 million homeowners for assistance.

The Hope Now Alliance was doing great work, but it was only dealing with a symptom of the crisis, not the cause. Of course, it was multifaceted, and there were systemic problems in the economy that were outside our wheelhouse, such as banking liquidity, private equity, and the auto industry. However, I knew that there was more we could do, at least in regard to the housing market and mortgages, and I wanted to push for change so that something like this could never happen again.

As a trade association, lobbying on behalf of our members was an integral part of both the FSR and the HPC. Now, though, with the bursting of the housing bubble, the subprime mortgage crisis, and now the 2008 recession tearing through the American economy, it took on a new layer of importance. We still lobbied on behalf of our members, of course, but we began to place greater importance on providing market expertise and policy suggestions on Capitol Hill on the legislation that would ultimately seek to address the weaknesses in the financial system. Paul Leonard, our senior vice president for government relations, spearheaded our efforts to speak with Senate and House committees. I joined him on a number of the Hill meetings as did Faith Schwartz, who briefed them on the progress of the Hope Now Alliance. Though a decade had passed since my time as Secretary of the Navy, I still had many acquaintances and friends in government. It was good to meet with them again, and they often helped open doors for us.

Our efforts shifted seismically when Barack Obama won the election in 2008.[15] With Democrats in control of the White House and Congress, we were now speaking with government that was more reform minded and inclined to a more meaningful government role in stabilizing the economy and regulating its participants.

My leadership approach during that crisis tracked a similar style to what I had employed as SECNAV, and those timeless traits of leadership continued to guide my actions. I coordinated closely with my boss at FSR, Steve Bartlett, and later, Tim Pawlenty, former governor of Minnesota, who took over from Steve in November 2012. Both were superb leaders, but their management styles were quite different from one another. Both gave me a lot of freedom to pursue our goal of sound policy reforms that would enable the industry to operate in a stable and responsible manner, and I in turn let my subordinates operate with a large degree of autonomy to work with all stakeholders on mortgage and housing policy. Paul and Faith had certainly earned my trust. Communication is vital, of course, to ensure that everyone is on the same page, and I usually had the final call on important or strategic decisions. We enjoyed considerable success.

The years 2007–2011 were tough, and for a while, it seemed that the tide of problems crashing down on us was endless. However, as we began to move into 2012, we finally began to see the light at the end of the tunnel. Fewer people were using the Hope Now Alliance and the HOPE Hotline as the effects of the mortgage crisis slowly began to recede. We had saved millions of households from foreclosure. Few things are more devastating for a family than losing a home, and I am grateful we helped spare so many people from that fate. The Hope Now Alliance and industry cooperation with our nonprofit partners

---

[15] Like so many others, I was overjoyed when Obama won the election in 2008. His election was a milestone for our country in so many ways, and I felt a sense of pride in our nation. In my lifetime, we had gone from segregation to the first African American president. Racism was not, and is not, dead, but this was an enormous testament to how far we had come. We still have a long way to go to address the racism issue.

stand as the greatest achievement of my presidency of the Housing Policy Council.

Not all of our members survived the crisis. Some went out of business, while others merged or went through significant reformations. Overall, though, most of them weathered the storm, and we even managed to steadily grow our membership from fifteen (when I started) to thirty-three by the time I left. Our efforts on the Hill had also met with modest success. While Congress was never going to act on all of our policy suggestions, they often turned to us for advice on the housing market and sometimes acted on our suggestions as they developed new legislation.

By 2014, things were largely back to normal, allowing me to happily oversee the running of the HPC without the looming dread of an economic disaster consuming all waking thoughts. Those last few years were not as eventful as the days of the crisis, but that was fine with me; I had had more than my fill of that kind of excitement! Besides, I was now in my seventies, and diverse and thrilling as my long career had been, I found my thoughts drifting toward retirement.

For a long time, I had played with the idea of retiring from full-time employment at the age of seventy-five. December 13, 2016, officially marked my seventy-fifth birthday, and after a terrific celebration with friends and family, I used the opportunity to revisit the idea. My time heading the HPC had been fantastic, and our family finances were healthy, but in my heart, I felt that I was ready to hang up my spurs. I visited with Governor Pawlenty, who completely understood, and we agreed that I would continue for another six months while my successor as president of HPC was chosen. But this is not where my story would end.

# CHAPTER 17

# NOT THE END, BUT A NEW BEGINNING

The two-hundred-strong crowd at the Park Hyatt Hotel in Georgetown applauded as Governor Tim Pawlenty introduced me to speak. A diverse collection of friends, family, and colleagues had come for my retirement party from the Housing Policy Council (HPC) at the Financial Services Roundtable in June 2017.

"I just want you to know how much I appreciate your being here, and how much I am grateful for your friendship," I began after I took my place at the podium.

It had been a great party, with plenty of good food, drink, and gifts for my wife Margaret and me. A long weekend at the Inn at Little Washington gift certificate, a framed personalized Washington Nationals jersey signed by the members of the Housing Policy Executive Council, and a framed Navy jersey signed by the members of the Housing Policy Council staff and head football coach Ken Niumatalolo were just three of these wonderful gifts. I have the last two proudly displayed in my home office.

I had been HPC's president since 2005, so this sendoff marked the end of twelve and a half years there. That was the longest I had ever worked anywhere. It had been a terrific time and, in my remarks, I reflected on how I had been convinced to take the helm after my tenure as president of IPG Photonics Corp. However, the party meant more than just my retirement from that organization. It was a celebration of my professional life.

My friends had reached out to many people I knew for the event. Some who came, like Governor Pawlenty, made speeches. Some not able to be there in person were kind enough to send videos wishing me well.

"I offer my sympathies to Margaret as John spends more time at home," President Carter joked as he smiled warmly.

"I wish I could be there in person as you're honored by your friends and colleagues, but I'm really glad to have this chance to offer my admiration and gratitude," said President Clinton. Most of the guests could not recall having two former presidents send a video to a retirement party, but they were not the only important figures to do so. Governor Terry McAuliffe of Virginia, Senator Joe Donnelly, Navy athletic director Chet Gladchuk, and Coach Ken Niumatalolo also made recordings and a House of Representatives resolution from Congresswoman Joyce Beatty was presented, and former President George W. Bush sent a letter that Governor Pawlenty read to all.

I was truly honored and humbled by their kind words for me. As I listened to the speeches, watched the videos, made my own remarks, and mingled with the guests, I reflected on everything that had brought me to this point. It represented a life that was often challenging but always rewarding.

Looking back, there have certainly been trials: the injury in high school that destroyed my dreams of a football scholarship, nearly having to declare bankruptcy when my savings-and-loan business in San Antonio failed, and scandals like Tailhook that I inherited when I became Secretary of the Navy. Those were tough times, but they taught me valuable and sometimes painful lessons, which I have put to good use.

However, my life has definitely been a blessed one, filled with great people and opportunities. Being appointed to the Naval Academy, serving on active duty on two submarines, working at Goldman Sachs, serving as Secretary of the Navy in the Clinton administration, as well as two positions related to housing in the Carter administration, living in Dallas, Washington, DC, and San Antonio, and working with the Hope Now Initiative, helping those facing foreclosure during the 2008 financial crisis are just a few. Beyond those experiences, I am especially grateful for my loving family and friends, who have always been there for me.

# CHAPTER 18

# WORTHY CAUSES

The humbling retirement party thrown for me was a line of demarcation from my working life to retirement. But it didn't mean I would sit in a rocking chair all day. For me, retirement meant giving back by focusing on my charitable work. But that also didn't mean I was starting from square one. Starting during the final days of my tenure as SEC-NAV, my participation with many organizations and charities only broadened with time. I deeply valued what these groups did and the sense of purpose they gave me, and retirement was no reason to end those commitments. In fact, I was just getting started!

Ranging from nonprofits to foundations and educational boards, they all provide a valuable service to society. Many also embody values I hold most precious and advocate for, such as faith and sports. For me these causes are a labor of love; it is never work if you love what you do! I continue to be a part of many of these organizations to this day, and it is a privilege to contribute to the impacts and changes they make.

Community Renewal International (CRI) was one of the first of the nonprofits I joined. In early 1999, after leaving the Pentagon, I was first contacted by Virginia Kilpatrick Shehee, a successful businesswoman, former Louisiana state senator, and also a Byrd alumna. We had a few things in common. Most notably, her father had owned Kilpatrick Life

Insurance Company in Shreveport, where my mother had worked for a number of years, so I was more than familiar with her family and her reputation, and it was a pleasant surprise to hear from her.

Virginia explained that she was the chairman of the National Advisory Board for an up-and-coming Shreveport-based charity called Community Renewal International, and that she and Mack McCarter, the founder and Byrd alumnus, were coming to DC to raise awareness for the cause and garner support. The fact that it was headquartered in my hometown, and that Virginia was a part of it, piqued my interest, and I did not hesitate to accept her invitation to dinner.

For the first couple years, I sat on their advisory board, providing advice on CRI's strategic initiatives and helping their community renewal projects whenever and however I could. Mack and I became very close friends. To this day, I admire his unshakable optimism and kindness, and the passion with which he leads CRI always amazes me. When Virginia retired as Chairman in 2002 due to illness, Mack surprisingly with no apparent deliberation asked me if I would take her place. I was humbled and moved by his request, and I accepted.

My efforts for CRI focused primarily on increasing the national profile of this inspiring, impressive charity. My decades living in Washington blessed me with an extensive list of contacts, so I proceeded to leverage this to CRI's benefit. That included inviting Mack to a couple Alfalfa Club dinners and even taking him to several Clinton Initiative events. At one such event in 2007, after the program, I asked Mack if he would like to meet President Clinton. He was stunned, but agreed excitedly, so we stood in the rope line. After President Clinton and I greeted each other warmly, I introduced Mack by telling the president that Mack was the founder and coordinator of CRI. As always, Clinton showed how well informed he is.

"Yes, I have heard about Community Renewal. I read that you are going to have the first completely energy-renewable office building in all of the south."

President Clinton never ceases to amaze me. Mack, always gregarious, was nearly lost for words and was simply blown away by the former president. We all spoke for another minute and President Clinton had to move on, though he did express a keen interest in CRI. Mack was over the moon! Those efforts helped CRI establish a bigger national presence and thus take on more significant projects. I worked to encourage support for its various initiatives, and, as CRI expanded, I convinced Mack to begin expanding this program into Washington, where each of the fifty states is represented and most of the world's nations have embassies.

The most impactful contribution I made was convincing President Jimmy Carter to speak at the CRI 2014 twentieth anniversary celebration in Shreveport. Mack and I went to Atlanta to encourage him to be with us on that occasion. Being one of the most famous patrons of Habitat for Humanity,[16] President Carter was happy to speak to an organization that shared a similar mission. I introduced him saying that he personified Matthew 25 and how proud I was of him. As of the writing of this memoir, he is also the only president ever to spend a whole day in our hometown. People turned out in droves to see him. All in all, it was an iconic event, and it is always a privilege to spend time with President Carter. Margaret and I also had the privilege to attend his and Rosalynn's seventy-fifth wedding anniversary in Plains, Georgia, in July 2021.

In 1999, soon after I had joined CRI, but before I became the new chairman of the national advisory board, I was also introduced to the Wesley Theological Seminary. My introduction began at St. John's Episcopal Church, often referred to as the Church of the Presidents, where we were then members of the congregation. I had had the privilege of serving there as a groomsman in the wedding of John and Jan Cope

[16] We had a few connections to Habitat for Humanity ourselves. Margaret spent a year working in its congressional offices shortly after I left government, and we had lunch with its founder, the late Millard Fuller, on a trip to Americus, Georgia. We continue to support Habitat for Humanity.

*President Jimmy Carter at his 75th anniversary weekend at Maranatha Baptist Church in Plains, GA.*

in 1993 before my swearing-in ceremony. My good friend John Cope urged to me to serve on that seminary board and introduced me to the president of the seminary. As someone of faith, I saw an exciting chance to deepen my understanding regarding how it is taught. Wesley is one of the country's most prestigious seminaries and located just down the block from our home. Historically Methodist, it is very ecumenical and has taught priests and members of the clergy across numerous denominations. If nothing else, a visit there would be a learning experience. Finding Wesley was inspirational, and without hesitation I wanted to be a part of it. I was delighted to discover that there was a vacancy on their board, and I was asked to join. They seemed as eager to have me as I was to join, and in no time at all, I joined the Board of Governors of the seminary in October of that year.

The twelve years, three terms, I had served on the board of Wesley Theological Seminary have only deepened my theological understanding of our faith, and it's been a blessing to help that organization continue its educational mission. Beyond the usual duties expected of a board member, I was able to help the Seminary expand its relationship with the armed forces that they had wanted to do for some time, and my background with the Department of Defense allowed me to be a big help.

David McAllister-Wilson, the president of Wesley Seminary, and I called on the Chief of Chaplains of the Navy Department and his staff, and that paid rich dividends. As someone who holds faith and public service in such high esteem, I thought this collaboration proposal was a fantastic idea. Thanks to our mutual resolve to this day, military chaplains of all stripes come to Wesley to study and deepen the understanding of their faith.

We at the Wesley Seminary also joined and assisted with the Yellow Ribbon Program, which was formed in 2008, to increase educational benefits for veterans who had served our country since 9/11/01. We felt strongly that veterans who wanted to study at Wesley Theological Seminary should not be turned away simply because they lacked the financial means. It took some lobbying and a little arm twisting, but those in charge soon saw the merits of including Wesley in the Yellow Ribbon Program.

I have also been privileged to work with and on behalf of the Washington National Cathedral. Margaret and I loved our time as part of the St. John's Episcopal Church congregation.[17] The rector of that parish, my true friend the Reverend Luis Leon, was the only minister of the cloth to do the invocation at the inauguration of both parties, Republican and Democrat, Presidents Barack Obama and George W. Bush.

---

[17] I have many fond memories of St. John's Church. One of those occurred soon after our first grandson, Antonio, was born and the lay reader blessed him in his prayer. President Bush and First Lady Laura Bush were at that service. Laura went out of her way to congratulate us at the end of the service. I was so touched by her kindness!

In 2005, my good friend the Reverend John R. Claypool, whom I had known from Christ Episcopal Church in San Antonio, called me. He was coming to Washington for the installation of the new dean of the Cathedral, his close friend the Reverend Sam Lloyd. He invited Margaret and me to join him and his wife, Ann, for the installation ceremony. We were so impressed with the Reverend Sam Lloyd and his sermon, we decided to join the congregation of the National Cathedral and started attending services there.

The Cathedral was much closer to our home, and we liked the new dean immensely, in part because the dean was a close friend of John Claypool, and we thought so highly of John. It was also because the National Cathedral represented a crossroads between the sacred and the civic in America, and that spoke to me on a deep and meaningful level. It is also a truly magnificent cathedral building, one of the largest churches in the United States and stunningly beautiful to behold. Standing in its grand nave, it is hard not to feel the love and greatness of God!

After some time, I was invited to join the chapter, the Cathedral's governing board, where I served two four-year terms. I had served on the vestry at my last three churches and was glad to serve on the governing board of the National Cathedral and enjoyed that experience immensely. I was involved in setting up the Veterans Committee and acting as a liaison between the church and the government. I also serve on the development committee. In 2010, the Cathedral's vicar left to become the rector of a large church in California, so the dean was tasked to bring a new vicar on board. The position was very much up for grabs; however, I could think of one person who would be perfect for it: my dear friend Jan Cope, the same one who had recommended me to become the president of the Housing Policy Council and had officiated at the wedding of our son Chris.[18]

---

[18] The wedding was held on August 16, 2008, at a military chapel at a Naval station in San Diego, CA. Thanks to my friend Craig Clark, we also held the rehearsal dinner at the prestigious University Club. The wedding was a beautiful ceremony, with our other son, John, taking the role of best man.

Jan had closed her own executive search business some years before, choosing to heed the call to the ministry. She studied and earned her degree at Wesley Theological Seminary while I was on the board and had spent her first three years as a priest at a smaller church in the capital, St. David's Church. I visited with Jan, and in a reversal of our meeting six years before, I told her about the vacancy and urged her to apply. Jan, ever humble, did not have much confidence in her chances, but she agreed. After the interview, which went well, I spoke to Dean Sam Lloyd and fervently argued Jan's case. It seems our efforts were not in vain, and Jan joined the National Cathedral as its new vicar in 2010.

Things went well at the Cathedral for several years, though the coffers were never as full as we would have liked, and we had deficits several years in a row, thanks in part to the lingering fallout from the great recession and the damage caused by the earthquake that hit Washington in August 2011. In 2015, Jan was promoted to Provost, the second-highest position at the National Cathedral. She conceived of a bold but potentially risky new plan to raise resources for the Cathedral: the Dean's Council. Intended as a new advisory body that would be "limited in size, but national in scope," the Dean's Council would bring together a selection of philanthropists with an interest in the preservation and the future of the National Cathedral. When Jan asked me if I would help her establish the Council, I could think of no more worthy use of my time. We did not even have a dean at the time that we started recruiting people for it.

I thought about who would be appropriate for the Council and who could meet the criteria. Jan did the same, and after some time, we had created a promising shortlist of potential members across the country, from DC to Dallas to San Francisco. About that time, the search committee did an outstanding job of calling the Reverend Randy Hollerith to be our new dean. I remember that we were on vacation in 2016 at the Big Bend National Park in Texas when I got a call from Jan that Randy had accepted the call, and he was totally committed to the National

Cathedral. The job of recruiting the Dean's Council became much easier with him in place. Jan and I met with each prospect, sometimes together and sometimes separately, until we had successfully convinced about three dozen of them on the merits of our cause. The premise of the Dean's Council was simple: members would serve for a three-year term, paying an annual pledge to the Cathedral and agreeing that they would attend at least one of the two meetings a year.

In exchange, they would hear from the Dean himself about everything that the Cathedral was doing, provide advice if they chose, and have access to virtually any event on the calendar. When the obligations were met and the three-year term on the council concluded, they were more than welcome to sign up again, either for another full three years or occasionally on an annual basis. Overall, I think the founding of the Dean's Council was a resounding success. Of course, not everyone said yes when we first approached them, and not everyone signed on for a second term. However, we were always successful in finding new members to fill any seats that were vacated. To this day, the Dean's Council is still going strong, and has been invaluable to the Cathedral. I am so happy for Jan's success in establishing it. It was definitely a gamble, but it has more than paid off.

Soon after, our relatively new Dean Hollerith asked me to represent the Washington National Cathedral as a trustee on the Protestant Episcopal Cathedral Foundation (PECF), which is like a holding company that encompasses the National Cathedral and its related institutions: Beauvoir School (for children in pre-kindergarten through the third grade), the National Cathedral School (for girls in grades four through twelve), and Saint Alban's School (for boys also in grades four through twelve). The Cathedral and those schools are all located on the fifty-six-acre Cathedral close.

The National Cathedral means a great deal to me, and it has always been a privilege to help serve it. I never did it out of a desire to be recognized or honored but simply to assist the institution I love. Because of that, I was completely speechless when the Cathedral bestowed upon me the title of an honorary Canon in 2017.[19] It came with a name plate on a seat in the great choir of the Cathedral. Receiving this recognition was truly one of the greatest honors of my life, and it means the world to me that the Cathedral would acknowledge me in that way. In 2019 we decided to do a comprehensive capital campaign with the goal of raising $150 million over five years. I am serving as one of the three co-chairman of the major gifts committee. Working with the National Cathedral, and being a part of its congregation, has been one of the most spiritually fulfilling experiences of my life.

I have previously mentioned my leading two festivals for the Luis Palau Association in San Antonio in 1991 and the event on the mall in Washington, DC, in 2005. So far, I am the only person to chair two festivals. Margaret and I are part of the Palau Association President's Club and also went with Luis and his team to Vietnam in 2011. The effort was focused on the one hundredth anniversary of the establishment of the first Protestant church in that nation. The gatherings were the first of their kind since the country's reunification in 1975. We were meeting with the leaders of government and members of the clergy. From there we went to Beijing, China, and met with government officials and church leaders there. Sadly, Luis Palau passed away March 11, 2021. He was a great man and a wonderful evangelist, for whom we had the highest respect. The LPA is now run by his sons.

The Naval Academy remains an institution that means a great deal to me, including but well beyond their sports teams. While no longer their boss as of November 1998, I now have more freedom in my dealings with the Academy. Throughout the years, I have spoken to the midshipmen at many events, and I continue to remain invested in its success and prestige.

---

[19] Dean Hollerith recommended me to Bishop Mariann Budde, and she presented it to the chapter for approval. She stated in her recommendation that I had a long, well-documented and ongoing commitment to the Cathedral. (The letter that she gave me at the induction service is in the appendix.)

Two specific events merit mention here. The first is the tradition known as "Link in the Chain," which is a relationship between a current class and the class that graduated fifty years prior. For me, this was the class of 2014, and what a great class they were. They represented, in my opinion, some of the finest young men and women our country has to offer, and it was a privilege to share a small part of their journey with them. Some of our classmates attended their induction ceremony, the climbing of the Herndon Monument where they shed their status as plebes, their Ring Dance and their graduation. The link in the chain is a wonderful tradition that exists between graduates across generations. I was part of the 1964 group of twelve who congratulated each of the graduates after receiving a diploma and presented them with their new insignia as they became ensigns in the Navy or second lieutenants in the Marine Corps. That was a genuine treat!

In 2016, the USNA presented to me the Distinguished Graduate Award. In the words of the Academy and the Alumni Association, the award was established to "honor graduates who have demonstrated a lifetime commitment to service, personal character, and distinguished contributions to our nation." To put it mildly, to be recognized in such a way by the institution I love so much means a tremendous amount to me.

Apart from faith and the Academy, I also found myself working with an organization that teaches and promotes something I have spoken about a good bit: good leadership and compatibility. PathNorth was founded by a close friend of mine, Doug Holladay, in 2007. One of the realizations that Doug had when he created PathNorth was that many people, men and women, spend most of their adult lives dedicating themselves to their professions. At some point, they become aware that there is much more to this life but are unsure how to become exposed to or involved in other areas. PathNorth is the perfect vehicle. There are wonderful trips all over the world, interesting and varied speakers, and mind-searching experiences, always with a wonderful group of other PathNorthers who are also interested in finding genuine meaning in life.

I met Doug in 1994 during my SECNAV days at a prayer breakfast we both belonged to. We helped each other from time to time and became good friends. We were both alumni of Goldman Sachs and each served in government. In essence, PathNorth is dedicated to bringing people together, facilitating the exchange of leadership techniques and ideas, and fostering lifelong friendships. Doug asked me to be a founding member of the board. From the outset, I thought it was a terrific idea, and I readily accepted his invitation.

Since that time, I have been an active member of the board and also led a couple of my own initiatives. First, I have gone out of my way to visit with or write to each new member who joins PathNorth. I want them to know that they are welcomed, that we care, and that we value any experience they wish to share. It is a small, personal touch, but it helps everyone feel like they are part of a more tight-knit community. Some other board members also send emails to welcome them to the organization.

The other effort I have co-led with Margaret is our Civility Series: a bi-monthly series of workshops where we encourage respect and courtesy in public discourse. This came about in 2017, in response to what we felt was a decline in the quality of civil discourse that was so apparent in our federal government and beyond. We started this effort in an attempt to repair interpersonal damage caused by the corrosive forces of the time. We can disagree without being disagreeable and still be respectful and friendly to each other; that is what we are trying to encourage. We have been fortunate to be graced by some fantastic speakers who have participated at these events, and I believe they have helped make a difference in restoring the social fabric of our society among those who have joined. There is a better way to act toward one another, and I think most of the attendees agree with us.

Additionally, beginning in 2002 about once a year, I began taking a group of twelve people on an aircraft carrier embark. Typically, I would invite people with whom I was working or serving with on boards of directors. When PathNorth was formed, I began taking six members of that organization along. Beyond these professional endeavors, Path-North has been a wonderful organization in terms of just having some good, old-fashioned fun. As a board member, I am lucky enough to be invited on all the trips, which have been universally excellent. From Cuba to the Orient Express and from Paris to London, our adventures have been diverse and exciting. Chances are, we would not have done many of these things by ourselves, and we had a great time sharing these experiences with PathNorth friends. On one of the PathNorth trips to London, the theme of the experience was Winston Churchill. We stayed at a club to which he belonged, visited his birthplace, Blenheim Palace, went to the House of Commons in the parliament, and had dinner in the Churchill War Rooms. Our speakers were his grandson Nicholas Soames, a then-member of Parliament, Lord John Gilbert from the House of Lords, and Ambassador Phil Lader, one of the Clinton administration ambassadors to the Court of Saint James. They were all excellent speeches. Touring the Churchill War Rooms in London and smoking cigars one lazy afternoon in Havana while competing over who could keep the longest ash before it fell off (Margaret won!) are just a couple of these fond memories.

Friendship Place, which serves the homeless, is another organization we have been supporting. It is their mission to help those experiencing homelessness attain stable housing and rebuild their lives, and it includes a very robust veterans' program. In addition to housing, they assist with food, supplies, job attainment, medical/psychological care, a street ministry, and other outreach initiatives.

With the exception of the COVID shutdown, their Welcome Center has been open for those needing breakfast or lunch. Pre-COVID, Margaret and two other ladies, Rosalie Berk and Gretchen Theobald, met early in Rosalie's kitchen most Wednesdays for the greater part of a decade to prepare and deliver a hot breakfast to those who arrived early at the center. It is an honor to help those less fortunate in our community.

I have also had the good fortune to be involved with another foundation——this one focusing on the intersection between two of my most important interests: public service and sports. I was introduced to the Bob Feller Act of Valor Award sometime in 2015 through an associate of mine from the Pentagon, Admiral Hank Chiles. He introduced me to Peter Fertig, its founder and president, who explained to me the purpose of the foundation. The Bob Feller Act of Valor Award was an initiative dedicated to raising recognition of service members, major leaguers, and Hall of Famers past and present, for their public and community service and dedication to our country.

They did this through the medium of baseball. Bob Feller, the only pitcher in the history of baseball to pitch a no-hitter on Opening Day, had served in the Navy during World War II and is regarded as one of baseball's best pitchers ever. He was the first of all the professional athletes in this country to volunteer on December 8, 1941, to serve in World War II. Needless the say, this foundation checked all the right boxes for me. When invited on board, I agreed without a moment's hesitation.

Unlike other organizations and nonprofits I have worked with, the Bob Feller Act of Valor Foundation is mostly a volunteer initiative, which is something I deeply respect. Every year they name a major league player, a baseball Hall of Fame member, a chief petty officer from the Navy, and a sergeant from the Marine Corps who have contributed significantly to their community. It is a passion project, dedicated to recognizing the efforts of some of our model men and women in uniform and teaching younger generations about the merits of public service through the power of example. I always have been happy to support them, especially when they went through some financial turbulence in 2015, and I was able to help them look for new donors during that time.

In 2014, I became involved in another nonprofit organization, this time dedicated to the preservation of history connected to the highest office in the land, the presidency: the White House Historical Association (WHHA). First Lady Jackie Kennedy founded this organization in 1961. My connection with the WHHA came about almost by accident. In 2014, the WHHA merged with the Decatur House, asking four members of the board including Gail West, Janet Howard, Bob McGee, and me to join WHHA's board. Jan Cope had invited me to join the board of the Decatur House in 2010. As the former home of Commodore Stephen Decatur, it had a relevance to naval history that I wanted to help preserve. I can still recall memorizing one of the commodore's quotes in my Reef Points when a plebe at the Academy. Jan had been Chair of the Decatur House board, but we both were very happy to be part of the WHHA when the two foundations merged.

In hindsight, I am glad we made the choice; our work with the WHHA has been fascinating. Learning more about the history of the White House and its long list of occupants and preserving some of that legacy has been marvelous. I helped with several marketing projects in order to raise funds, including some communications with the Washington Nationals for collaboration on the limited edition of the Christmas ornaments. As I have also been fortunate to serve in two separate presidential administrations, the WHHA often turned to me when looking for speakers.

However, despite the presidential focus of the WHHA, I did appreciate that they did not ignore the separate and rich history of the Decatur House. When I broached the subject of holding a yearly observance in honor of the late and influential Commodore Decatur, they were right on board with the idea. Every year on January 5, I host the observance of his birthday in the Decatur Carriage House, where most events are now held, honoring Decatur's memory while promoting the overall work of WHHA. I have had a great time working with the WHHA and its president, Stewart McLaurin, and I look forward to what is in store for this association of history and education enthusiasts.

The most recent organization I have had the privilege to be a part of is WETA. Based in Washington, DC, WETA is the second-largest PBS station in the country, responsible for helping create and broadcast fantastic programs like the *PBS Newshour*, Ken Burns

*Michelle Obama receiving from WHHA board members the painting of Alma Thomas, the first African-American painter to have a painting in the White House.*

documentaries and other TV and radio shows. I have always been a staunch believer in the value of good public broadcasting as an educational and entertainment tool which is accessible to all. I have had some earlier experience with the medium back in San Antonio with KLRN, on whose board of directors I served. When Sharon Rockefeller, the Chairman and CEO of WETA, invited me to be on the board of trustees, it was my hope that, in my own small way, I could contribute to WETA's continued success.

Sharon was grateful that I was interested in being a part of it and readily welcomed me into the WETA family. Even after my dear friend Jim Lehrer had passed away, it remained exciting to see how everything worked behind the scenes. Like any PBS or NPR station, a substantial slice of WETA's budget comes from donations from individuals or organizations. Many of us work to support WETA. I also have assisted with WETA's organization on their capital campaign. I have not been with them for long, but I am eager to see where my experiences with WETA will take me in the future.

I urged that Sharon hire someone I knew could be of great help to WETA, Richard Bland. I knew Rich well from the National Cathedral, where he was the chief operating officer, but due to the tragedy of the COVID-19 pandemic, the Cathedral was forced to let him go. I knew he was a very smart and talented man, because we had also worked together on the chapter of the Cathedral. There happened to be an opening at WETA that I thought Rich would be a perfect fit for, so I called Sharon to convince her of the merits of hiring him. He came on as vice president for foundation and government development in January 2021, and I cannot wait to see all the good he will do for WETA in that position. Sharon recently called me to sing Rich Bland's praises.

There is another group I treasure, which is unlike the others I have spoken about, because it is more a breakfast event than a charity and has been an important staple of my life for nearly three decades. However, I think it deserves an honorable mention, because it has been so meaningful to my life in Washington. A group of people of faith with some federal experience gather weekly to discuss scripture, events in our lives, and lessons learned we wish to pass on through the Cedars Breakfast.

I have been a part of this group since the early days of the Clinton administration. Members who are in town and can attend meet every Thursday morning. Comprised of over twenty-five individuals, it is mainly an inclusive Christian gathering with Catholics, Orthodox, Episcopalians, Baptists, and a number of other denominations accounted for in the membership. We often have had guests from other faiths, such as Muslims, Buddhists, Hindus, and Jews. It has been rewarding and refreshing to hear the perspective that different faiths bring to the table. Each member normally speaks twice a year on their chosen topic, which for me is often lessons I have learned from my family, other experiences, or one of John Claypool's books.

The Cedars Breakfast also includes my dear Army friend, former Under Secretary of the Army Joe Reeder. Joe and I met during the Clinton administration, working together on a number of issues confronting the military at that time, like increasing representation of minorities and discussing broader disciplinary frameworks for the military in the wake of Tailhook. A veteran like me, Joe is a graduate of West Point and a very impressive man. Our relationship quickly grew into a genuine friendship, which included a competitive but friendly tennis rivalry. Just after his good friend, Secretary of Commerce Ron Brown, tragically died in a plane crash in 1996 while visiting US troops in Bosnia, I invited Joe to join us at the Cedars Breakfast, so that he could have a circle of supportive friends to count on. Joe quickly took to the Cedars Breakfast, where he has remained quite active to this day.

Over the years I have devoted time and treasure to these and other groups because they all have missions I believe in. They encompass key issues like community, public service, faith, sports, and my desire to give back. All of us have had our share of ups and downs, but overall I have been truly blessed with a wonderful family, terrific friends, and a deep and abiding faith that gives me purpose.

Life has been good to me, and showing gratitude is important to me. I want to give back to society in the best way I know how and in a manner that honors my ethics and principles. I want to do what I can to leave this a better world for my grandchildren and the future generations to inherit. Besides, I am one who always needs something to do, a project to sink my teeth into. Retirement is nice, but I think I would drive myself and Margaret crazy without something to work on.

I believe all of us should immerse ourselves in organizations and the causes we believe in. Whether it is on their board or on the ground, offering our time and energy will make a difference in our lives. You will feel a sense of fulfillment that you will not find in your career alone, and you can do your part in making the world better for all of us.

# CONCLUSION

As I have been writing this memoir, much has transpired, both personally and in the world at large. COVID-19 has ravaged the world, claiming millions of lives and completely changing life as we once knew it. I am thankful that most of my friends and family were not seriously affected by the pandemic, which is a reminder that we can take nothing for granted. Our hearts go out to all those who have suffered or lost loved ones. Of course, we are also horrified by Russia's invasion into Ukraine. We so hope that the war will terminate soon and peace will prevail.

Despite these unusual times, I continue to indulge in my hobbies as much as I am able, and I always keep an eye out for new opportunities. The coronavirus made it almost impossible to travel or to take part in the annual baseball trip with my friends John Peavy and Ralph Severson. John Peavy was Rex Jennings's partner at Goldman Sachs in Dallas and was very helpful to his widow, Sue, when Rex passed away. Now that we are all vaccinated, however, we plan to pick up right where we left off. I cannot wait to get back into the ballparks to watch America's favorite pastime and Navy football.

We have been planning another pilgrimage to the Holy Land. Margaret and I had a great experience with the Cathedral tour when we went to Israel in 2017 and asked our guide about arranging another trip. He was happy to accommodate but told us the group needed to be at least twenty people. Over the next couple of years, we gathered together a collection of family and friends who were interested in joining us and planned it for the New Year of 2020–21. We had hoped to spend our fiftieth wedding anniversary in Jerusalem, but the COVID-19 pandemic intervened. With vaccination efforts not yet arresting the coronavirus in the US and Israel, we are now aiming 2022–23 instead. As our Jewish friends say: "Next year in Jerusalem!"

Our sons, John and Chris, have been living full, rewarding lives. After graduation from Davidson, John spent a year in Jamaica teaching and coaching in a program similar to the Peace Corps before he went to Officer Candidate School (OCS) and joined the Navy. He spent seven years and served on two ships, where he was a surface warfare officer. When his service ended, he took a position at the Chicago Transit Authority and attended night school at DePaul University to earn his MBA degree. He spent three years in Dubai consulting on their rapid transit system and today is the project manager for the Green Line Extension of the Massachusetts Bay Transit Authority, a $2.5 billion project. He and his wife, Yasmin, live in Newton, MA, with their two sons, Antonio and Mateus, who are now eighteen and fifteen.

As for Chris, during the four years he spent at W&L, he played football the first year and switched to rugby the last three years. Between high school and college during an exchange year in England at Denstone College, he had played and greatly enjoyed rugby, making good friends in the process. He studied hard at W&L and graduated magna cum laude, after which he attended OCS and became an officer in the Marine Corps. He loved the nine years he spent in the Marines, choosing to attend flight school in Pensacola, Florida, where he trained as a helicopter pilot for the CH-53 Sea Stallion. He was deployed to Iraq twice and served in combat. He looks back on those years and experiences with pride and satisfaction. After leaving the Marine Corps, he attended Georgetown University Law School. Since then, he worked as a litigator for three different firms before becoming the General Counsel for Air Center Helicopters near Fort Worth, Texas. He and his wife, Kelly, have two sons: Brian, twelve, and Charlie, eight.

*At the Navy Memorial before the Lone Sailor statue with our two sons when they were on active duty. We are very proud of them!*

Since my retirement, each morning I enjoy breakfast with Margaret while we watch the morning prayer service from the National Cathedral. After breakfast, I go down to my basement office, close the door and start my day with a period of reflection. This is something I do daily, and it provides me with a sense of grounding and spiritual sustenance. I read Abraham Lincoln's daily devotional among others, some scripture, and I spend some time in prayer, focusing on adoration, thanksgiving, confession, intercession, and petition. I recommend this practice to everyone.

My life is not all leisure, family time, and pent-up desires to travel. Pandemic or not, I still keep up with most of my commitments, especially with the nonprofits I have previously talked about. I've also joined additional corporate boards, including Xactus, Crius Technology Group, and Trustar Bank.

From my childhood in Louisiana until my retirement in 2017, I often have had the privilege and responsibility of being a leader. Those have been some of the most rewarding events of my life, and it is my hope that the lessons I have learned in those positions might be useful to others. I believe good leadership is important in any organization, and I know there are many ideas of what it takes to make a good leader. For my part, much of what has shaped my approach has come from the key pillars of my life: family, faith, friends, dedication to public service, involvement in the private sector, and a love of sports.

It has been those, more than anything else, that have been my moral bedrock and have given me strength through thick and thin. Those things honed by my experiences, have taught me the most important traits I believe anyone in leadership should possess: integrity, responsibility, perseverance, principle, and compassion. I have tried to live by those traits, and it is my hope that through the events in my life, others will see their value. If you lead by example, with those principles in mind, I believe you will be successful and respected when it is your turn to lead.

I would like to share part of the poem "Sermons We See" by Edgar Guest. It means a great deal to me because it captures much of what I believe to be important, especially in matters of faith and leadership.

*I'd rather see a sermon than hear one any day;*
*I'd rather one should walk with me than merely tell the way.*
*The eye's a better pupil and more willing than the ear,*
*Fine counsel is confusing, but example is always clear;*
*And the best of all the preachers are those who live their creeds,*
*For to see good put in action is what everybody needs.*

*I soon can learn to do it if you'll let me see it done;*
*I can watch your hands in action, but your tongue too fast may run.*
*And the lecture you deliver may be very wise and true,*
*But I'd rather get my lessons by observing what you do;*
*For I might misunderstand you and the high advice you give,*
*But there's no misunderstanding how you act and how you live.*

*My 1967 MGB, which I have owned since it was new.*

Which memories are the sweetest or which ones do I cherish most? There are too many contenders for that honor. However, there are a few that were the most pivotal or significant in bringing me to today, and I treasure these moments very dearly. Those would be my time at Byrd, LSU, the Naval Academy, the Navy, the golden years spent in Texas (excluding my S&L financial tumult), my work as Secretary of the Navy and other positions of public service, and the births of our two wonderful sons and four precious grandsons. Most importantly: my wedding and marriage to Margaret. We have spent over fifty-two amazing years together. Margaret has been an endless source of love, inspiration, motivation, and support. Truly, I cannot imagine my life without her.

If there is any last wisdom or final shred of advice to offer, it would be this: always cherish family and friends; find ways to serve your country, state, or community; treat everyone you meet with dignity and respect; strive for self-improvement; remain humble and trust in God.

I wish you many blessings, fair winds, and following seas.

# APPENDIX

# Midshipman's Prayer

Almighty Father, whose way is in the sea, whose paths are in the great waters, whose command is over all and whose love never faileth; let me be aware of Thy presence and obedient to Thy will. Keep me true to my best self, guarding me against dishonesty in purpose and in deed, and helping me so to live that I can stand unashamed and unafraid before my shipmates, my loved ones, and thee. Protect those in whose love I live. Give me the will to do my best and to accept my share of responsibilities with a strong heart and a cheerful mind. Make me considerate of those entrusted to my leadership and faithful to the duties my country has entrusted in me. Let my uniform remind me daily of the traditions of the service of which I am a part. If I am inclined to doubt, steady my faith; if I am tempted, make me strong to resist; if I should miss the mark, give me courage to try again. Guide me with the light of truth and keep before me the life of Him by whose example and help I trust to obtain the answer to my prayer, Jesus Christ our Lord. Amen.

# President Carter's Letter

THE WHITE HOUSE

WASHINGTON

April 28, 1978

To John Dalton

After years of difficult negotiations and months of Senate debate, new Treaties between the United States and Panama were recently approved.

I want to thank you for your participation in this deliberative process. The active interest that you and many other Americans took in this vital issue resulted in a broad public discussion of the Treaties.

It is part of the greatness of America that people everywhere can have an influence over the great decisions which face our nation. Your willingness to take the time to be involved sets an excellent example for all Americans. I hope you will continue to let your voice be heard on other issues in the future.

Sincerely,

Jimmy Carter

Mr. John H. Dalton
2303 Creek Drive
Alexandria, Virginia 22308

# Swearing-in Ceremony Remarks

Remarks delivered by
The Honorable John H. Dalton
Secretary of the Navy
Swearing-in Ceremony
Annapolis, MD
August 14, 1993

### TAKING THE HELM

Thirty-three years ago last month, I stood right here at
Tecumseh Court and took that same oath of office. It was a day I
will always remember. I was proud and I was scared. Today, I am
proud and grateful. As proud as I am to be Secretary of the
Navy, I'm even more proud of--and, indeed my claim to fame is my
wonderful wife Margaret and my fine sons John and Chris. I would
like for them to stand. I am also very proud and grateful to my
brother and sister, William and Margaret. I would like for you
both to please stand. As a matter of fact I have a lot of family
and relatives here, and I would like for all of my relatives to
please stand.

I have relatives here from Texas, Louisiana, and Arkansas.
I lived in Maryland and Virginia and have relatives there. At my
confirmation hearing, Senator Hutchison said that if I continue
to claim so many home states, I am going to be known as the
"George Bush of the Democratic Party."

There are many people to whom I am very grateful today, and
first of all I am grateful to President Clinton, who I think is
an outstanding Commander-in-Chief.

As Dr. Perry said, he and I were with the President
yesterday aboard the USS CARL VINSON, a nuclear power aircraft
carrier in Oakland, CA. I have been with him at the Marine
Barracks, and Tuesday night we had a nice dinner at the White
House with the Joint Chiefs of Staff and all the Commanders-in-
Chief of the Unified Commands from around the world. I can tell
you from first hand experience that from Seamen Recruits to four-
star Admirals and Generals, our president is respected and
admired and has a great rapport with all the Armed Services.

I met with General Powell recently. We had breakfast the
Saturday morning after the Tomahawk missile strike on Iraq, and
General Powell said this about our Commander in Chief, "This guy
really gets it. I have worked with a number of Presidents in my
career but none is a finer Commander-in-Chief than President
Clinton." I am proud of him; I'm grateful to be in the Clinton
administration and I am particular grateful to him for the
confidence he expressed in me by appointing me to serve as
Secretary of the Navy.

1

## Swearing-in Ceremony Remarks (continued)

I am also very grateful to Secretary Les Aspin, and Deputy Secretary William J. Perry--very fine men who are great to work with and work for. They are true giants in National Security. They have forgotten more about national security than most military experts will ever know. I am also very grateful to President Jimmy Carter for giving me the opportunity for my first public service. Because of that public service in the executive branch of government during his administration, I feel very comfortable and very much at peace in taking this job.

I want to thank Admiral Arleigh Burke. Truly a legend, he was Chief of Naval Operations that day when my class was sworn-in. He has done so much for the Naval Service. And, Admiral I really appreciate your being here today. I want to thank two fine clergy men on the stage who have meant so much in my life, my brother-in-law Bob Ratelle, and my good friend Rick Lobs.

You know I have had many of my friends ask me when I was being considered for this job: why in the world would I want to leave San Antonio, Texas--one of the garden spots in the country, where I was with an outstanding investment banking firm and enjoyed some success with that firm--to come up to Washington and take on the issues of Tailhook, gays in the military, and women in combat, and building down and closing bases? Well after being here a few weeks, I feel a little bit like the guy who was arrested for being drunk and setting his bed on fire, and who stood before the judge and said, "Your honor I plead guilty to being drunk, but that bed was on fire when I got in it."

Well, I took this job because I love the Naval Service, and I welcome the challenges that confront me. I'm particularly grateful to my friends--so many of you who are here today. First of all, my classmates from the Class of 64--men such as Tom Lynch. I am proud of him for being our Superintendent. I'm grateful for my shipmates on the BLUEBACK and JOHN C. CALHOUN who are here. Lord Nelson said that classmates and shipmates are like "a band of brothers" and many of you have been brothers to me.

I am grateful to my friends that are here from the Carter Administration, and friends that I have worked with politically in campaigns for Gephardt, Ann Richards and in the Clinton campaign. I am grateful to my friends who are here from Stephens and my friends from home.

You know Washington is a tough town. People are not at all adverse to stabbing you in the back if they think that it is to their advantage. Harry Truman once said that "If you want a friend in Washington, buy a dog." Well, I have a dog and those of you who know me now how special my Pepper is to me, but I also

2

## Swearing-in Ceremony Remarks (continued)

have many friends. Friends that have been with me in good times and in times that were tough. Friends who have been with me long before I had any kind of position of responsibility. And I am grateful for my friends.

And I say to my friends that you may not always agree with what I do or decisions that I make in this office. But I want you to always know that whatever I do, I will do because I think that it is right, honest, fair, and in the best interest of the Naval Service and consistent with the policies of the Clinton Administration.

When the President called me and offered me this job, he said we have the finest Naval Service in the history of our country in quality of people. Well, the few weeks that I have been here I have found that that is indeed the case. Our sailors, Marines and civil servants are smart, dedicated, hardworking, committed, and do an outstanding job and you should be very, very proud of them. It is a great honor for me to serve as their Secretary.

They are standing watch around the globe. For example, First Class Petty Officer Donald Heffentrager is aboard the USS THEODORE ROOSEVELT off the shores of Bosnia. Corporal Charles Moreno is in a Company in Somalia. Our sailors and Marines are standing watch, defending our freedom, standing up for us. My job is to lead them. The world has changed in the last few years. The Iron Curtain is no more, the Soviet Union is no longer there and the Cold War is over. The President has charged Secretary Aspin and Bill Perry to do a "bottom up" review--to look at the world as it exists and see what our defense requirements are, what the needs are; and see what we have and go from ground zero or do what we call a "bottom up review."

It is important to me as we do this build-down--and we do need a smaller service then we have--that we do it in the right manner. And I like to refer to it as "right-sizing." It is important that we get it right, that we do it right, and that we treat our people right in the process. We need to be innovative and creative, do our business in a cost effective manner and always remember that the taxpayer is our customer. It is our job to deliver the highest quality Naval Service that we possibly can and to give value to the taxpayers.

I will continually emphasize the values of honor, courage, commitment and leadership. As was pointed out earlier, John Paul Jones is buried in his crypt below the Naval Academy chapel, and I welcome you to go by and see that on you way over to the reception after the ceremony. He is known as the father of our Navy, and during the American Revolution he set down the qualifications of a Naval Officer. He said an officer of the Navy must be a capable mariner of course, but also a great deal

3

## Swearing-in Ceremony Remarks (continued)

more. He must be a gentlemen of liberal education, refined manners, punctilious courtesy and the nicest sense of personal honor. I'm sure today he would include women as well. And that's the standard to which men and women of the Naval Service are committed.

The Navy and Marine Corps are precious resources that the American people entrust to their civilian leadership. The role of the Secretary of the Navy, along with the Chief of Naval Operations and Commandant of the Marine Corps is to safeguard these assets--to lead. To shape them so that they can achieve excellence. ...To ensure that they are ready in all aspects and all respects to carry out their mission. ...To ensure that they remain strong. ...To ensure they are constituted in a way that inspires outstanding performance by each sailor, Marine and civil servant. ...To ensure that they treat all their members with dignity and respect.

I have always been moved by President John F. Kennedy's reflection on naval service and what he said in his graduation address here in my plebe year. "Any man who may be asked this century what he did to make his life worthwhile...can respond with a great deal of pride and satisfaction, 'I served in the United States Navy.'" I would say the same about our heroic United States Marine Corps. I am determined as Secretary to retain and enhance this sense of pride and satisfaction for all our people, and continue the legacy into the next century.

I want you to know how very much I appreciate each one of your being here today. Thank you very much for sharing this very, very special day with me. There is no other job I would rather have, and there is no other place that I would rather be. I thank the Lord for this wonderful opportunity to serve my country.

God Bless you. God Bless the United States Navy and the United States Marine Corps. And God Bless America.

Thank you very much.

4

# The *New York Times* Tailhook Editorial

## The Tailhook Fiasco

The new Secretary of Defense, William J. Perry, must have thought he was making the best of a bad situation by crafting a deal to entice Adm. Frank B. Kelso 2d into retiring with full rank and pay. Alas, it was a dishonorable deal announced with language that insults public intelligence. So in his first weeks in office, Secretary Perry has joined former Defense Secretary Les Aspin, former Navy Secretary H. Lawrence Garrett 3d, the Naval Investigative Service and the Pentagon as shareholders in an episode of utter disgrace.

The current Secretary of the Navy, John H. Dalton, was correct in urging Admiral Kelso's removal as Chief of Naval Operations for failing to show proper leadership at the Tailhook convention. Former Secretary Aspin was wrong to overrule Mr. Dalton.

And now the Navy's Tailhook inquiry has ended as ignominiously as it began. Admiral Kelso refused to step down unless Mr. Perry issued a statement calling him "a man of highest integrity and honor." Yet the Navy's own judge, Capt. William T. Vest Jr., concluded that Admiral Kelso had lied about his activities at the Tailhook convention and then used his rank to impede the investigation.

Only one of them is right, and Secretary Perry has no way of knowing whether it is he — or Captain Vest and Mr. Dalton, who assert that the Navy's top admiral failed in his duty. Now, of course, the public will never know either, since Admiral Kelso's retirement ends any review of his conduct.

•

More than two years ago the now-infamous Tailhook convention was the scene of physical assaults in which unwilling women were grabbed, fondled and partially disrobed. The Navy says 140 Navy and Marine pilots assaulted 83 women. No one was convicted because scores of commissioned officers lied about what they had witnessed.

In the final development Captain Vest, the judge, dismissed the last three naval cases on the grounds that Admiral Kelso had lied about his own knowledge of bawdy activities and actively manipulated the investigation to shield his personal involvement.

From all accounts, Captain Vest is a responsible jurist. He was forced to weigh evidence of the admiral's involvement because the three defendants challenged the whole proceeding as tainted. The theme that weaves most strikingly through his 111-page opinion is his deep skepticism about the truthfulness of Admiral Kelso and those who testified for him.

The admiral said, for example, that he had never witnessed any improper activities and never set foot in the suites or hallway where the assaults took place. Other officers corroborated his assertions. Yet the judge chose to believe a vice admiral who testified that he had led Admiral Kelso through those suites and a personal aide who said the admiral had at least passed close to a key suite. The judge also believed the undisputed testimony of an officer who said he was talking to the admiral on a patio when both witnessed and commented on a scene in which male officers surrounded a woman, yelled for her to display her breasts, and held high the top of her bathing suit.

Similarly, Admiral Kelso denied even being present on the patio on the night when the worst assaults occurred nearby, and some officers corroborated his account by saying he was with them elsewhere. Yet the judge chose to believe other officers who testified that they had seen Admiral Kelso on the patio in the company of then-Navy Secretary Garrett, a pairing that could only have happened that night.

The judge's opinion is flawed in some respects. It occasionally speculates on what Admiral Kelso must have known or seen. Some officials complain that their remarks were taken out of context. The conclusion that Admiral Kelso tried to manipulate the investigation is largely inferred. And the judge erred in charging that Admiral Kelso had received incriminating files on himself and other flag officers and failed to pass them on to prosecutors. Those files were apparently held by the Pentagon's civilian leadership and never delivered to Admiral Kelso.

But the indisputable bottom line in this tangle of conflicting tales is that a judge of known professionalism, the chief judge for his particular district, has carefully weighed the evidence and declared the Navy's investigation tainted.

Over and against that is the Defense Secretary's exonerating statement that was based not on a detailed inquiry but on a bargaining among top civilian and military officials inside the Pentagon. One of the effects of that statement was to curtail formation of a special court of inquiry composed of retired generals and admirals to assess Admiral Kelso's performance.

Mr. Perry assures us that all's well that ends well. In fact, a fiasco has ended with a charade.

251

# USNA Class of 1995 Commencement Address

Remarks as delivered by
The Honorable John H. Dalton
Secretary of the Navy
USNA Graduation
Annapolis, MD
31 May 1995

## TIMELESS TRAITS OF LEADERSHIP

Thank you, Chuck [Admiral Larson]. I want to congratulate you on the outstanding job you have done here at the Academy. One of the decisions I am most proud of was my decision to make Admiral Chuck Larson Superintendent of the Naval Academy. He has stepped in and demonstrated once again his extraordinary leadership ability. I thank you, the Academy thanks you, the Naval Service thanks you, and, above all, America thanks you for producing such outstanding young officers as we have graduating here today.

I am very pleased today to have two people—who are very special to me—here with us. First of all, my claim to fame—the first lady of the Navy, my wife, Margaret...and sitting with her is a young man who graduated with honors last year from Davidson College and taught for a year at a Peace Corps-related service in Jamaica—teaching kids in the third world—and who is going to be entering Officer Candidate School this August to become a Naval Officer of the United States Navy: my son John.

We are also very pleased to have with us today an outstanding Member of Congress, who has been a strong support and friend of the naval service, Congressman Steny Hoyer.

I have a letter I would like to read to you from our Commander-in-Chief. He wanted to be here today, but was called to that other

Academy out in Colorado. I took the first prize and came here. The letter reads:

> *Congratulations to the class of 1995 as you complete your studies at the United States Naval Academy. You can take great pride in the skills and character you have developed, knowing that you are well prepared to meet the tremendous challenge of leadership. Through the past 150 years, more than 60 thousand Naval Academy men and women have helped to keep our nation great.*
>
> *Today, America looks to you to maintain this tradition of excellence. I am confident that you will be equal to the task. As you establish new standards of able performance and lead the Naval and Marine Corps into the 21st Century, you will stand as a beacon of liberty and democracy for nations around the world. On behalf of all Americans, thank you for your dedication to the idea of freedom and your commitment for defending the Constitution of the United States. Best wishes to each of you for every future success.*
>
> *Signed... Bill Clinton*

It is simply not possible to describe what a great honor and privilege it is for me to be the principal speaker at the sesquicentennial graduation ceremony of this great institution that I love. I'm proud to be a graduate of the United States Naval Academy, and I know how proud and excited you are today because I remember so well how I felt as I sat where you now sit on graduation day in 1964. The speaker was Congressman Carl Vinson, Chairman of the House Armed Services Committee. Due to the day's excitement, I remember very little of what he said.

Three decades from now, you probably won't remember much of what I say either. But, I hope that you get the main point. Actually, in preparation for this speech I went back to review Carl Vinson's text. He said, "During your Navy careers there not only will continue to be Secretaries of the Navy, but these Secretaries will also continue to shoulder heavy responsibilities." Those words did not have any significance to me at that time. They certainly do now! Paul Nitze was Secretary of the Navy then and handed me my diploma as I will have the honor to present yours to you today.

At graduation last year President Clinton said, "I came here today because I want America to know there remains no finer Navy in the world than the United States Navy, and no finer training ground for naval leadership than the United States Naval Academy." I could not agree more. Today, I want to talk to you about naval leadership and my experience here as a midshipman.

When I was a sophomore at Byrd High School in Shreveport, Louisiana, we had a guest speaker who said that in his opinion the finest overall education that anyone could get in our country was at the United States Naval Academy. My mother always taught me to "hitch my wagon to a star," so I decided right then the Academy was where I wanted to go. That was the only place I applied, but in the spring of my senior year, I learned that I had not been accepted. I was devastated! So, I went to LSU for a year, which I enjoyed, but my heart was still set on the Naval Academy. The next year I was admitted into the Class of 1964.

I got off to a rocky start as a plebe and continued to have some painful and humbling experiences. I wanted to row crew, but got cut plebe summer. The first time they published an unsat list for academics my name was on it. I wanted to fly, but my eyes deteriorated. I competed for a Rhodes Scholarship and was not selected.

But, I also had many great and memorable experiences here. I marched with the whole brigade in John F. Kennedy's inaugural parade. Sadly, I later led a special honor company that marched in his funeral procession to Arlington National Cemetery. I spent first class summer on a foreign exchange cruise with Her Majesty's Royal Navy in Singapore. I had the privilege to serve as a striper in one of the truly great classes ever to graduate from here. For four years in a row, we "beat Army" in football...and I am confident that come the first Saturday in December, we are going to start that habit one more time!

The greatest lesson I learned came from our Superintendent, Rear Admiral Charles C. Kirkpatrick. He repeatedly told us, "You can do anything you set your mind to do, and don't you forget it." I pass that on to you. You can do anything you set your mind to do, and don't you forget it.

I know that right now your minds are on the end of your long voyage here…and the pride and joy you feel in what you have accomplished. Your family and friends share that pride and so do I. But along with the celebration, this is also a moment for each of you to think seriously about the challenges you will face in the future.

As you move forward in life, the one thing you will always need is a framework on which to base your approach to leadership. I have given much thought over the years to my own framework. It helped me with the leadership challenges I faced—as a midshipman, an active duty submarine officer, a Naval reservist, a community leader, and government official.

Recently an acquaintance of mine, a theologian from California, sent me a list of eight specific leadership traits that he drew from chapter 27 of the book of Acts in the Bible. In a succinct way, he has caught traits essential to my leadership framework. Now I'm not a preacher and this is not a sermon. But you certainly don't have to be a religious person to appreciate the value of these traits, and you don't have to be a Biblical scholar to interpret them.

These traits have stood the test of time. The list is as follows: A leader is trusted, a leader takes the initiative, a leader uses good judgment, a leader speaks with authority, a leader strengthens others, is optimistic and enthusiastic, never compromises absolutes, and leads by example.

This list can be exemplified by predecessors of yours from this Academy who have captured the essence of these leadership traits.

The first trait is trust. I am told by Admiral Larson that your class admires President Jimmy Carter, Class of 1947, and so do I. He personifies trust. He was successful with the Camp David Accords and the Middle East Peace Treaty, and he continues to serve the cause of peace in the world, because he is so honest and straightforward that he is genuinely trusted.

As plebes, you memorized a great example of trust. At the Battle of Manila Bay, Admiral George Dewey (Class of 1859) turned to the captain of his flagship and said, "You may fire when ready, Gridley." This Academy teaches trust and Admiral Dewey trusted each captain and crew to fight without need for his personal direction.

A leader takes the initiative. *Carpe Diem*, Latin for "seize the day," has always been a fundamental tenet of leadership.

I find inspiration in this regard in the deeds of Vice Admiral Jim Stockdale, a classmate of President Carter, who took command of his fellow Prisoners of War in Hanoi at the height of the Vietnam conflict. Admiral Stockdale initiated and led cohesive resistance to torture and abuse despite the daily uncertainty of his own fate.

Good judgment is also critical to good leadership. Good judgment is not just evident in success, it can be most evident in defeat and disappointment.

In the Battle of the Coral Sea, the carrier USS *Lexington*—one of our few assets following Pearl Harbor—took multiple hits that caused her to list and burn. Rear Admiral Aubrey Fitch (Class of 1906), commander of the carrier group—and later a Superintendent of the Naval Academy—calmly assessed damage control efforts. He then turned to the *Lexington*'s captain and said, "It's time to get the men off this thing." Twenty-seven hundred lives were saved by that one judgment call. A good leader needs to make tough decisions especially when things are going wrong.

The next trait is at the heart of a leader's personality. A leader speaks with authority. A leader needs to have sufficient confidence in what he is saying so that potential followers will be convinced. The best way to convince people is to speak with authority. And if that authority is matched by knowledge then the chances for leadership are greatly enhanced.

The development of the concept of amphibious warfare was initiated by Marine Corps Commandants who combined authority with conviction and knowledge. From its origins during the tenures of Commandants John Lejeune, Wendell Neville, and Benjamin Fuller, through the establishment of the Fleet Marine Force under General John H. Russell, all Naval Academy graduates, the development of the Marine Corps as America's expeditionary force was the result of leadership. It was backed by the experience of campaigns in the Caribbean, Central America, the Pacific, and China. These leaders spoke with authority in directing new ideas because they had experienced the old ideas and borne the scars.

Likewise, when Chief of Naval Operations Admiral Arleigh Burke (Class of 1923) began the project to build the first fleet ballistic missile submarine, he needed to convince both the civilian leadership and the Navy itself that the program required top priority. The authority of his presentation was fortified with his combat experience—and his reflections about the deterrence implications of that experience.

A leader strengthens others. A good leader does not seek to impose his or her own attitudes or solutions on others. Rather, the leader provides the support and guidance that prompts others to have confidence in their own abilities and decision-making.

When Fleet Admiral Chester Nimitz (Class of 1905) arrived to take command of the remnants of the Pacific Fleet at Pearl Harbor, his first effort was to renew the confidence of the staff and the commanding officers that they could go on to victory. Rather than making heads roll, he made them think. Rather than emphasizing the mistakes, he convinced his subordinates that they were the ones to overcome the past. Those who served under him recalled that his very "presence" seemed to give confidence wherever he was. He strengthened others to believe their abilities could achieve the crucial victory that they sought.

A leader remains optimistic and enthusiastic. To lead effectively, see the glass as half-full, not half-empty. Believe, every morning, that things are going to be better than before. Attitudes are infectious. Optimism and enthusiasm overcome the greatest challenges.

Captain John Paul Jones captured this idea with the immortal quote, "I have not yet begun to fight." I have a painting of that famous battle between the Bonhomme Richard and Serapis hanging in my office and it inspires me every day. John Paul Jones's spirit of optimism and enthusiasm has been a part of our Navy since the American Revolution.

A leader never compromises absolutes. Defense of American freedom and obedience to the Constitution of the United States are two absolutes the Naval Service lives by, and for which our Sailors and Marines may face death.

Admiral Hyman Rickover (Class of 1922), the father of the nuclear Navy—by whom I was interviewed for the Navy's nuclear program—vividly demonstrated this commitment to absolutes. He wanted to ensure there was no compromise in the safety of our submarines. And he did this by setting an example. Most Americans don't know that Admiral Rickover went on the first trial dive of every nuclear submarine the Navy built. He knew that it wasn't enough to simply certify on paper that a new submarine was safe. If Sailors were going to trust their lives to an untested submarine, he would go with them. If something seemed like it was going wrong during the dive, he would calmly go to the compartment where the problem appeared and sit to watch the crew handle it. How could you be afraid when this small, wrinkled old man was not? How could you treat safety as anything but an absolute?

This leads to the final quality on this list of traits: example. The best leaders need fewer words than most, because they lead with their lives. In the sports world, example is not just ability, but both the willingness to lead and the humility to support a team effort that is stronger than one skilled individual. Roger Staubach class of '65 and David Robinson class of '87 are competitors who set the example as both leaders and teammates.

Among today's Naval leaders, Rear Admiral Anthony Watson, class of 1970, has set an example that many young Americans have decided to follow. Raised in a public housing project in Chicago, he was a recognized leader in every position from midshipman to Commanding Officer to Deputy Commandant here, and became the first African-American submariner to make flag rank. He takes over soon as Commander of the Navy Recruiting Command, a position that demands a very public example.

And finally, I want to mention an academy graduate who exemplifies the fact that women in the Navy and Marine Corps no longer face any limits to their dreams. Since the age of ten, LCDR Wendy Lawrence, class of 1981, dreamed of becoming an astronaut. Three years ago she fulfilled that childhood dream. She became the first female naval aviator chosen by NASA for the astronaut program and was a mission specialist on the shuttle *Endeavour*'s last mission. LCDR Lawrence demonstrates that what matters to the Naval service, above all else, is your performance as an officer. Man or woman, you will rise as high as your abilities will take you.

These eight traits of leadership provide a path, a course that has been marked for almost two thousand years.

There is a long line of Naval heroes before you…men and women tried by history. Your turn has come. That's what you were trained for. That is why the Naval Academy has existed for 150 years. Not just to educate…not just to train you in the arts of war…not just to provide competent officers. But to instill you with a commitment and tradition of service and leadership that will remain with you forever.

In character and in deed, you will always be the ones to set the example. This institution is unique because its mission is to ensure that in your hearts you are unique…that foremost and everywhere the defense of American liberty will remain your task…whether in the Naval Service or elsewhere. Those people behind you are counting on you. When you shake hands with me as you receive your diploma, let's regard it as a pact—a bond between two graduates of this extraordinary institution—to be as worthy as we can possibly be of those who have gone before us…of those who march with us today…and of those who will follow us. In a few moments, your diploma and our handshake will seal that bond. And then the real challenge will begin.

God bless you. God bless the United States Navy and United States Marine Corps. And God bless America.

# Episcopal Diocese of Washington Recommendation

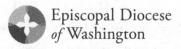

Episcopal Diocese
*of* Washington

May 23, 2017

Mr. John Donoghue
Chair, Cathedral Chapter
Washington National Cathedral
Mount St. Alban
Washington, DC 20016

Dear John,

At Dean Hollerith's excellent suggestion, I am thrilled to recommend the election of The Honorable John H. Dalton as Honorary Canon of the Cathedral Church of St. Peter and St. Paul, pursuant to the provisions of Article III, Section 2(c) of the Cathedral Bylaws.

John's commitment to the Cathedral is long, well documented, and ongoing. He is not only a generous supporter of the Cathedral; he works diligently to promote its mission and work. A man of deep faith and passionate engagement, present in worship nearly every Sunday and at all significant Cathedral events, and an enthusiastic ambassador for the Cathedral and its Lord wherever he goes, John will take his place among Cathedral Canons with characteristic humility and a servant's heart.

I ask that you and the Chapter vote to approve John's nomination at the Cathedral Chapter meeting on Friday, June 2, 2017.

Faithfully,

The Rt. Rev. Mariann Edgar Budde
Bishop of Washington

cc:     The Very Rev. Randolph M. Hollerith

# Kelly's Letter

*Dear Mr. Dalton,*

*Yesterday was my last day as an active duty officer in the U.S. Navy. I can hardly believe how fast the time went, and I've been thinking a lot about my winging- and even earlier than that, to my time in college as a midshipman, and my commissioning. I wanted to share something with you that occurred to me as I reflected on the last nine years of my life.*

*I wrote a thesis my senior year at Georgetown, and the question it posed was what happens to our society's idea of what it means to be a woman, when women put on uniforms and perform what is traditionally considered "a man's job," as well as what happens, in particular, to those women is those uniforms. (You can imagine why this was of particular interest to me.) One of the books I used as a reference was Tailspin, about the Tailhook scandal and its aftermath. Chris has told me a few, brief stories about your experiences as Secretary of the Navy, and one of the things that sticks in my mind is imagining what it must've been like to accept a job with a stack of Tailhook investigation files waiting on the desk.*

*As difficult as it is for an organization to change a policy or a rule, it is clearly exponentially more difficult to go about changing a culture- especially when the culture defines itself by the very traditions you're trying to change. I can't imagine how professionally and personally taxing it must've been to make the difficult decisions you made.*

*So now, a little more than a decade and a half after Tailhook, and a little less than a decade after I received my commission, I wanted to say a personal thank you for those decisions. For me, the culture of naval aviation was not just a physically safe place to be, it was a place where I was able to succeed and excel to the very limits of my ambition, intellect, and talent. It was an organization that valued my contributions and efforts more than it counted the cost of "berthing issues." And that goes, as well, for so many* of my friends, amazing women whom I feel so lucky to have known and served with.

When I was about six years old, and told my parents that I wanted to "fly planes off of the big ship like Dad" when I grew up, my Dad had to tell me the truth- they didn't let girls do that.

Thank you so much for being a big part of the reason why it turned out that I could.

Very respectfully,

Kelly

# DGA Remarks

Admiral Carter, Admiral Natter, distinguished graduates in attendance.

The great class of 1964. Please stand. These guys are great, and I love 'em! I want to sincerely thank the selection committee. I am humbled, honored, and very grateful. I loved serving as the 70th Secretary of the Navy. I am convinced that that is the best job in government! I had the privilege of serving in that job for five and a half years, when the average tenure is less than three years.

My partner in that job was my best friend, the very best first lady the Naval Service ever had, who did more to enhance the quality of life for sailors and Marines than any other one person ever has…my wife of forty-five wonderful years and my claim to fame—Margaret.

Also, I am grateful to my older brother, sister-in-law, sister, and cousin William, Pam, Margaret, and Jean from Dallas are here. My family has showered me with love and support from the day I was born.

I'm also proud to have my two sons here. John Jr., who served seven years in the US Navy as a surface warfare officer is here from Chicago with his lovely wife and two fine sons, Antonio and Mateus. And my son Chris who served nine years as a CH 53 pilot in the US Marine Corps. He is married to a former Navy CH 60 pilot and has two fine sons who are too young to make the trip from San Diego. I am most grateful to have them and many friends who have come from far and wide to be with us today. I am a richly blessed man!

Now, I would like to address the Brigade of Midshipmen.

When I assumed office in 1993 there were some major issues that had to be addressed:

The Tailhook convention had occurred less than two years before. Some historians have said that that event was the biggest blow the Navy had taken since the Pearl Harbor attack. The discipline to those involved had yet to be resolved and was on my desk for action. The biggest cheating scandal in the history of the Naval Academy had occurred the year before. I'm told it was the biggest in the history of any service Academy. My decision was required for those involved. The Congress had just changed the law with respect to women in combat and gays in the military. These changes were a huge shock to the culture of the Navy Department! The significant drawdown as result of the end of the Cold War was underway and advancement rates were MUCH slower than normal. After I had been an office for a few weeks, I was about to leave the Pentagon to visit sailors and Marines in the fleet, there was a huge banner headline of *Navy Times* which read:

*"Navy Morale at All Time Low!"*

Well, I had a major leadership challenge on my hands. About that time I received in the mail unsolicited, a lovely framed list of the timeless traits of leadership from Dr. John MacArthur, Jr. I want to share with you this list of traits that was VERY helpful to me, and I hope they will be for you, also. They are:

*A leader is trusted*
*A leader takes the initiative*
*A leader uses good judgment*
*A leader speaks with authority*
*A leader strengthens others*
*A leader is optimistic and enthusiastic*
*A leader never compromises absolutes*
*A leader leads by example*

Leadership is the ability to start from anywhere and influence everybody that comes into your path! This Academy is all about developing leaders.

I want to share some thoughts on just a few of these traits with you:

A leader is trusted. President Jimmy Carter, a distinguished graduate, personifies trust. He tells it like it is and is genuinely trusted around the world.

A leader strengthens others. When I was a midshipman, we had a Superintendent named Rear Admiral Charles C. Kirkpatrick. Whenever he spoke to a group of assembled midshipmen, he would always tell us, "You can do anything you set your mind to do, and don't you forget it!" He made us believe in ourselves and was a great leader. Sir Winston Churchill said, "There is nothing that man cannot do, if he wills it with enough resolution." That is something I want you to know, "You can do anything you set your mind to do!" I hope that you will not forget it!

A leader never compromises absolutes. You may say, "What is an absolute?" Our personal integrity is an absolute. Our core values of honor, courage, and commitment are absolutes. Treating every individual with dignity and respect is an absolute.

A leader leads by example. The best leaders need fewer words than most, because they lead with their lives. In the sports world, Roger Staubach, a distinguished graduate, leads by example. David Robinson, a distinguished graduate, leads by example. In the brigade today, Midshipman Keenan Reynolds leads by example in establishing all kinds of records and by leading the Navy team to the first eleven win season in the history of this Academy.

A shorthand version of these timeless traits for a lesson in leadership is simply this: "Know your stuff. Be a person of character. Take care of your people."

I will close with a Psalm that is very special to me. I hope it will be a blessing to each one of you. It will be familiar to the football team because I have shared it with them every year for many years. It is Psalm 20, the 20th Psalm.

*May the Lord answer you when you are in distress.*

*May he send you help from his sanctuary.*

*May he give you the desire of your heart and make all your plans succeed.*

*We will shout for joy when you are victorious and will lift up our banners in the name of our God.*

*May the Lord grant all your requests.*

*Now I know that the Lord saves his anointed; he answers him from his holy heaven with the saving power of his right hand.*

*Some trust in chariots and some in horses, but we trust in the name of the Lord our God.*

*They are brought to their knees and fall, but we rise up and stand firm.*

*Oh Lord, answer us when we call.*

I wish each one of you fair winds and following seas.
God bless you. God bless this great institution. God bless America!
And one more thing…BEAT ARMY!!!

# ACKNOWLEDGMENTS

*I would like to thank each of these gracious people
who helped me with the book. I am indebted to them!*

**Colonel Wayman Bishop**, USMC (Ret.), was my first Military
Assistant as SECNAV and very helpful to me in my early days at the
Pentagon. **Colonel Rusty Blackman**, USMC, served as my third Military
Assistant and had a great sense of humor. **Rich Bland** was on
the Chapter with me at the Washington National Cathedral and most
helpful to me in remembering things that happened on our watch, and
is now an official at WETA, the second largest public television station
in the USA. **Hon. Bill Cassidy** was the Deputy Assistant Secretary
of the Navy (Conversion and Redevelopment) who helped me a great
deal with BRAC and remembered much that I had forgotten. **Captain
Chuck Connor**, USN (Ret.), was my second Public Affairs Officer
and was of meaningful assistance to me. The **Reverend Canon Jan
Cope**, a superb preacher, was responsible for my joining the Housing
Policy Council, and is now the outstanding provost at the Washington
National Cathedral. **Hon. Richard Danzig** served as Under Secretary
of the Navy while I was SECNAV; an immensely intelligent man,
excellent deputy, and a natural choice to replace me when I left office.
**Hon. Carol DiBattiste** was my first deputy general counsel of the Navy
Department and was very helpful to me in the Tailhook scandal. **Peter
Fertig** was the founder of the Bob Feller Act of Valor Foundation, in

which I have been very active. **Ens. Peter Graef** was a fellow ensign on the USS *Blueback*; we were both promoted to Lieutenant junior grade on the same day. **Hon. Hubert "Herky" Harris** is a good friend and was a senior official at the Office of Management and Budget (OMB) in the Carter administration. **Ambassador J. Douglas Holladay** is the founder of PathNorth in which Margaret and I are very active, and I serve on the board. **Hon. Steve Honigman** was the first general counsel of the Navy Department during my tenure and conducted the program for my official swearing in. **Ron Kessler** has been a dear friend since 1976 when I became active in politics. **Paul Leonard** was the chief of legislative affairs at the Housing Policy Council and was my right-hand man, being of great assistance for the twelve and a half years I was at HPC. **RADM Tom Lynch,USN** (Ret.), was captain of the Navy football team in 1963 which played for the national championship and a prominent alumnus of the US Naval Academy. **Major General Joe Lynch**, USAF (Ret.), was a senior official in the legal counsel's office at the Navy Department and very helpful to me when I was in the Pentagon. **David McAllister-Wilson** is the long-serving President of the Wesley Theological Seminary and is a wise man with whom I enjoyed serving on the board of governors. **Mack McCarter** is the founder of Community Renewal International, where I serve as the chair of the National Advisory Board. **Stewart McLaurin** became President of the White House Historical Association in 2014; we worked together on numerous initiatives. **Jim Metzger**, USN (Ret.), was the Executive Assistant for the Vice Chief of Naval Operations from 1995–96 before he became my EA. **Frank Moore** was the National Finance Director for the Carter Campaign, and worked with him to raise funds for Governor Carter's first campaign for president and who later became the Chief of the Legislative Affairs for the Carter administration. **Mike Murray** was my roommate all four years when we were midshipmen at the Naval Academy and a great friend since 1960. **RADM Robert Natter** worked closely with Danzig, especially on the 3rd Seawolf submarine and BRAC, and was in charge of legislative affairs for the Navy.

Colonel Greg Newbold, USMC, became my second Military Assistant during my tenure as SECNAV, and served me well by providing counsel on many issues. Honorable Fred Pang was the first Assistant Secretary for Manpower and Reserve Affairs. David Pierson is the son of an old friend and fraternity brother, Clint. I serve on the board of directors for David's innovative company, Crius Technology Group. RADM Joe Prueher, USN. Joe's last job when I was at the Pentagon was CINCPAC, and he later became Ambassador to China. Governor Tim Pawlenty, the 39th Governor of Minnesota and was the CEO of the Financial Services Roundtable. Rick Perry served ably as my assistant while I was a member and chairman of the Federal Home Loan Bank Board during the Carter Administration. Under Secretary of the Army Joe Reeder and I worked together on issues concerning the military broadly. Lt. Dan Richardson was a very accomplished officer and a colleague and friend during my service on the USS *Blueback*. RADM Norb Ryan, USN, was in charge of the Office of Legislative Affairs from 1996–97 while I was SECNAV and helped lobby on Capitol Hill to get resources for the department. Captain Bill Schmidt, USN, was my first Executive Assistant and aided me greatly in reviewing reports from Tailhook and suggesting appropriate solutions. Faith Schwartz worked at Option One before we recruited her to work for HPC and played a decisive role in the Hope Now Alliance. I met Perry Steiner through Governor Pawlenty, and worked with him to grow this dynamic company, Xactus, where I serve on the board. Lt. David Stryker and I became good friends during the seventy days on patrol at sea, serving together on the USS *John C. Calhoun*. Dan Tate was President Carter's chief lobbyist in the Senate and we collaborated to get the Panama Canal Treaty passed.

# INDEX OF NAMES